END OF THE LINE:

A HISTORY OF RAILWAYS IN PAPUA NEW GUINEA

BOB MCKILLOP
AND MICHAEL PEARSON

PORT MORESBY :
UNIVERSITY OF PAPUA NEW GUINEA PRESS
1997

End of the Line: A History of Railways in Papua New Guinea

ISBN 9980-84-096-X

University of Papua New Guinea Press and Bookshop
PO Box 413
University PO, NCD
Papua New Guinea

TABLE OF CONTENTS

FOREWORD

I have always advocated the introduction of Railways to Papua New Guinea as a mode of Transport. This was because I know that one or two railways had existed in the country since 1884.

This book demonstrates beyond doubt that railways have made a significant contribution to the development of Papua New Guinea and could in the future advance economic and social development.

Messrs McKillop and Pearson are both enthusiastic railway historians. Their constant probing and penetrating questions has uncovered a surprising number of railways that existed in Papua New Guinea and provided insight into their construction and operation.

This history by its character is a history of the colonial efforts to develop Papua New Guinea. However, it has been written with the future concerns of Papua New Guineans coming to the fore in the last chapters. Normally foreign histories of Papua New Guinea leave out much of what really happened to Papua New Guineans, but this history attempts to show what happened from both sides of the track.

Because of its nation wide perspective many of the areas studied have not been done in depth. Therefore, there is scope for Papua New Guineans to take up the challenge of discovering our own history and recording it in detail. Woodlark Island mentioned in this book is one area which had the earliest contact with Europeans and the effects of foreign mining. Nevertheless, it is an area sadly lacking in history records and interpretation from the Papua New Guinean perspective. I hope that Papua New Guineans will take up the quest to record our history from our point of view.

This book is a valuable contribution to the economic history of Papua New Guinea. It confirms my belief that railways can be a successful mode of transport and a mechanism for building our nation.

Hon. Dr. John Waiko, MP
Minister for Education

PREFACE

Papua New Guinea is commonly thought to be a land without railways. At the very least, railways do not immediately come to mind as a topic for historical research in Papua New Guinea. Nevertheless, we set out to document and record something of the history of local railways in 1971, initially as individual projects. Inevitably, our interest in the topic of railways brought us together and we have been working collaboratively on our research since 1980.

At first the task was to identify and document the railways which have operated in Papua New Guinea. To our surprise, we now have records of some 150 railways lines, many of them small hand-pushed operations from a jetty to a copra store or around a sawmill. Others have yielded fascinating stories of more substantial enterprises and the endeavours of colonial pioneers at the frontier.

As we brought the material together we began to realise that we not only had stories about small railway operations around the country, but we also had the basis for a new look at some basic elements of Papua New Guinea economic history. Through the story of railways we had identified important themes which helped us learn about the economic conditions of today from the experience of the past.

Many people have assisted us with information over the past 25 years. These contributions have been acknowledged in the footnotes. Particular thanks are extended to Professor Ron Huch (History Department, University of PNG), Professor Donald Denoon and Dr. Hank Nelson (Pacific History, Australian National University), Father Theo Aerts (Bomana Seminary), John Millett (Institute of National Affairs), James Sinclair, Jerry Kuhena and Phil Wallens for their constructive comments on our draft manuscript prepared in late 1995. And a special vote of appreciation is extended to Rita Mamavi Pearson for her tolerance of train-crazy men who left her alone while they searched the bush in remote corners of the country in pursuit of "rusty rails".

Finally, our thanks go to the Prime Minister of the Independent State of Papua New Guinea, Sir Julius Chan, for agreeing to an element of subsidy for this book, and to the Department of the Prime Minister and National Executive Council for making the arrangements. This has allowed for a wider range of illustrations to be included.

R F McKillop
Michael Pearson

August 1996

CHAPTER 1. RAILWAYS AND SOCIETY

Railways in History - Industrialism

Railways provided the foundation stone for the *Industrial Revolution* which swept Europe and North America in the nineteenth century. Through railway construction, European people experienced rapid technological advancement, unified themselves into strong nations and broke down the barriers of time, distance and delay. Many scholars argue that the introduction of railways was the single most powerful initiator of economic *takeoffs* which allowed European societies (and later North America and Japan) to provide their people with improved living standards[1].

Railways built their own industrial base, absorbing vast quantities of capital, men and natural resources to forge rails, build locomotives and rolling stock, and keep their equipment maintained in vast workshops. As railways expanded to new frontiers, they generated local industrial capacity. In Australian colonies, railway workshops at Eveleigh in Sydney, Newport in Melbourne and Islington in Adelaide, provided the initial impetus for industrialisation, including the capacity to build locomotives and carriages. Railways were also pioneers of industrial synergy [2]. They greatly increased the effect of other inventions such as the Wheatstone telegraph, electric traction and micro-electronics.

The wealth and power generated by the Industrial Revolution enabled European nations in turn to expand their influence around the globe. Eventually this expansion encompassed the people living in the mainland and islands now known as Papua New Guinea (PNG). This is the story of that process, initiated by the invention of steam locomotives operating on iron (and subsequently steel) rails and expanding through the capital, industrial might and technological expertise of railway engineers to the most remote outposts of colonial empires.

Time and Discipline

Through their requirement for punctuality and discipline, railways greatly contributed to the social transformation from rural to industrial society. In this transformation, railways scheduled the arrival and departure of trains according to strict timetables, thereby disciplining the citizens of industrial societies to time[3]. The discipline of the railway pervaded the whole society. To travel by train, members of the public had to queue for tickets, present the correct tickets to officials, follow company rules and above all, to become a servant to *railway time*. At village, town and city alike, the railway guided the daily habits of citizens. Natural time, the pattern of activities dictated by the sun's progress through the heavens and the peasant's age-old rhythm of life no longer sufficed. The train did not wait and those who did not adjust to the new discipline were left behind.Moreover, railways standardised time. In the pre-railway age, towns prided themselves in keeping their own times, a few minutes different from a neighbour a few miles away. This would not do the railways, who required a precise, standard time to schedule their operations. In England, Greenwich Mean Time, colloquially known as *Railway Time*, was established in the 1840s to solve the problem[4]. Other countries followed suit and International Standard Time emerged in 1884.

The Railway as Social Exchange

In providing new opportunities for people to travel, railways helped break down old cultural divisions and expand social exchange for ordinary people. The railway station emerged as the place where people met and mingled, the starting and arrival point for journeys to work, the country, the city and the wider world. The station was a gateway through which individuals could expand their network of social exchange beyond their town and village to the wider world. In industrial society, railway stations became:

> cathedrals of the new humanity [which were] the meeting points of nations, the centre where all converges, the nucleus of the huge stars whose iron rays stretch out to the ends of the earth[5].

Railways brought diverse communities and regions together. In this process, they helped to diminish regional differences and, at the same time, they advanced the process of urbanisation by breaking down the distinction between town and country.

Suburban railways and street tramways enabled mass transportation to come into existence for the first time in history[6]. Walking distance no longer set the limits to urban growth and city growth followed railway lines into the hinterland. Mass transport made mass suburbia possible. In Australia, railways shaped settlement patterns and helped create the world's most urbanised nation. Vast metropolis' developed around the opportunities offered by cheap mass transport which funnelled people and goods into a central place. Cultural activities and mass media emerged to shape a sense of national identity.

Institutional Development

Through railways, the first modern business corporations were born. Railway organisation required the effective organisation of multi-disciplined work units covering many thousands of employees on a national basis. At first, they were organised along military lines as armies were the only other organisations of such size spread over so broad a canvas[7]. The early railway organisations imposed tight discipline, long hours, strict hierarchy and military-style regulations. In Germany in particular, respect for authority and strict observance of the rules dominated railway operations. This discipline brought with it an efficiency and safety record which characterised the German ethos[8].

However, railways soon became the pioneers of modern management techniques, particularly in North America and England where private companies operated the enterprises. Railway companies were the first corporations run by professional managers who did not necessarily control the company's shares[9]. They established new organisation patterns with clear functions between departments and they forged new cultures of customer service.

This institutional base built by railways was a fundamental step toward modern international market economies. At the dawn of the railway age, European economies were in the process of evolving from the city state with some specialisation into capital markets with secure property rights over time and complex governance structures. For the first time, the problems faced by traditional institutions in achieving secure, low-cost market transactions were overcome[10]. With the railway age, new institutions developed to facilitate measurement (quality control) and enforcement of contracts. These institutions safeguard property rights and provide certainty in transactions. In contrast, non-industrial economies found that transaction costs increased sharply and the productivity of the traditional groups had difficulty competing with the specialist commercial institutions of industrial societies[11].

Railways not only created the first large-scale economic organisations which operated over vast distances, but also introduced innovative solutions for regularised, low-cost transactions. Travel was procured by the purchase of tickets covering journeys for clearly specified prices; goods were shipped according to publicly advertised charging rates. Other means of transport were pushed aside by the certainty, convenience and price advantage of railway transactions.

In Australia, where the state was seen as a benevolent provider of railway services (Chapter 3), the need to distance railway management from political interference for sound commercial operation resulted in the railways founding the model for the modern state corporation[12].

The technical expertise, discipline and work ethic of the railway culture was an important factor influencing the adventurers and colonialists who extended the influence of industrial powers to Africa, Asia and the Pacific in the 19th and early 20th centuries. However, the response to technological change and new competition at home was too often to seek regulatory protection. Accordingly railway management became ossified and failed to move with the times through the mid-20th century.

Nationalism and Imperialism

Industrial expansion and the rise of nationalism in Europe generated imperial rivalry for new spheres of influence in the Americas, Africa, Asia and the far off Pacific. Nineteenth century imperialism was profoundly influenced by railways. Railways created colonies like Kenya and enabled small groups of foreigners, like the British in India, to rule large subject populations[13]. The Russian Czar built the Trans-Siberian Railway to open up Siberia and colonise it with millions of Russians.

The impact of railways was viewed with ambivalence by the colonised. On the one hand, local leaders saw railways as symbols of modernity and power; on the other, they were part of an alien culture who treated them as inferior people. Moreover, railway stations and carriages were designed to segregate the colonial masters from their indigenous subjects[14]. Strict segregation was seen as fundamental to the strength of imperial rule and reinforced the sense of inferiority imposed on the indigenous people.

Imperialists sought to modernise their colonies through the work discipline and institutions of industrial societies. In this process, the "backwardness" of the old societies would give way to new cultures in their own image. Significantly, it was in Japan which enthusiastically adopted railways without becoming subject to imperial powers, that this modernisation was most effectively achieved.

When Captain Perry arrived in Japan in 1853, the country had never seen a wheeled vehicle and there was no tradition of industrial discipline. Unpunctuality was accepted as a Japanese cultural trait[15]. Within twenty years, the Japanese were building railways to modernise the country. Through its railways, Japan established a strong industrial base and, from this, an international reputation for its disciplined industrial work force. Japan is now a major industrial nation where *railway time* is paramount. In to-day's Japan, split-second timing to change trains on Tokyo's complex network is a common theme of popular crime fiction.

Foreign Intrusion in PNG

Europeans began to arrive in the New Guinea islands from 1794. Industrial expansion and imperial rivalry in far off Europe made it inevitable that foreign intrusion would intensify over the following century. Traders, missionaries and adventurers arrived from Britain, France, Germany and Australia to promote their various interests.

Statesman in Europe were primarily concerned with the strategic and diplomatic advantages of the acquisition of colonial possession might bring: economic benefits were of secondary importance[16]. The spur to British colonial expansion in the Pacific Islands came from Australian settlers who sought British domination of the region. German ambitions were driven by expansionist business opinion and national pride back in Europe.

French Marist missionaries first began working on Woodlark Island from 1847. English Methodist missionaries established a station in the Duke of York Islands in 1875, while German Catholic and Lutheran missionaries commenced their work in mainland New Guinea in

1886. Australian traders had established bases by 1875 and the German trading firm JC Godeffroy & Sohn expanded its operations into the Bismarck Archipelago from a base in the Duke of York Islands the following year. The stations enabled Godeffroy's successor, *Deutsche Handels-und Plantagen Gesellschaft* (DH&PG), to recruit labourers for German plantations in Samoa. Competition from Queensland recruiters was deeply resented by DH&PG, who urged annexation of New Guinea by Germany to monopolise access to labour. [17]

In 1884 Bismarck decided to make Germany a colonial power, prompted by a claim that the Reich would incur little expense if the territories were administered by chartered companies modelled on the East India companies of the 17th and 18th century. Germany proclaimed north-eastern New Guinea as a protectorate on 3 November, 1884. Britain responded to pressures from Australian colonies with a similar claim over south-eastern New Guinea two days later.

Britain and Germany agreed on the partition of New Guinea by April, 1885, when a charter was granted to the *Neuguinea Kompagnie* (NGK) to administer German New Guinea (GNG). Initially the company established its main station at Finschhafen on the mainland (*Kaiser Wilhelmsland*), but conditions were unsatisfactory for European settlement and the hopes of many settlers succumbed to early mortality.

German New Guinea was expanded to include Buka, Bougainville, Choisel and the Shortland Islands in 1886. Isabel and Ontong Java were added in 1889. In 1899 New Guinea became an imperial German colony which covered the Carolines, Marianas and Palau, but Isabel, Choisel, the Shortlands and Ontong Java were transferred to the British Solomon Islands.

Pre-colonial PNG Society

Traditional PNG societies were based on local exchange within the village. Families relied on agriculture, supplemented by hunting, gathering and fishing activities, to meet their subsistence needs. Territory and institutions were generally confined to small localised areas, although some extensive trading patterns were established.

Land provides clan members with a sense of identity and security, while serving as a store of wealth for past, present and future generations. Customary law and order was maintained by each clan. Clan members came together to defend their territory against threats from outside groups. Endemic warfare was a feature in many areas, particularly in the Highlands.

Politics and decision-making in Melanesian society usually revolved around big men (rarely women) who acquire their position through economic largess to clan members. While women were primarily responsible for growing food and generating surpluses, men dominated decisions on the allocation of resources. The emphasis was on the distribution of wealth, not its acquisition and transfer to future generations. Leadership is constantly under challenge from emerging *big men*, a situation which can lead to considerable instability.

Pre-colonial Transport

Physical, tribal and language boundaries restricted social interaction and exchange to small social groups. There were few goods to transport and travel was restricted to nearby villages. Most land transport was handled by women. Journeys were made by foot, with the men walking ahead carrying weapons to guard against surprise attacks. The women laboured behind with heavy loads.

Only in selected coastal areas were wider patterns of trade established. Water transport required canoes which varied greatly in their manner of construction. Some of these canoes were very large, and it was in their manufacture, always by men, that the first organisation of land transport emerged. Large trees, up to 30 metres tall and 4 metres in girth, were cut in the forest and transported to the coast. Often whole clan groups were required to pull the log. Saplings were cut and placed as rollers under the log, and vines were used to pull it to the shore where the log was carved into a canoe.

Railways in PNG History

Papua New Guinea is a land of rugged terrain, broad rivers, swamps and jungles which are not inviting to the railway engineer. Nevertheless, as the following chapters amply demonstrate, many small railways were constructed in PNG over the years. On the one hand, these railways represent the efforts of pioneers and innovators to gain access to resources and improve their quality of life; on the other, they symbolise the fleeting and insubstantial impact of industrial civilisations on the forces of nature in the tropics.

As the case studies demonstrate, imperial power was reduced to impotence in the remote tropical outposts of Papua and New Guinea. Here, the steel rails which conquered Europe and the American prairie did not march forward with vision and boldness to modernise the country. Instead, numerous short lines marked the hopes of an individual or a company to master an unknown environment. Only rarely did the whistle of a locomotive announce that the frontier was being tackled with confidence: in most cases trucks pushed by local labourers or pulled by animal power sufficed to demonstrate the continued struggle of man over nature. It was very much the "end of the line" where few resources of the industrial metropolitan powers penetrated and local impacts were minor.

Chapters 2 and 3 trace the policies and performance of German and Australian colonialists building and operating railways in New Guinea and Papua. Chapter 4 traces the efforts of the Australian administration in the Mandated Territory of New Guinea to build on the base German infrastructure and the decision to bypass a railway in favour of air transport to open up the Bulolo goldfields in the 1930s. The chapters examine the impact of railways and their associated commercial ventures on the economy and on the lives of Papua New Guineans.

The power and conflict of industrial society was to be thrust upon PNG in the turmoil of the Pacific War from 1942 to 1945. Railways were to play only a minor role in PNG during this conflict, though their important function behind the war machines of the combatants is often overlooked. Chapter 5 examines the war years from a railway perspective.

The post-war era was initially dominated by the motor vehicle and the aeroplane rather than the railway. The limited railway operations in PNG during this period are examined in chapters 6 and 7.

Chapter 8 draws together the conclusions of preceding chapters into an economic history of PNG. It looks at the role of railways in establishing the infrastructure and building the institutions of modern commerce. It also highlights the implications of the historical failure to establish this base in PNG.

The threads of this experience, including today's international railway revival, are brought together in a final chapter which examines the potential future roles for railways in PNG.

The account represents the product of 25 years research by the authors. Yet the record is by no means complete. The ravages of war, tropical mould and carelessness in maintaining and storing records have made the task of tracking the fortunes of various railway ventures, many of them in remote locations, a difficult one. A listing of the 150 railways identified by the authors is presented in the Appendix, including known details of the gauge, length, purpose and mode of operation.

Notes for Chapter 1

1   Rostow, WW, *The process of economic growth,* Cambridge, 1960. p. 302

2   Faith, N, *Locomotion: the railway revolution*, London, BBC Books, 1993, p. 141.

3   *Ibid.,* p. 20; Richards, J and MacKenzie, JM, *The railway station: a social history,* Oxford University Press, 1988, p. 94.

4   *Ibid.,* p. 94-5.

5   Gautier, T, in Jean Dethier (ed), *All Stations,* London 1981, p. 6.

6   Mumford, L, *The city in history,* London, Secker, 1961, p. 429.

7   Richards and MacKenzie, *op. cit.,* p. 62.

8   *Ibid.,* p. 99.

9   Faith, *op. cit.,* p. 62-3.

10 North, DC, "Institutions", *Journal of Economic Perspectives.* Vol. 5:1, 1991, p. 101.

11 *Ibid.,* p. 99.

12 McKillop, RF, "Railways in Australian history: a preliminary reconnaissance. Part 3: building institutions." *ARHS Bulletin,* No. 558, April 1984, p. 92.

13 Faith, *op. cit.,* p. 96.

14 *Ibid.,* p. 139.

15 *Ibid.,* p. 29.

16 McKillop, RF, and Firth, SG, "Foreign intrusion: the first fifty years", D Denoon & C Snowden (eds), *A time to plant and a time to uproot: a history of agriculture in Papua New Guinea*, Port Moresby, Institute PNG Studies, nd, p. 85.

17 *Ibid.,* p. 88.

GERMAN NEW GUINEA

Top - This short tramway from the jetty to a warehouse at the Godeffroy and Sohn station at Mioko in the Duke of Yorks Island group is believed to have been the first railway in PNG.

Deutish-Neuguinea und meine Erteigung (1891), p. 145.

Bottom - Neu Guinea Kompagnie plantation railway at Stephansort. The German official demonstrates his position riding an ox-drawn carriage in the 1890's attended by Javanese servant and driver.

CHAPTER 2. GERMAN NEW GUINEA

New Guinea came under Imperial German administration in 1884. Although it received less attention than the newly acquired African colonies, the Germans had ambitious plans to develop their new South Seas possession. It was intended that railways would play a significant role in this development. This chapter traces the development of railways under the Germans, commencing with an examination of factors which shaped colonial policy in the fatherland, followed by case studies of individual railway applications in New Guinea.

German Imperialism and Industrialism

Germany offers one of the most striking examples of an economy transformed by railways. German states entered the *Railway Age* as backward rural-based economies. Railways played a direct role in establishing industrial technology and stimulated coal mining, metallurgical and engineering industries. In the Ruhr, railways built on their original role of linking coal mines with navigable water founded one of the world's great industrial regions.

The growth and modernisation of the German iron industry and the engineering sector was a direct consequence of the railway. In the northern state of Prussia the bulk of locomotives and rails were imported up to 1842, but after 1850 almost all of these products were produced by local industry. In Germany as a whole, railways accounted for a quarter of total industrial investment[1] Railways served a central role in the rise of Prussia as a European military power. As early as 1843, the Prussian Chief of Staff wrote:

> Every new railway development is a military benefit, and for national defence it is far more profitable to spend a few million on completing our railways than on new fortresses.[2]

Military influences and interests dominated German railway development to a greater degree than elsewhere. A railway section was formed by the Prussian General Staff in 1864 and was upgraded to a Field Railway Section two years later. By 1867, regulations provided for military control of railways in wartime, and this facility was of vital importance in the Franco-Prussian war of 1870. A large proportion of positions on the Prussian railways were reserved for ex-military personnel and this resulted in "a noticeable orderliness and precision about everything connected with German railways." [3]

Colonialism

Industrialisation and militarism generated pressure to expand German trade and influence. German traders commenced operation in Africa and began to arrive in the South Pacific by 1850. The firms Johann Cesar Godeffroy & Sohn and Hersheim & Kompagnie were operating in the Bismark archipelago from 1873. In April 1884, Bismarck told the *Reichstag* that he was prepared:

> to provide Imperial protection against attacks from neighbouring territories or abuse by other European powers for those colonies that have not been artificially created, but result from spontaneous growth. [4]

On 22 June 1884 a German protectorate was proclaimed over *Luderitzland* (South West Africa), followed by Togo (5 July), Cameroon (14 July) and German East Africa (Tanganyika). In the South Seas, a protectorate was declared over German New Guinea on 3 November 1884. The intention was to limit colonial activities to the protection of the trading activities of Hamburg and Bremen companies under the principle, "the flag follows the trade". However, the reality was quite different and the German state was soon called to provide financial support for colonial activities.

Colonial Railway Policy

Agricultural potential and mineral deposits in the colonies constituted wealth only on paper. A good transport system was necessary to exploit this potential wealth. In Africa and New Guinea, navigable rivers were practically non existent, so that porterage was the only means of transport into the hinterland. Construction of railways created the opportunity for the authorities to extend their authority into the interior. In Africa, the first stage of colonial railway building was the penetration line inland from a port to carry minerals and agricultural products.[5] Metre gauge was chosen for railways in Togo, Cameroon and East Africa, while 3 ft 6 in was selected for South-West Africa with an eye to standardisation with South Africa. Light 600 mm gauge lines were constructed in South-West Africa and New Guinea.

Railway construction drew the state into investment in infrastructure. However, the *Reichstag* opposed colonial investment until late 1906 when an election resulted in delegates who were more willing to support railway bills. Rapid colonial railway construction followed and, by 1914 a total of 4,410 km of public railways had been constructed in Africa. The 1906-1914 period also saw significant investment in New Guinea.

Early lines were built to the rules and limitations of the secondary railways of Germany. Only in 1912 was the code of practice for building and operating colonial railways (the *Kolonialeisenbahn Bau-und Betriebsordnung* or KBO) laid down.[6] The KBO established loading gauges for locomotives and rolling stock, standards for permanent way earthworks, bridges and signalling, operating speeds, maintenance procedures and staff regulations. It influenced the construction of an extensive network of 600 mm gauge railways in the Belgian Congo.

Financially, the colonial railways were expected to attain a sufficient rate of return to allow for running expenses, 0.6 per cent repayment and 4.0 per cent interest charges on the initial investment, together with a financial reserve.[7]

Locomotives, rolling stock, rails and other railway equipment were built by metropolitan foundries. Orenstein & Koppell (O&K), Maffei and Hanomag provided locomotives and rolling stock for the standard (1435 mm) and metre gauge railways. For narrow-gauge plantation and construction railways, O&K, Arthur Koppell and Lokomotiv-Fabrik Krauss and Company provided rails, locomotives and rolling stock to lines in the colonies and to many other countries, including Australia.

Neuguinea Colonial Administration

Neuguinea Kompagnie

In 1884 a charter was granted to the *Neuguinea Kompagnie* (NGK) to enter into relations with the native people, to experiment with the cultivation of useful tropical crops, to prepare for settlement and to serve as a basis for administration when established.[8] The NGK was formed by a consortium of Berlin financiers headed by Adolph von Hansemann of the *Disconto-Gellschaft*, one of the largest private banks in the city.[9] Initially the company established its main trading station at Finschhafen on the mainland (*Kaiser Wilhelmsland*), with sub-stations at Hatzfeldthafen, Constantinhafen and Matupit, the latter on the Gazelle Peninsula.

The initial intention of the NGK was to bring thousands of settlers to the colony. However, conditions at Finschhafen were unsatisfactory for European settlement and operations were hampered by excessive red tape from Berlin.[10] The NGK was unable to attract suitable migrants and turned to the establishment of large-scale plantation enterprises using Asian labour.[11]

The company spent lavishly in its attempts to establish new agricultural industries on the mainland. By 1898, the NGK had invested 11 million marks with little return.[12] Tropical pests and disease, an inability to handle the new environment and local hostility, generated by colonial arrogance, brought failure for the German colonising effort. They persisted, with more success, in the islands where the cultivation of coconuts proved more rewarding.

The NGK faced competition from other German trading companies, individual traders and entrepreneurial missionaries. The legendary Emma Forsayth, who was to become widely known as *Queen Emma*, arrived from German Samoa in 1879 to establish a trading station adjacent to the Godeffroy head station at Mioko in the Duke of Yorks islands. In partnership with her brother-in-law, Richard Parkinson, *Queen Emma* established a prosperous business empire with numerous plantations on the Gazelle Peninsula. Parkinson was a pioneer in establishing a scientific approach to agriculture in the new colony.[13] Other German trading houses, notably *Deutsche Handels-und Plantagen Gesellschaft* (DH&PG), which took over Godeffroy & Sohn in 1884, *Nord Deutsche Lloyd* (NDL) and Hernstein & Company, also established plantations and trading enterprises.

Imperial Administration

With the heavy financial losses of the NGK, the German government stepped in to take over the burden of civil administration in 1899. The Imperial government headquarters were established at Herbertshohe (Kokopo), moving to Simpsonhafen (Rabaul) in 1909. The administration sought to encourage villagers to produce copra in order to "train the natives in the habits of work" and overcome their "natural tendency to indolence."[14]

The period from 1900 to 1914 was one of relative prosperity for the German colony. Plantations expanded rapidly in response to strong demand for copra in Europe and good shipping links by NDL steamers.[15] The companies began to make profits and individuals were encouraged to become planters. Land for plantations was purchased from villagers and confirmed as freehold title by the administration.[16] It was widely believed that the welfare of the local people could best be promoted in European-managed enterprises.[17] The Germans demanded strict discipline by labourers and any breach led to punishment such as caning. Medical services and schools were established for the local population. Through the provision of these social services, it was hoped to "coax the natives into becoming part of this expanding economic empire."[18]

Plantation Railways

To provide transport for their trading, plantation and industrial ventures, the Germans laid down light, narrow-gauge railways using materials imported from Germany. Case studies of the most significant lines are presented in the following sections.

The first recorded railway in German New Guinea was a short line from a warehouse to a jetty on Mioko Island in the Duke of York Island group. Godeffroy & Sohn established the trading station there in 1876 although a precise date for the tramway has not been established. A light railway between the wharf and store is depicted in an etching published in 1891[19] and a photograph of 1900.[20] Trucks were apparently hand-pushed on the line. No other references to this operation have been located, although the plantation was listed in the expropriated properties. Nearby on Manuan plantation, there was a narrow-gauge railway, some 1200 metre in length in 1927 with two trucks.[21] This line is reported to be still in operation.[22]

Erimahafen-Stephansort Railway

The NGK established substantial light railway systems of 600 mm gauge to transport produce on their extensive plantations. In 1888, they opened a new tobacco station at Stephansort on Astrolabe Bay, some 40 km south of Friedrich Wilhelmshafen (now Madang) and the station became a focus of company operations in 1891. With the backing of von Hansemann in Berlin, the NGK established the subsidiary Astrolabe Company to take over tobacco growing activities at Stephansort and at Erima a short distance away.

Over the next five years the tobacco growing ventures of the Astrolabe Company constituted the main commercial activity of the German colonial effort in New Guinea. An extensive narrow gauge (600 mm) railway system was established to provide transport on the plantations. The railway equipment, imported from Germany, was operational by 1893.[23]

Initially, a railway line was constructed from Stephansort plantation, north-west though forest country to Erima on the left bank of the Jori (or Gori) River, a distance of some 4.5 km. At Erima, a "big administrative building, drying rooms and secondary buildings" were established.[24] The line then ran north-east for 4 km to port facilities at Erimahafen.

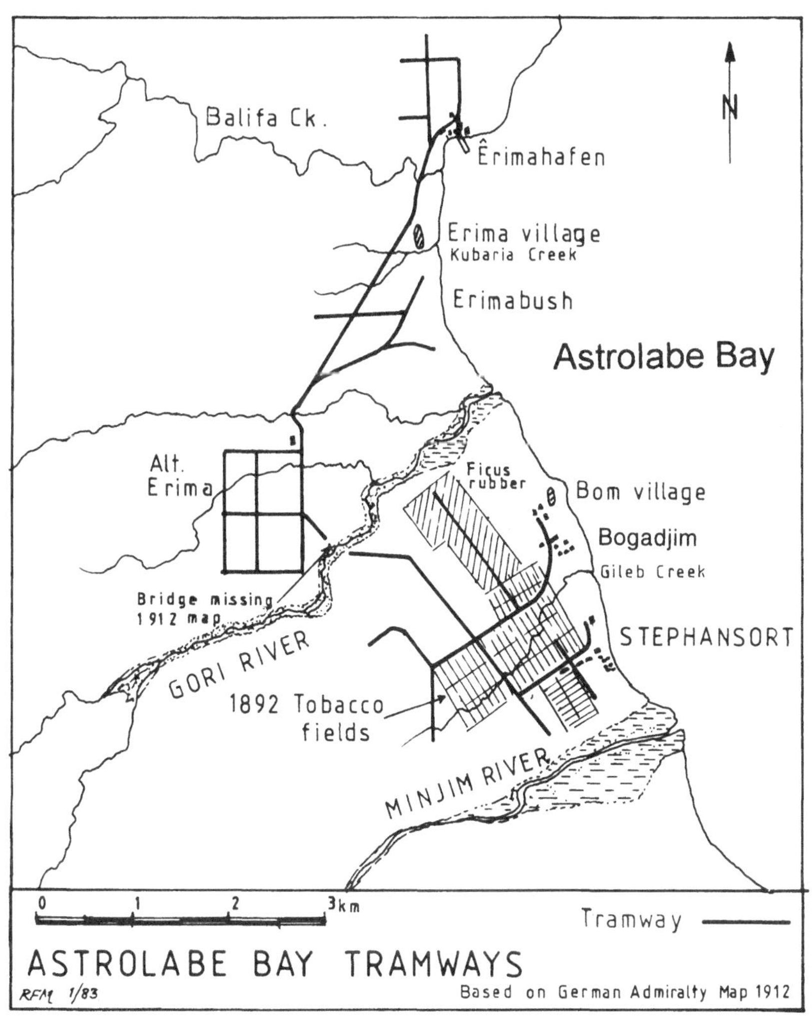

Above - Map of Astrolabe Bay Tramways

Top - Ox-drawn bogie carriage on Erimahafen-Stephansort railway with Javanese driver.
Kreiger, M. *Neu Guinea: bibliothek der landerkunde*, 1899.

Bottom - Tobacco proceesing facilities and railway at Stephansort. Note loaded trucks in background behind ox-drawn carriage.

The Leader, 25 June 1898

There were several extensions to the system. To support planned expansion of tobacco planting on the right bank of the Jori River at Erima in 1895, rail tracks were laid along the main paths through the plantations, bringing the total length of the system to 16 km.[25] The system may have totalled 24 km by 1897.[26]

Although light railway technology was employed, the local environment required investment in significant infrastructure. A large bridge was required to cross the Jori River, but it was inadequate to match the fury of the flash floods of 1897 and was washed away.[27] Thus severed, the Stephansort and Erima railways were subsequently operated as individual systems. Other structures were more enduring. In 1927, seven bridges were listed on the Erima system, including a 43 metre suspension bridge, and there were also seven bridges on the Stephansort system (by then known as Bogadjim plantation). [28]

Operating power for the railway was provided by oxen. It was reported in 1898 that:

> [t]he oxen are much cheaper and more easily managed than engines, and, on the whole, answer very well for a road with so little business, especially as all engines used in the tropics need great care and many repairs.[29]

Rolling stock consisted of bogie wagons for the transport of tobacco (16 remained in 1927) and several bogie carriages for management personnel. The German managers, their families and visitors rode in these well-furnished, ox-drawn carriages while driven by Malay drivers.[30] For the European *mastas*, at least, the railway provided the opportunity of movement in a style which upheld their status.

The NGK established the tobacco venture as a foreign enclave. New Guineans were generally not encouraged as labourers, Asians being preferred for this role. By 1894, there were 450 Chinese, 324 Malay and 664 Melanesian labourers in the fields.[31] Another 173 Javanese and 87 Chinese filled semi-skilled positions.

In 1898 Erima was described as "an insignificant place", with a few dwellings built in Sumatra style for the manager and other officials and the recent addition of a sawmill and furniture manufacturing plant.[32] Most of the field work was undertaken by Chinese labourers. District Commissioner Stuckardt reported a more active scene when he travelled from Stephansort to Erima by railway on 15 November, 1901.[33] He noted that the sawmill at Erima "was a hub of activity".

Astrolabe tobacco leaf sold quite well on the Bremen market, but at grievous cost in men and money. The annual death rate of indentured labourers employed by the Germans between 1887 and 1903 has been estimated at 28 per cent. Production peaked in 1894, when 73 tonnes of tobacco were exported to Bremen, but drought, pests and flash floods affected production in subsequent years. By 1897, the expenses of the tobacco ventures had crippled the Astrolabe Company and it was merged with the parent NGK. The "poor quality of the Asiatic coolies" was claimed to be a contributing factor in the company's demise.[34] Tobacco growing continued at Stephansort on a declining scale until 1901 when the fields were planted to coconuts, cautchouc, guttapercha and ficus rubber.

With the conversion of the plantations to coconuts and ficus rubber after 1901, the railway systems continued to serve the new mode of production. Following World War I, German properties were expropriated and sold to Australian settlers in 1927. There were three lots: Erimahafen plantation with 215 ha planted and 1.6 km of railway; Erimabush plantation, 245 ha planted, 5.6 km of railway and 5 bogie trucks; and Bogadjim plantation, 717 ha and 8 km of railway.[35] The plantations were to come under rival ownership with differing approaches to maintenance of the railway lines. In 1943, Allied Army intelligence reported that the railways were still in existence.[36] However, the lines were destroyed in subsequent fighting and were not restored after the Pacific War.

Friedrick Wilhelmshafen Railways

With the death of officials, the NGK abandoned Finschhafen as their headquarters in 1891 and transferred operations to Friedrich Wilhelmshafen (now Madang). By 1892, some 200 metres of light 600 mm gauge railway was in operation linking the wharf to warehouses.

In 1888, the *Kaiser Wilhelmsland Plantagen-Gesellschaft* was formed in Hamburg for the purpose of growing cocoa and coffee on a plantation at Jomba, 5 km south-west of Friedrich Wilhelmshafen. The NGK established tobacco trials on Jomba in the early 1890s, but these were closed in 1893 when a smallpox epidemic decimated workers. By 1899, a new 60 metre pier had been constructed at Friedrick Wilhelmshafen and the 600 mm gauge light railway was extended 4.5 km from the wharf, through Modilon plantation to Jomba plantation.[37] Kapok, coconuts and cocoa were being grown at Jomba.

Despite the failure of the Astrolabe Company's ventures, von Hansemann in Berlin was reluctant to forsake his vision of vast tobacco estates.[38] In 1900, a further tobacco growing enterprise was initiated on Jomba and Modilon plantations and 270 Chinese coolies were recruited for the enterprise. To upgrade the railway from Jomba to port facilities at Friedrich Wilhelmshafen, railway equipment was to be relocated from Erimahafen.[39] This did not prove practical, so new equipment was probably obtained from Germany. It was planned to continue the line a further 23 km to link up with the railway system at Erimahafen. [40]

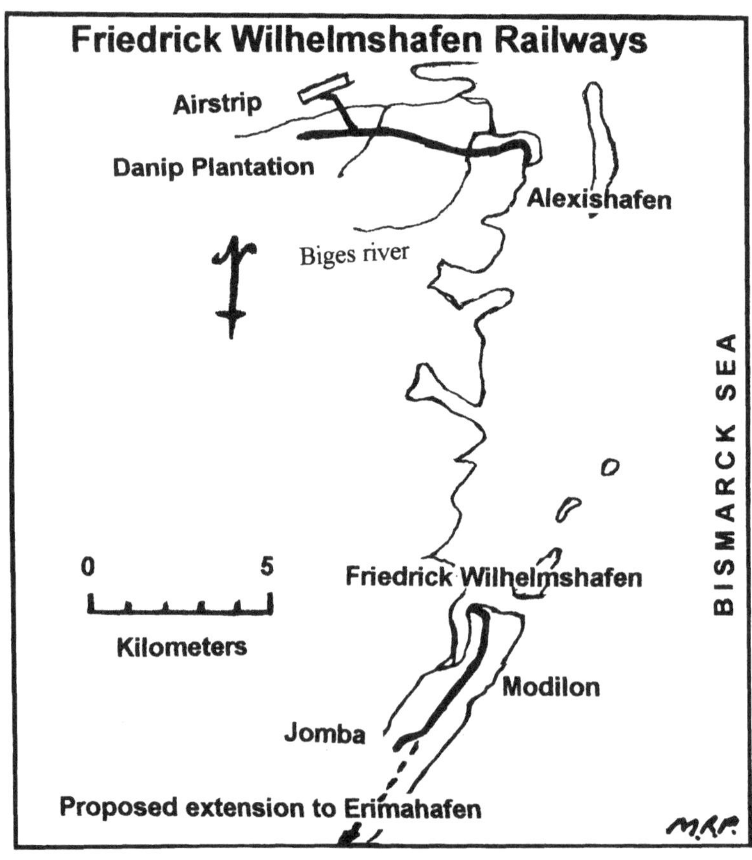

Above - Map of Friedrick Wilhelmshafen Railways

Top - Railway and overseas wharf at Friedrich Wihelmshafen, c. 1892.
Alexander Pfluger, *Samoa und Inselen de Sudsee.* Berlin: Susseroll, nd. (National Library)

Middle - German residence in Friedrich Wihelmshafen with railway line in foreground.
Kreiger, M. *Neu Guinea: bibliothek der landerkunde,* 1899.

Bottom - Large bogie truck hauling coconuts on Modilon Plantation in 1927.
Catalogue of New Guinea Properties, 1927.

Steam locomotives may have been imported in 1901 to operate the upgraded line (and the proposed extension to Erimahafen).[41] An 0-6-0TT locomotive purchased by the Moreton Sugar Mill at Nambour, Queensland in 1904, reputedly came from "a German New Guinea plantation". The NGK abandoned tobacco growing at Jomba in 1903 and with it hopes for an extension of the railway. Accordingly, locomotives would have been surplus to the traffic then offering. Two historians have reported photographs of a steam locomotive among German records.[42] Information recently published in Australia indicates that it is most unlikely that the locomotive at Moreton Mill came from German New Guinea. The identity of the any locomotives at Jomba remains a mystery.

The plantations at Jomba and Modilon were planted to coconuts and ficus rubber after 1903. Three large bogie trucks, each with a capacity of 1000 coconuts, and two 4-wheel trucks were in service in 1927.[43] They were hauled by two oxen.

A substantial new pier was completed at Friedrich Wilhelmshafen in 1902 allowing "the Imperial Mail Steamer to tie up without difficulty and unload from both hatches."[44] The railway laid by the NGK helped to simplify the loading and unloading. The line ran from the large plantation copra shed, through the plantation and alongside the road to the Madang wharf.

The alienation of land by the Germans for their plantation ventures generated deep resentment among the local villagers. The villages of the Madang area comprised seafaring and trading people whose land holdings were confined to the narrow coastal strip and small offshore islands. Large amounts of their land were taken over for plantations in transactions which they little understood.

The dam of resentment broke in July, 1904, when the villagers decided to kill off the foreigners who had disrupted their lives. The plot was uncovered and the ringleaders were captured as they tried to storm the arms depot.[45] One man was shot dead and nine were later executed. Others were exiled to remote government stations.

Gazelle Peninsula Plantations

German pioneers found the rich volcanic soil of the Gazelle Peninsula on the island of New Britain more suited to agriculture and European settlement than the harsh, disease-ridden cond-itions of the mainland. The Emma Forsayth-Richard Parkinson partnership purchased extensive areas of agricultural land on the Gazelle Peninsula to establish coconut plantations from 1882. By 1884 DH & PG had claimed five stations and Hernsheim & Company four stations on the Gazelle Peninsula. The following year the NGK established a head station at Herbertshohe (Kokopo) and set about establishing extensive coconut plantations.

A narrow-gauge railway, 300 metres in length, was constructed at the NGKs Herbertshohe station to link the landing place with a cotton store by 1893.[46] The line was extended to 1000 metres the following year when a new jetty was opened. The railway was listed in the expropriated properties in 1927 as Timbur Concentration Depot.

Nearby, Emma Forsayth was developing Ralum plantation into one of the largest and most impressive in the colony. By 1900, 1050 hectares had been planted to coconuts on Ralum and some 90 tonnes of cotton were also produced.[47] The famous residence of *Gunantambu* was established at Ralum Point. A large two-story office block administered the dealings of the trading empire, there were many stores and copra sheds, residences and a substantial jetty.[48] Dual railway lines ran from the jetty, some 30 metres in length, for about 300 metres to three large copra stores, with a tramway shelter, known as Ralum Depot.[49] This small railway system was still in place in 1943.

Some of the early railway operations symbolise the ingenuity of the new settlers in solving difficult transport problems. Forsayth's Raniolo Plantation on the Gazelle Peninsula was recorded as having a funicular railway across a steep sided valley to the plantation in 1898. A short railway was also established on Forsayth's Kabakaul plantation, linking the jetty to warehouses. After the Pacific War the Production Control Board (predecessor of the Copra Marketing Board) opened a copra-buying depot at Kabakaul and restored the wharf and tramways.[50] The depot was closed in the mid 1960s and the line and sheds left to rust away.[51]

Pondo Plantation

The only German property on the west coast of New Britain was the 500 ha plantation at Pondo. It came under the ownership of the WR Carpenter & Company subsidiary, Coconut Products Ltd (CPL). Plantation railways were operating in the early 1930s.

CPL established a desiccated coconut factory at Pondo, the products of which were marketed under the *Desikoko* brand. Photographs from 1933 depict operations on the railway, with European travellers on trucks being pushed by New Guineans.[52] A report in the *Rabaul Times* in 1936 covered a journey over a well maintained narrow-gauge railway inland to the factory.[53] The enterprise employed nine Europeans and 600 labourers.

The railway system, reputedly of 700 mm gauge, comprised some 8-10 km of lines through the plantation prior to the Pacific War, but was being dismantled by 1963.[54] Rolling stock then comprised a diesel locomotive and about "a dozen" flat wagons. The last section was closed in 1970.

Bougainville Plantation Railways

The islands of Bougainville and Buka (now North Solomons Province) were transferred from the British administered Solomon Islands to German New Guinea in 1886. Initially, German contact was purely nominal and Europeans who ventured into the area did so at their own risk. A number of the plantations on Bougainville were established by Australian or British companies. Numa Numa plantation, originally established by a Dutch planter and later owned by Buka Plantations, was to become the country's largest. Choisel Plantations commenced the first clearing at Soraken in January 1913, with Banin, Arigua and Teopasino being established soon afterwards.[55] By 1914, 30,000 hectares had been alienated for plantations.

These plantations used extensive light railways for the transport of green copra from the fields and processed copra to their wharves. The Numa Numa railway bears the most distinct German heritage. Light railway lines with a total length of 6.5 km were constructed from the wharf through the plantation with four branches in a "H" pattern.[56]

Few reports of railway operations at Numa Numa have been located although there is evidence that a steam locomotive operated there.[57]. The line gained brief media attention in 1927 when an accident occurred on the line. As a result of brake failure, a truck loaded with labourers returning from work tore along the track at increasing speed until it left the rails, "capsizing its human freight and causing some alarming injuries."[58] The manager attended to the injured.

The lines are reported to have been lifted by the Japanese in 1943 and used to mount heavy guns in the mountains.[59] Rails were also used at Asitavi sawmill and to build a copra drier at Tenakau. These rails are of German origin and bear the inscription GHH -11B.[60] A wheelset collected from Numa Numa observed at Wakunai was of 600 mm gauge and bore O&K inscription.[61].

Top left - Pondo Plantation railway, New Britain. Mrs Wood, Mrs. Evensen and Patricia Wood being escorted to the Pondo wharf on the railway, 9 December 1933.

Mrs M Ferguson

Top Right - SVD 700 mm gauge plantation railway, St. Anna Mission, Aitape.

UPNG Library, Fryer Collection

Bottom - Railway line through Taveliai village near Kaliai Catholic Mission, West New Britain.

Curriculum Unit, Department of Education

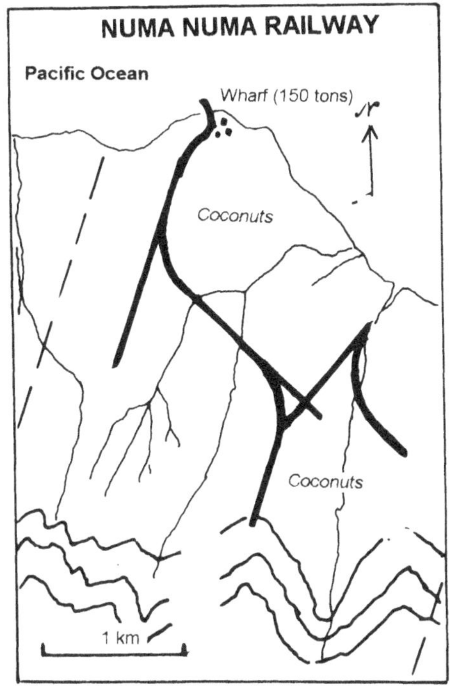

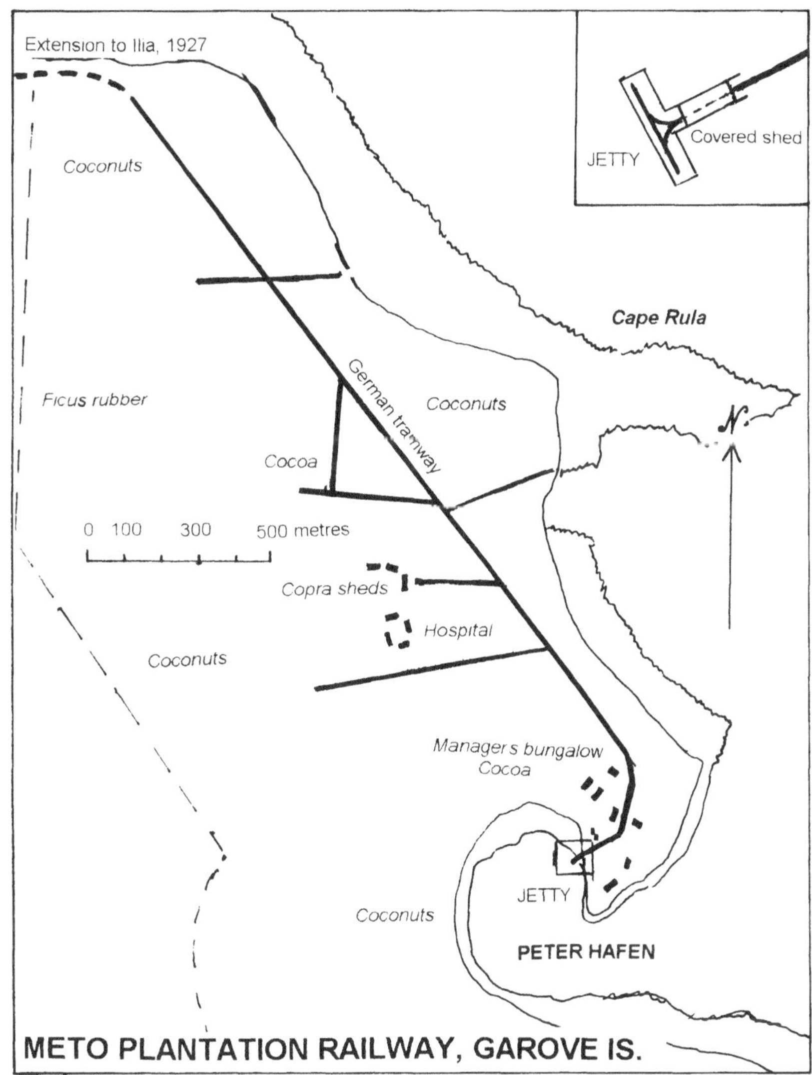

Above - Maps of Numa Numa and Meto Railways

Soraken, Kunua, Baniu, Arigua and Teopasino all had extensive systems by the 1930s, but these probably post-date the German era. They are discussed in chapters 4 and 6.

Other German Plantation Railways

On Garowe Island in the Witu Group of West New Britain, Meto plantation was served by a railway which dates from German times.[62]. The plantation and trading station at Peterhafen was established by Captain Peter Hansen, a Forsayth trader, in the 1890's.[63] A railway line ran from a wharf at Peterhafen, through Meto plantation.[64] It is believed there were several branches on a herring-bone pattern bringing the total length of the system to 4.5 km. The T-jetty had a rail line across the face with a "Y" joining this line to the line on the jetty. A section of the line was operational by 1909.[65] Reports indicate that the railway was operated by oxen or buffalos. The line was subsequently extended to Ilia plantation (Chapter 4). In 1927, the Australian Minister for Territories, Hon. CW Marr, visited Garove Island on the SY *Franklin*.[66]

The islands which now comprise Manus Province were far from the centre of administration and few records are available of German colonial activities in the area. On clusters of atolls, known as the Northwest Islands, Heinrich Rudolph Wahlen took over the rights of Hernsheim & Company and established coconut plantations and a trochus shell venture[67]/. At Longan plantation in the Niningo Group there was a 100 metre railway line from the wharf[68]/. There were three bogie trucks. On nearby Pelleluhu plantation, a light railway from the wharf to plantation buildings was still in operation in 1943[69]/. A 600 mm gauge is likely. No other records have been located.

Mining Railways

Although the Germans actively explored and researched the natural resources of their new colony in the hope of finding new riches, they failed to find mineral wealth. Consequently, there were few mines and associated railways. Phosphate mining was the only significant mining activity.

The Neuguinea Kompagnie established an early phosphate mining venture on Mole Island in the Purdy Group south of Manus Island. In 1888, it was reported that track and rails had been completed for conveying phosphate across the reef surrounding the island for loading onto ships.[70] The venture was short lived. A tropical storm in March 1891 wrecked the installation and the mining operation closed.[71]

Phosphate mining was also carried out in the Micronesian islands administered as part of German New Guinea. Guano rock brought from the island of Nauru to Sydney in 1899 was found to be rich in phosphate. The Pacific Islands Company made a secret assessment of the resource and formed the Pacific Phosphate Company to mine the island in 1902.

To gain German support for the Nauru operation, the company ordered Orenstein & Koppell 610 mm gauge locomotives for their initial mining operations on the British-administered Ocean Island in 1905.[72] Eventually eleven O&K 0-4-0T 610 mm gauge locomotives were to operate on Ocean island. German cooperation to mine the Nauru phosphate was secured through a joint-venture with *Jaluit Gesellschaft* and the use of German engineers to install the mining equipment and 610 mm gauge railway. It is believed three 0-4-0WT Krauss locomotives (B/N 5671-3/1907) were supplied through Arthur Koppell for the railway.[73] Three O&K locomotives followed in 1908-09. Nauru came under Australian control following World War I. The mining and railway operation was taken over by the British Phosphate Commission.

Public Railways

The German state stepped in to provide infrastructure and services in 1899. The level of investment was modest until 1906, when the Reichstag began supporting more lavish colonial investment. In New Guinea, the administration commenced a visionary program for development of transport infrastructure based on the necessary railway network to support a more modern economy. The vision was grand, but well beyond the capacity of budgetary support in this remote economy. Nevertheless, considerable investment was made in roads planned for conversion to narrow-gauge railways with traction by bullocks or by locomotive once plantations were established. The intention was to build bridges over major rivers when the railway was laid. Consequently, roads followed routes that in many cases would come to what seemed an abrupt stop at a river or gorge.[74]   On the east coast of New Ireland the German administration established a network of fine roads under the colourful district officer, Bulominski. Due to difficult navigation conditions, greater emphasis was given to land transport from the junction point at *Nusa* (Kavieng). The main public road, 6 metres wide on average, connected the trading stations on the north and north-east coasts by 1902.[75] The surfaced road extended some 180 km by 1911.

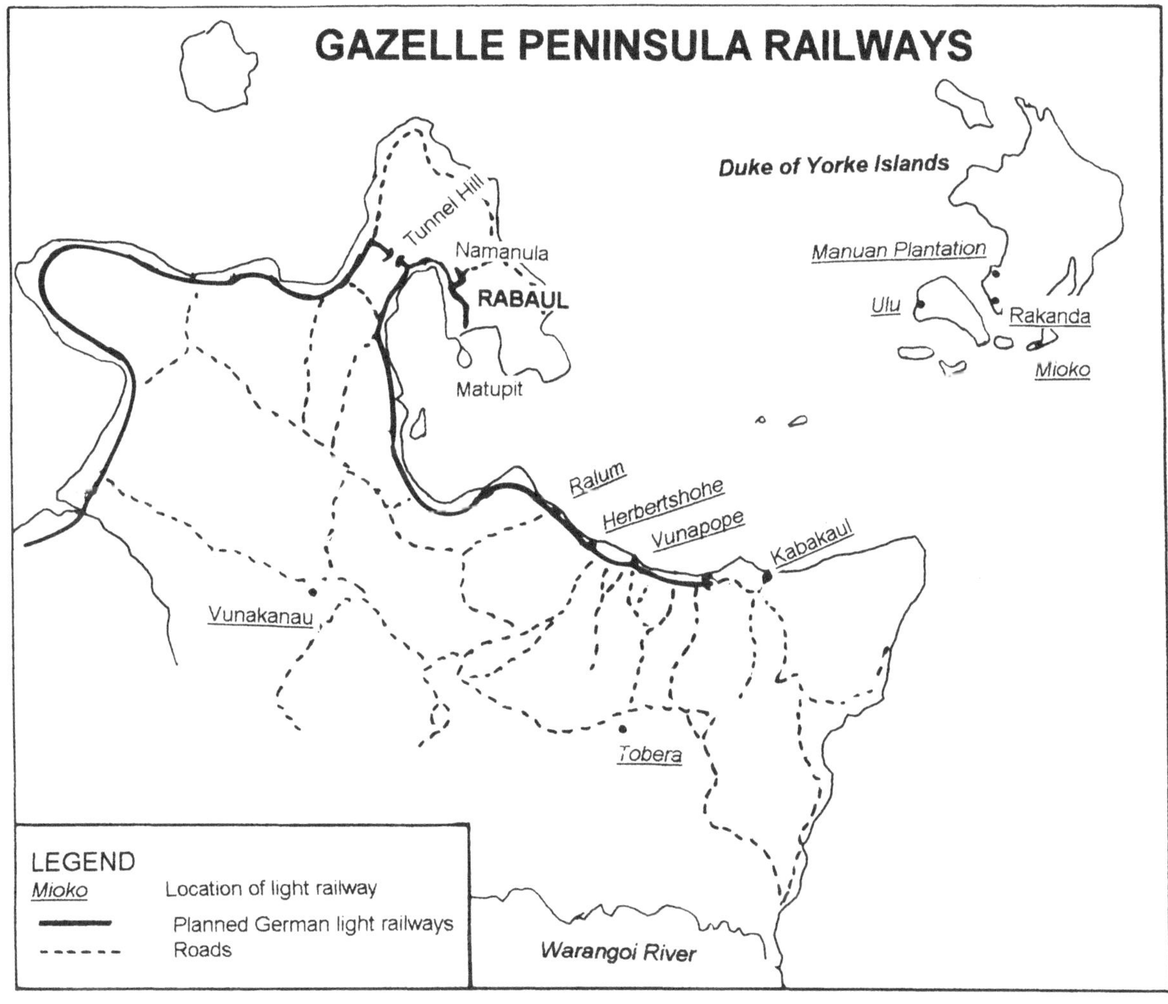

Above - Map of Gazelle Peninsula Railways

Top - Railway tracks at main NDL wharf, SS *Marsina* and *Mindini* are berthed following takeover by Australian occupational force in 1914.

PNG National Archives

Bottom - Mango Avenue, Rabaul with a flatcar on the line to the Botanic Gardens.
National Library, PNG Collection, Photo 317 from *Historishes Bildmaterial our dem Archives des stoatlichen Museums fur Volkerkunde*, Dresden.

On the Gazelle Peninsula a tunnel was built for a railway out of Rabaul. The intention was a continuous line of railway extending for 200 km from the mouth of the Warangoi River to the Baining country. Apart from light street tramways in Simpsonhafen (see below), Tunnel Hill and transport infrastructure on the Gazelle remained as roads.[76]

Railways were also planned for the Friedrich Wilhelmshafen and Aitape districts. In addition to the planned 23 km railway link from the Friedrich Wilhelmshafen to the Stephansort systems, evidence has recently emerged that the Germans planned to extend the railway from Stephansort to the Lower Ramu flats where they hoped to tap alluvial gold washed down from the hills. [77]

Significantly for PNG, this bold vision for an extensive narrow-gauge railway network was never realised due to the European War of 1914. However, public railways were established in Simpsonhafen (Rabaul) and *Nusa* (Kavieng).

Rabaul Tramway

In 1905, *Norddeutscher Lloyd* (NDL) established a settlement and wharf at Simpsonhafen (Rabaul) on Blanche Bay. The German administration moved their headquarters to Simpsonhafen in 1909 and a flourishing town soon took shape as a trading and service centre for the colony. The town plan included wide tree-lined avenues which provided space for footpaths, a tramline and roadway under the shady trees. The *Neuguinea Kompagnie* (NGK) built a jetty and large warehouse 300 metres north of the main NDL wharf, while Hernstein & Company established a smaller jetty 150 metres south of the main wharf. A coaling jetty, copra wharf and Tobai wharf on the western shore were also built during German times.

A narrow gauge tramway network was constructed to connect the wharves of the NDL, NGK and Hernsheim & Company to their business houses, administration offices, post office, Chinatown and hospital. The purpose of the Rabaul tramways was to facilitate the transport of goods to the German business houses. As urban street tramways, it appears that the lines were built to the German standard narrow gauge of 750 mm.

Records suggest that wagons were hand-pushed on the tramway. The role of the local Tolai people in railway operation was to provide the manpower for pushing wagons. In 1914 the *Sydney Mail* reported.[78]:

> it is a curious fact that each residence in the settlement has a line like this [photograph of a hand-pushed wagon conveying mail] connecting it with the wharf, so that goods can be conveyed direct from the boat side.

As the seat of German administration and the focus of Australian occupational forces, the Rabaul tramway system is well documented in photographs. They depict a complex pattern of light rail lines on the wharves and into large warehouses, with lines along the sides of most major streets. A recently located photograph provides evidence that the system included a branch line up Namanula Hill to the Governor's residence.[79] In 1996, a section of this line was uncovered by erosion associated with Rabaul's volcanic eruption of 1994.[80] Reconstruction of this evidence indicates that the line from the NDL wharf, along Namanula Street and up Namanula Road to Government House was 3.3 km in length, while other street lines added 1.3 km, making a total system of 4.6 km.

In September 1914 an Australian Expeditionary force captured Rabaul. German New Guinea became an occupied territory. This brought a reordering in the relationship between colonial *masta* and Tolai labourer, as evidenced in this description of unloading operations from ship to tramway trucks:

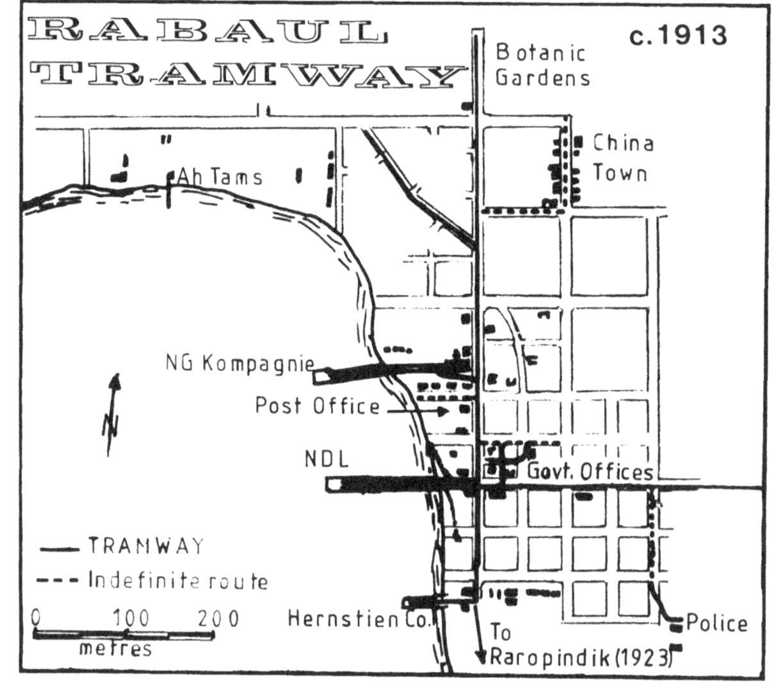

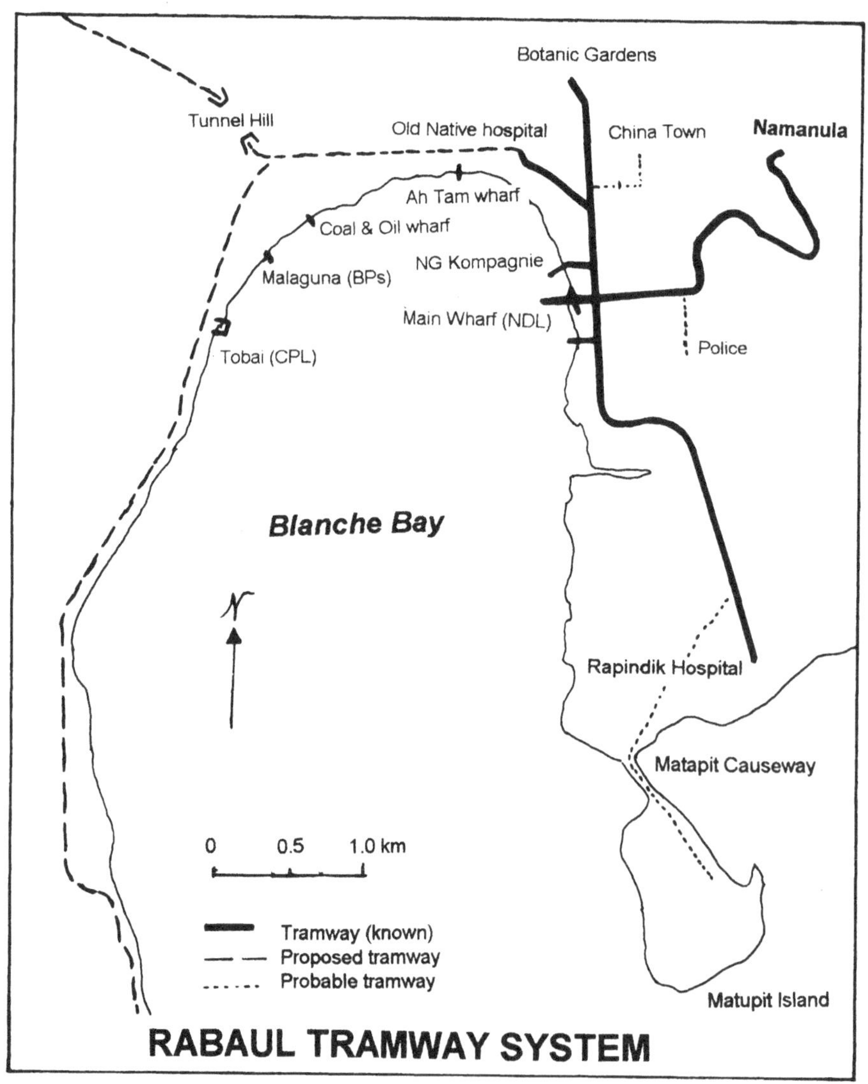

Above - Maps of Rabaul tramways

Top - Railway lines from Neu Guinea Kompagnie wharf to wharehouse, Rabaul

Mackenzie

Bottom - Japanese Naval officers inspecting Australian guard of honour on Rabaul wharf amid railway tracks in 1914.

Australasian Post, 22 September 1960

One fatigue party has been detailed to take out the cargo, and another to transport it to the stores. They are - unaccustomed to wharf lumping - battling with heavy boxes of foodstuffs - dragging along heavy truck loads of necessaries - perspiring till the sweat runs in streams almost down into their boots, but, nevertheless, cheerful - shouting, yelling, and cracking jokes at the stupid *kanakas*, who are supposed to help, but can do nothing from amazement at seeing so much *kai-kai* - much more than they ever dreamt could possibly exist - and taken completely off their feet by observing the funny white fellows from Australia doing manual labour.[81]

During the occupation no further development of railways took place. The Rabaul tramlines continued to operate for the next 12 years under German ownership, but without any more capital investment. Because the Germans were unsure of their future they were both unable and unwilling to make any improvements to the capital assets of their businesses. The assets were eventually expropriated for Australian companies and new lines were built by the administration. The subsequent history of the system is discussed in chapter 4.

Kavieng Tramways

The port of Kavieng was the second most important after Rabaul, shipping about 1000 tonnes of copra per month from plantations on both the east and west coasts.[82] A short section of narrow-gauge railway was established from the wharf to the customs house and bulk copra store in Kavieng township.[83] A set of railway wheels recently located in Kavieng which were used on the railway are of 600 mm gauge.

Photographs of the Kavieng wharf in the 1930s depict a double tramline with branches, operated by hand-pushed flatcars. Another photograph, dated 1937, shows a labour line standing on a tramline leading away from a jetty.

Mission Railways

Missionaries were a key force in the efforts of colonialists to forge their subjective people into their own likeness. While their attention was focused on pastoral care, education and health, a commercial base from plantation development or exploitation of forest resources served to fund God's work. Thus, missionaries followed as their commercial competitors and established railways to transport their produce from field and forest. From 1901 through to the Second World War, sawmilling in New Guinea was dominated by missionaries who were prepared to work for higher goals than mere commercial profit. Isolation from external markets limited sawmilling activities to the small domestic market. Under these circumstances, the returns to logging and sawmilling were not attractive and few commercial ventures lasted for more than the initial period of hope. Logging and timber enterprises were left to German missionaries.

The movement of large logs from the forest to a central sawmill and the dispatch of sawn timber required efficient transport. The use of rivers to float logs downstream was rarely practical because of New Guinea's shallow, fast flowing streams, while some of the most valuable species (*kwila* for instance) were too heavy to float. Railways were therefore indispensable for the early timber operations. Compared with the plantation railways, the missionaries chose heavier lines of 700 mm gauge for hauling heavy logs. However, they initially relied on manpower for the haulage task.

Methodists

Methodist missionaries were the first to establish themselves in New Guinea. George Brown founded a station at Port Hunter in the Duke of York Islands in 1875. They established Ulu plantation to generate income for their work. A light railway, about 300 metres in length and of 600 or 610 mm gauge was constructed from the copra shed to the wharf. Plantation workers pushed flat trucks over the line[84]. The construction date of the railway is not known, although the plantation is believed to date from 1875. It was probably destroyed by heavy fighting in the area during 1944. The line was rebuilt during the 1950s and was still in operation in 1982.

Lutheran Immanuel Synod

The Methodists were established prior to the German proclamation, but were seen as foreigners. A more German spiritual presence was favoured. In 1886 the Lutheran Immanuel Synod of Adelaide sent Johann Flierl to commence mission work in *Kaiser Wilhelmsland.* He initially established a station (Simbang) at Finschhafen.[85] Despite suffering from malaria, Flierl stayed on after the NGK withdrew its administration from the area. To escape the disease problems of the coast, Flierl established an inland station on Sattelberg mountain in 1892.

The primary intent of the Lutheran missionaries was evangelical, although coconut plantations and sawmills were also established. A photograph exists of the Rev. Pilhofer with "mission-helpers" posing in front of a light railway line at Sattelberg.[86] No further information on this operation has been located.

German Lutheran missionaries in Morobe established a small sawmill at Butawung, near Finschhafen in the early 1920s. It operated through the 1930s, cutting 15-30,000 super feet of timber per year. A railway for the transport of logs and/or timber is reported. [87]

Sacred Heart Mission Railways

The first Catholic missionaries, from the French Most Sacred Heart of Jesus order, arrived at Matupit Island in Simpsonhafen in September 1882 and established a mission station at Vunapope, near Herbertshoehe (Kokopo) in 1889. Under the leadership of Monseigneur Couppe, the *Vicariate Apostolic* of the Bismarck Archipelago, they actively sought commercial ventures.[88] The mission established plantations, undertook sawmilling and investigated the possibility of starting a brewery. By 1900, they had planted 460 ha to coconuts on three Gazelle plantations and they dominated the sawmilling industry in the Islands region for over 70 years. Sacred Heart missionaries also played an important role in mobilising labour for other plantations. In 1902, the German administration reported:

> Thanks to the service of the Mission of the Most Sacred Heart of Jesus, a large new area has been opened up for labour recruiting in the territory of the Sulka tribes around Cape Orford. [89]

At the Sacred Heart Mandres plantation at Weberhafen, in the Wide Bay area of New Britain, it was reported in 1901 that the "the jungle is full of magnificent Eucalyptus trees" and that the Bishop planned to start a sawmill there.[90] The Toriu River sawmill and a 700 mm gauge timber logging railway was operational by 1902.

Photographs of the Toriu River operation depict a substantial steam-operated sawmill.[91] One photograph shows at least 14 local labourers hauling a "record Eucalypt trunk" by rope over a bridge on the railway. [92] Four Europeans pose in front of the log dressed in white safari suits and pith helmets. The Toriu River operation closed in 1917. The railway and sawmill was moved to Kurindal a few miles north. [93] This mill cut 800,000 super feet of timber in 1923-24.

In 1928 the operation moved west again to Ulamona mission, in the shadow of Mount Ulawan, an active volcano known as *The Father.*[94] Here, a 700 mm gauge logging railway was constructed from the sawmill inland behind Sule for approximately 10 km. [95] A line of lighter construction was laid over 100 metres from the mill down to the jetty to carry the sawn timber for loading onto ships.

Top left - Road through Tunnel Hill at Rabaul. This was to form part of an extensive light rail network on the Gazelle Peninsula.
Historishes Bildmaterial our dem Archives des staatlichen Museums fur Volkerkunde, Dresden.
PNG National Library photo 332.

Top right - Kavieng wharf with tramlines and flat cars.
Courtesy: Burns Philp.

Bottom - Boluminski Highway, New Ireland 1914.

MacKenzie, p. 294.

Sacred Heart Mission Logging Railways

Top - Mission labourers hauling a record Eucalyptus deglupta log on the Toriu River logging railway, c. 1910. German missionaries supervise.

Historishes Bildmaterial our dem Archives des staatlichen Museums fur Volkerkunde, Dresden.
PNG National Library photo 314.

Bottom - View of the Toriu River sawmill, c. 1910.

Ibid. PNG National Library Photo 313

A steam locomotive was imported for the Kuriendal logging tramway in 1928. It was transferred to Ulamona with other equipment shortly afterward. A second steam locomotive, reported to be Arn. Jung Locomotivfabrik B/No. 8644/1938, arrived in 1938/39. This was an 0-6-0WT of 700 mm gauge supplied to "Emile Nolting Oliva". A diesel-powered locomotive was reported at Ulamona in 1943. It is known that the Jung locomotive was converted to an 0-6-0 diesel mechanical unit. It was still in service at Ulamona in 1986. Post-war, a steam locomotive was reported to be abandoned with shrapnel holes in the boiler. [96]

By 1966, logging was taken over by tractors, skidders and trucks. The logging railway was abandoned, but railway operations continued at the sawmill. The diesel locomotive and about 500 metres of track remained in operation into the 1990s.

At their Vunapope headquarters, the Sacred Heart Mission established a sawmill and timber dressing shops where timber from the Toriu River, Kurindal and Ulamona operations was prepared for the domestic market.[97] The complex was in operation by 1921, and was progressively expanded over the years. It was served by a 700 mm gauge railway system from the jetty to copra sheds and timber yards, over which trucks were hand-pushed. The origins of the railway have not been identified, but it was reported in 1943.[98]

A new jetty, some 100 metres in length, was opened in 1962.[99] Field inspections by the authors 1980 and in 1991 identified some 550 metres of railway with several branches serving a ship repair yard, timber dressing facilities, timber storage sheds and a copra store. In 1980, a bogie wagon was still in use for moving timber around the yard and there were four wagons in storage. Two flat wagons were still there in 1991, although the railway was no longer in use.

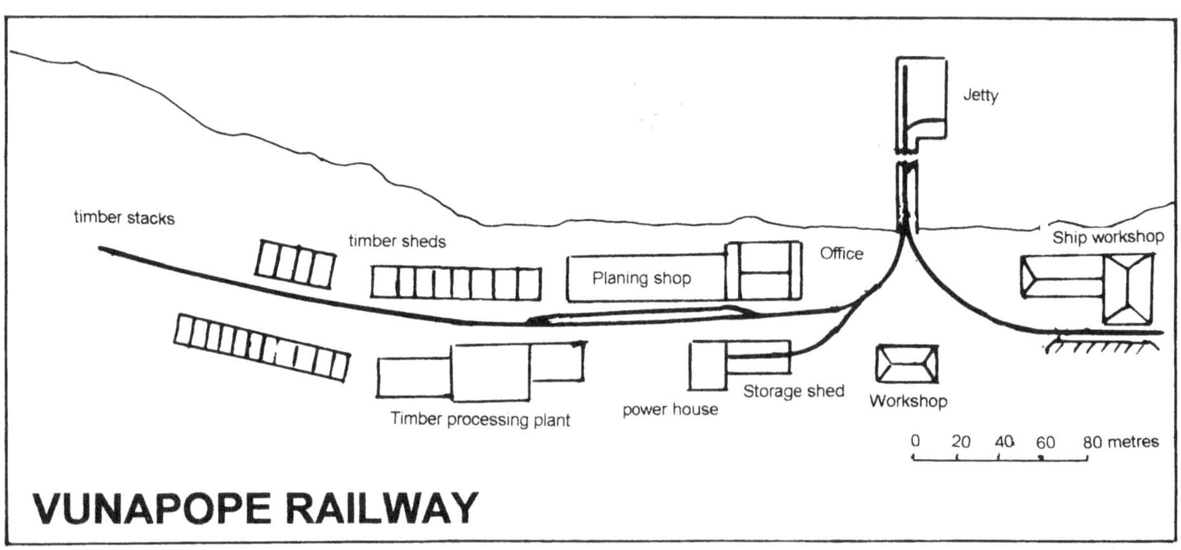

Above - Map of Vunapope Railway

Top - Ulamona sawmill, West New Britain. Diesel 0-6-0 locomotive built on frame of Arn Jung steam locomotive and logging trucks, c. 1960.

PNG National Archives

Bottom - Timber stacks and railway yard, Ulamona sawmill,c. 1960.

PNG National Archives

Societas Verbi Divini

The most commercially active mission was the Catholic Society of the Divine Word (*Societas Verbi Divini,* SVD). Bishop Eberhard Limbrock arrived at Friedrich Wilhelmshafen in 1896 as Apostolic Prefect. The SVD combined commerce with missionary work in order to make their operations as independent as possible from overseas financial sources.[100] Limbrock believed that the mission could not fulfil its spiritual aims without the "civilising" influence of industrial work habits. By 1914 the SVD had 18 mission stations in the Sepik-Ramu area with more land under coconuts than the NGK. They also operated significant sawmilling ventures.

The SVD expansion into plantations included the venture at Saint Anna mission, near Aitape in today's West Sepik Province. In accordance with SVD policy to become self-reliant, the station head, Br Edward Irlenbush initiated a program to clear virgin forest at St. Anna on July 27, 1903, for a large plantation.[101]

Plantation railways, probably to the SVD "standard" gauge of 700 mm, were constructed to service the fields. A 1935 photograph of the plantation depicts a substantial railway line through well-maintained coconut palms.[102]. A 1 mile (1.6 km) line running from the St Anna boathouse to the plantation drier was reported in 1939. There were four 4-wheel light trucks.

Alexishafen Railways

German New Guinea's most ambitious industrial enterprise was established in 1905 by the SVD mission at Alexishafen, on Sek Harbour, 15 km north of Friedrich Wilhelmshafen. Father Limbrock purchased what was described as swampland at Alexishafen, where a large steam-powered sawmill was in operation by the end of 1905. [103] Its initial purpose was to cut timber for mission houses and schools for what was to become the SVDs headquarters in 1909. A school for catechists was established, together with a boarding school for boys and girls. A huge timber cathedral was completed in 1932.

The equipment for the sawmill and railway, including a steam engine, were ordered from Germany. They arrived in Friedrich Wilhelmshafen in October 1905 and were transported to Alexishafen on lighters borrowed from the NGK. [104] The steam engine, weighing 4.5 tonnes, was the centre of much attention when it commenced operations on 5 December, 1905:

> the utmost excitement prevailed amongst the black helpers ... though they had no idea what the 'strange objects' were for. They were especially bewildered as to what the "great pot" - as they called the locomotive - would do. All were gathered about this enigma, when suddenly the whistle sounded for the fist time. At first they opened their mouths and eyes to their utmost, holding their ears, while some ran away in terror. The astonishment, however, reached its height when the locomotive was set in motion, and all the other machines were likewise started. The natives regarded it as a great honour to be assigned to assist at a machine, and made it their ambition to learn everything necessary about it as quickly as possible.

At first logs were cut within the immediate area of the mill, but it was soon necessary for a 700 mm gauge railway to be constructed some 4 km into the forest to haul logs to the mill. There were a number of substantial bridges including a roofed bridge spanning the Biges River. Log bogies were hauled by oxen. Other photographs depict German colonial officials riding on 4-wheel flatcars hauled by donkeys or mules, while buffalo are shown hauling V-hoppers for the haulage of sand and gravel for construction projects. The SVD owned 37 railway trucks in 1919.[105] In 1921-22, the sawmill cut over a million super feet of timber. [106]

Passenger transport on the railway was improved in the 1920s. To give an example, in 1929, District Officer A J Hunter travelled from Alexishafen to Danip, the mission outstation, on a

Top - This classic photo depicts a group of SVD missionaries on a flatcar hauled by a donkey team crossing a substantial bridge at Alexishafen, c. 1914.

Courtesy, Missionaries of St. Michael, Germany

Bottom - A buffalo-drawn hopper wagon transports material from a construction site at Alexishafen.

Word - SVD Mission

rail car provided by Bishop Wolff. [107]. In 1935, the SVD imported an aeroplane from MIVA in Germany to service its outlying mission stations.[108] An airstrip was constructed 3.8 km from Sek and was linked to the station by a tramline.[109] The rail motor was presumably a boon to those with the privilege of travelling by air.

Alexishafen mission, the sawmill and the railway were destroyed by bombing during World War II. The railway was not rebuilt, any salvageable equipment being transferred to Marienberg. [110]

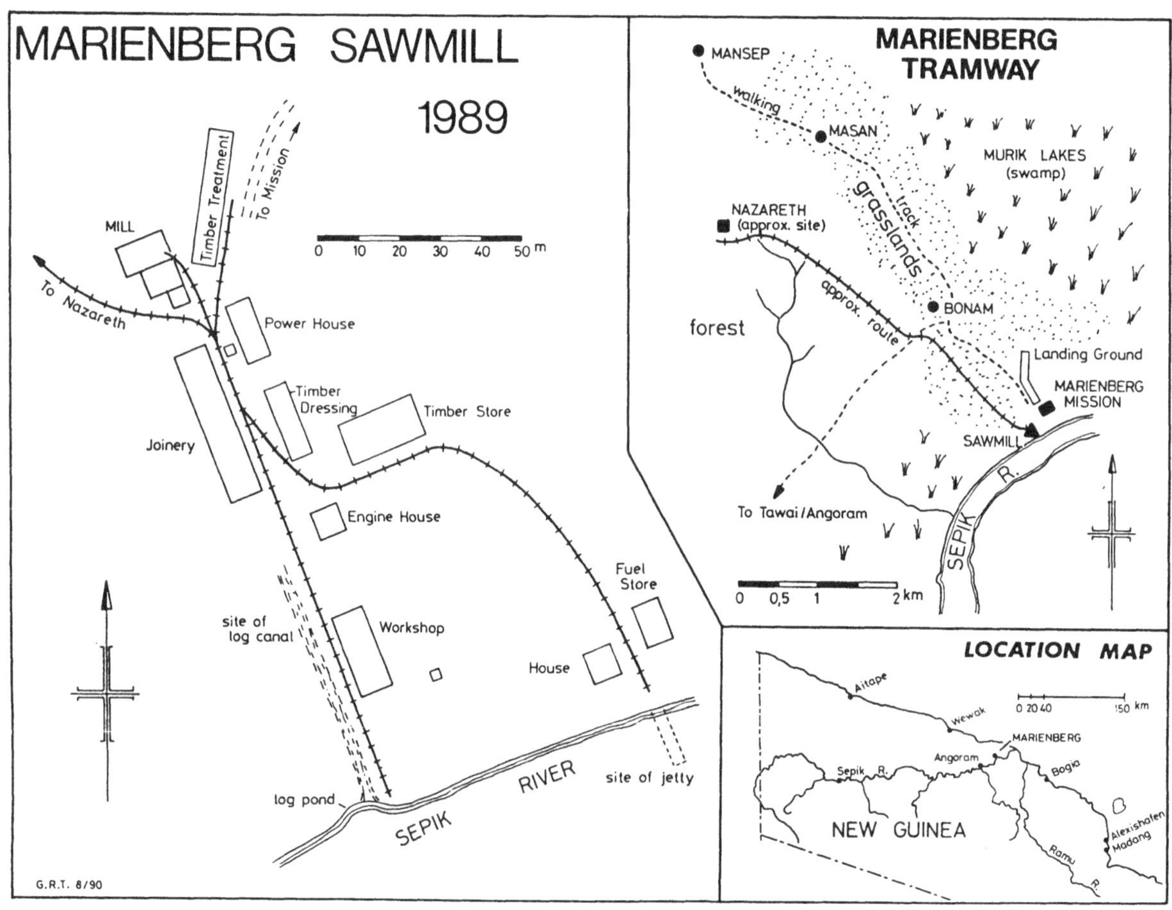

Above - Map of Marienberg Railway

Marienberg Sawmill and Railway

SVD missionaries, led by Father Franz Kirschbaum, established a station at Marienberg on the lower Sepik River in 1913. They selected a prominent hill overlooking the mighty river, about 60 km from the mouth. It was the first European settlement on the Sepik.[111] The station was in its infancy when an Australian flotilla sailed up the Sepik and captured the German stations at Marienberg and Angoram. A sawmill was established to cut timber for station construction from an early date. A first-hand report in 1922 found an operating sawmill, a number of permanent houses. a large church and farm produce, including goat and mare's milk. [112].

By 1939, Marienberg was the service centre for a string of eight mission stations along the Sepik. Their timber needs were met by a steam sawmill located in the bush at Nazareth behind Bonam village. A 700 mm gauge railway, about 6 km in length, transported sawn timber from the mill to Marienberg station for shipment.[113] Motive power was by buffalos. However, grades were in favour of the load. Wagons were allowed to free-wheel downgrade and the buffalo were hitched up again at the bottom. Oral sources indicate that two trips were made from the mill to Marienberg each day.

In 1942, Japanese military forces occupied the Sepik region. They occupied Marienberg and Nazareth, although the sawmill was not made operational. Fierce battles and Allied bombing in 1944 resulted in the complete destruction of Marienberg station.

The SVD missionaries returned after the war and set about rebuilding their station. A new sawmill was established on the river bank adjacent to the station using salvaged equipment from Alexishafen and Japanese operations in the region. The logging railway survived the war, but all draught animals were killed. It saw limited post-war use, with local villagers employed to operate the line. They hauled log wagons up the grades, then rode them free-wheeling down the grades.[114] Forestry officers visiting the mill in 1951 report that most logs were brought in by truck or floated down the river, but the railway was used to bring in heavy kwila logs.[115] The sawmill complex at Marienberg was expanded into an extensive industrial enterprise during the 1960s. A network of railway lines was established to serve the various facilities: a log pond on the river, sawmill, joinery shop, workshops, timber storage sheds and jetty. However, rails from the Nazareth line were taken up to construct power poles at the station.

The missionaries sought to install industrial discipline among the local workers. Time discipline was promoted through strict working hours signalled by a siren. In the joinery shop, volunteer lay workers from Austria trained local workers in carpentry skills. For a brief period, Marienberg became an enclave of Western energy and efficiency, with 60-70 people employed in industrial endeavour.[116] Ships regularly called at the jetty to load timber for mission houses on the Sepik, the Wewak Hospital, private houses in Wewak town, mission stations in the Wewak Islands and Wuvulu Islands.

The thriving industrial operation at Marienberg came to a sudden end shortly before Independence.[117] The Sepik area was a focus for rising nationalist sentiments and long-standing resentments over the hierarchical power structures at Marienberg surfaced in a claim for increased wages. A strike resulted and management called in government Labour Officers to help resolve the conflict. Workers returned, but the underlying resentment of landowners over their lack of involvement in management and decisions affecting their future, remained.

The mission offered to hand over the business to the landowners. A 12 month trial period was initiated for landowners to carry out logging and operate the sawmill. However, they had not developed the expertise to manage such an enterprise. The sawmill and related industries collapsed.With the failure of the sawmilling enterprise, relations between the mission and surrounding villagers deteriorated. Claims were made for the return of mission land, stealing of mission property occurred and sabotage of mill equipment was alleged. In 1989, the sawmill, equipment, remaining railway lines and a single railway truck stood rusting as forest regrowth gradually reclaimed the area. Two Polish priests tended the spiritual needs of a declining flock and guarded the remaining mission property against an increasingly hostile community. On the manse walls, faded, fungus-ridden photographs and pith helmets bore testimony to the hopes and values of a colonial era. The mission community, despondent and reduced to bare subsistence living, hoped for an industry revival which might once more generate employment opportunities.

Marist Brothers

On the island of Bougainville the missionary zeal was in the hands of the Marist order, which had Franco-German origins and had links with Oceania rather than the rest of New Guinea. The Marist missionaries entered Bougainville from the Solomons and they generated a sense of affinity among their followers in the two areas.[118] Several short railway lines were established by Marist missionaries in the 1960s and these are covered in Chapter 6.

Top - Donkey-powered train on the Alexishafen railway. The train has just crossed the covered bridge over Biges River on the line to the airstrip.

Allied Forces South West Pacific, Geographical Section, Terrain .Study, Madang No., Vol. 2, photos

Bottom - Labourers pushing a log from the Sepik River to the sawmill at Marienberg, c. 1955.

PNG National Archives

Notes to Chapter 2

1 Fremdling, R, "Railroads and German economic growth: a leading sector analysis with a comparison to the United States and Great Britain", *Journal of Economic History*, 37 (1977), p. 585.

2 Quoted by Richards, J and MacKenzie, JM, *The railway station: a social history*, Oxford, Oxford UP, 1986, p. 257.

3 *Ibid.*, p. 99,

4 Quoted by Schoeter, H and Ramaer, R, *German colonial railways then and now*, Krefeld, Rohr Verlag, 1994, p. 8.

5 *Ibid.*, p. 11.

6 Schoeter, H and Ramaer, R, *op. cit.*, p. 15.

7 *Ibid*, p. 20.

8 Sack P and Clark, D (eds), *German New Guinea: the annual reports* (GNGAR), Canberra ANU Press, 1979; 1886-87 Report.

9 Jacobs, M, "German New Guinea", in P Ryan (ed), *Encyclopedia of Papua New Guinea.* Melbourne University Press, p. 486.

10 Souter, G, *New Guinea: the last unknown*, Sydney, 1963, p. 22.

11 GNGAR, 1886-87, p. 42.

12 Jacobs, *op. cit.*, p. 487.

13 McKillop, RF and Firth, S, "Foreign intrusion and the establishment of agricultural institutions" in D Denoon and C Snowden (eds), *A time to plant and a time to uproot: a history of agriculture in Papua New Guinea*, Port Moresby, Univ. of PNG, nd, p. 90.

14 GNGAR, 1900-01, p. 217.

15 MacKenzie, SS, *The Australians at Rabaul,* 1932, p. 112.

16 *Ibid.*, p. 273.

17 Rowley, CD, *The Australians in German New Guinea: 1914-21*, Melbourne, 1958, p. 106.

18 Quoted by Douglas, J, "Taim bilong ol Jeman", *Paradise* magazine, No. 30, July, 1981, p. 27.

19 *Deutich - Neuguinea und meine Ersteigung des Finisterre = Gebirgen.* Hugo Boller , Union Deutshe Yerlagsgesellschaft. 1891, p. 145 (etching) & p. 285 text (in German).

20 Hesse Wartegg, E, *Samoa, Bismardarchipel und Neuguinea: drei deutsche kolonien in der Sudsee*, Leipzig, Weber, 1902 p. 184

21 *Rabaul Times*, August 5th 1927.

22 Iseop Jason, interview Kavieng, September 1995

23 GNGAR, 1893-94. p. 96.

24 Kreiger, M, *Neu Guinea: Bibliothek der Landerkunder*, Berlin, Alfred Schall, 1899, p. 238. Translation by Mrs H Zalazar.

25 GNGAR, 1895-96, p. 120.

26 McKillop, RF, "Tramways and oxen: the Neu Guinea Kompagnie tramways of Astrolabe Bay, Papua New Guinea", *Light Railways*, No. 81, July 1983, p.14-16, based on German maps.

27 GNGAR, 1897-98, p. 131.

28 *Catalogue of New Guinea properties*, Expropriation Board, Comm. of Aust., Melbourne, 1927.

29 *The Leader*, 25 June, 1898, p. 5.

30 Kreiger, M, *op. cit.*, p. 238. Hesse-Wartegg, E, *op. cit.,,* p. 61 (translation R Moser).

31 GNGAR, 1893-94, p. 95.

32 *The Leader*, 25 June, 1898, p. 5.

33 *Deutsches Kolonialblatt* 1902 Vol XII p71-72 (Translation by Fr Tschauder - 1975)

34 GNGAR, 1895-96, p. 120.

35 *Catalogue of New Guinea properties*, Expropriation Board, Comm. of Aust., Melbourne, 1927.

36 Allied Geographical Section, South West Pacific Area, Terrain Study (AGS SWPA TS), No. 59, 6/8/1943. Area Study of Madang Volume 1 text and Maps p 29, 40, 140.

37 *Deutsches Kolonialblatt* 1899; Translation by Fr Tschauder 1975. The GNG AR of 1896-97 reports plans for construction of the line, but in 1898-99 it states that the cost was too high. The following year it was reported that one third of the track had been laid and it was apparently completed in 1900-01.

38 Jacobs, *op. cit.*, p. p. 487.

39 GNGAR, 1898-99, p. 165.

40 GNGAR, 1900-01, p. 216.

41 From correspondence among locomotive historians (Peter Hodge to Charles Small, April 1964). Krauss 4679/1900 was delivered to *Auswartiges Amt. Kolonial Abteilung* and shipped from Hamburg to Neu Guinea on 10 April, 1901. However Krauss record show 4679 went to South West Africa. Five Krauss locomotives (four 610 mm guage and one 600 mm guage) delivered to Arthur Koppel in 1900-01 have unknown destinations.

42 Pers. com., W Gammage and SW Firth.

43 *Catalogue of New Guinea properties*, Expropriation Board, Comm. of Aust., Melbourne, 1927.

44 GNGAR, 1902-03. p 11

45 Douglas, J, *op. cit.*, p. 27.

46 GNGAR, 1893-94, p. 94.

47 *Ibid*, 1899-1900.

48 Robson, RW, *Queen Emma*, Brisbane, Robt. Brown, 1994, p. 153.

49 Catalogue of New Guinea Properties - First group p 216 -217.

50 Neville Threlfall, letter, 10 April, 1984.

51 Field observation by author in 1981.

52 Correspondence and photographs from Mrs Ferguson, 6 March 1979.

53 *Rabaul Times* August 14th 1936, "Around the group (continued) on SS *Montoro*" by Gordon Thomas.

54 M B Hart, Manager Coconut Products Ltd, letters 6 June 1978 and 9 March 1984..

55 *Rabaul Times*, Friday July 10 1931, "Some Reminiscences of Buka" by Gordon Thomas.

56 AGS SWPA TS, No. 41, Mandated Solomons, Map No. 4844, 1943.

57 Numa Numa Manager, Mr Campbell, interview 1981. Reports a photograph of a steam locomotive.

58 *Rabaul Times*, 4 November, 1927.

59 M Havine and villagers, interview along Numa Numa Trail, April 1986.

60 Field observation, M Pearson, 1980, 1981 and 1983. Correspondence Mrs Stewart.

61 M Pearson, 1983.

62 New Guinea - Report on Expropriated Properties and Businesses. The Parliament of the Commonwealth of Australia 6/8/1924. Photograph of Peterhafen wharf showing 7 railway trucks.

63 Robson, RW, *op. cit.*, p. 201-2.

64   AGS SWPA TS, No. 57, Study of West New Britain, 1943, Map 11, based on German charts and local informants. Map courtesy Burns Philp.

65   German Admirality chart of Peter Hafen dated 1909.

66   Henley, T, *New Guinea and Australia's Pacific Islands Mandate*, Sydney, John Sands, 1927, p. 24. Photographs of the visit depict rail tracks on the wharf.

67   Robson, RW, *op. cit.*, 203.

68   Catalogue of New Properties Vol 3, p45 - 47.

69   Allied Forces Geographical Section Terrain Study. No 43. Area Study of Manus and Western Islands. p15

70   GNGAR, 1888-1889, p. 37.

71   Firth, S, *New Guinea under the Germans*, p. 31.

72   Williams, M and MacDonald, B, *The Phosphateers: a history of the British Phosphate Commissioners and the Christmas Islands Phosphate Commission*, Melbourne Univ. Press, 1985.

73   Ellis, RF, "The steam locomotives of Nauru and Ocean islands", *Light Railways* , No 88, April 1985, p. 10.

74   Interview, Fr Tschauder, SVD, Madang, 1990

75   GNGAR, 1901-02, p. 230.

76   Rowley, CD, "The area taken over from Germans and controlled by the ANMEF", *South Pacific*, April 1954, p. 828.

77   *South Pacific Post*, 19 August, 1968, p. 7, article by Noel Staggs; confirmed by Fr Tschauder, SVD, Madang.

78   *The Sydney Mail*, September 2, 1914 p 24.

79   *Historishes Bildmaterial aus dem Archives des stoatlicken Museums fur Volkerkunde*, Dresden. Copy held PNG National Library NG Collection.

80   *Post Courier*, 15 April 1996.

81   J. Lyng, *Our New Possession*. (location UPNG C995.4 L988). Chapter IX "Garrision Life". p 102-103.

82   Hilder, Capt. B, "The port of Kavieng", *Walkabout*, January 1950, p. 36.

83   *New Guinea Gazette* No 152 15th October 1926, p. 956, list of expropriated properties. Interview Alfred Takapi, Kavieng, September 1995.

84   Neville Threlfall, *op. cit.*

85   Wagner, H and Reim, H (eds), *The Lutheran Church in Papua New Guinea: the first hundred years, 1886-1986*, Adelaide, Lutheran Publishing House, 1986, p. 37.

86   Flierl, J, *Wunder der gottlichen Grande Evangelisten aus Menschenfressern*, Tanunda, Lutheran Mission, 1931. p. 222.

87   AMF II, *Industrial Reports of Lutheran Mission, Finschhafen, 1920-1939*, (PMB 642); Letter by J Lindner, 20 August 1925; Also *Rot bilong Kamapim Haus Tru bilong God: Piska Histori bilong ELC-PNG, 1886-1986*, Madang, Kristen Press, 1986, photo 1, p. 64.

88   McKellar, CD, *Scented isles and coral gardens*, London, 1912, p. 77-79.

89   GNGAR, 1901-02.

90   *Deutsches Kolonialblatt* 1901; Translation by Fr Tschauder 1975, p. 681.

91   Photos 313/4 of *Historishes Bildmaterial aus dem Archives des staatlicken Museums fur Volkerkunde*, Dresden. Copy held PNG National Library NG Collection.

92   It would appear that extensive *Eucalyptus deglupta* stands were being logged.

93   Mandated Territory of New Guinea Annual Report (MTNG AR) 1921-1922, p. 69-70.

94   MTNG AR 1928-1929 p. 94 p. 280.

95   AGS SWPA TS, No. 51, 28/2/1943. Area Study of East New Britain p. 22.

96   LJ Low, Bulolo, letter, 9 June 1978

97   MTNG AR, 1921-22, p. 69-70.

98   AGS SWPA, Terrain Study No. 22, Gazelle Peninsula and Rabaul p 16.

99   *PIM* September 1962 p 109

100   Wiltgen, RM, "SVD Catholic mission plantations: their origins and purpose," *The History of Melanesia: proceedings of the Second Waigani Seminar.* Canberra, 1969, p. 329.

101   Sr Joan Walker (Ed), *A Story of Christianity in Papua New Guinea.* Liturgical Catechetical Institute - Goroka, Wirui Press - Wewak, p. 34. (Br Irlenbush died of blackwater fever 1905).

102   UPNG Library HAJ Fryer Collection, negative L. 362.

103   Gash, N and Whittaker, J, *A pictorial history of New Guinea*, Brisbane, Jacaranda, p. 175.

104   Hagspiel, B, *Along the mission trail: III New Guinea*, Mission Press, Tech, Illinois, 1926, p. 117-119. The reference to a "locomotive" is believed to be a translation error as photographic evidence shows logs and other wagons on the railway hauled by animal power.

105   Lyng, L, *Our new possessions (late German New Guinea)*, Melbourne Publishing Coy, 1919. Some of these wagons may have been at Marienberg.

106   MTNG AR 1923-1924, p. 80.

107   *Rabaul Times*, Friday June 7th 1929.

108   *The First 75 years - Divine Word Missionaries 1896 to 1971.*

109   *Pacific Islands Monthly*, February 1938, p 4.

110   Interview, Br Roland, CM Angoram, 20/4/1989.

111   McKillop, RF, "Mosquito coast II: Marienberg sawmill and Tramway, Papua New Guinea", *Light Railways,*, 110, October, 1990, pp. 7-15.

112   GWL Townsend, *District Officer: from untamed New Guinea to take success, 1921-1946*, Sydney, Pacific Publications, 1968.

113   McKillop, RF, *op. cit.,* p. 10.

114   Joachim Onol, interview Bonom village, 16/5/1989.

115   Jim Cavanaugh, interview 7/7/1989.

116   Interview, Br Roland, *op. cit.*

117   McKillop, RF, *op. cit.,* p. 13-14.

118   Griffin, J, "Bougainville - a challenge for the churches", *The Independent*, 10 May 1996, p. 10.

CHAPTER 3. AUSTRALIAN TERRITORY OF PAPUA

Railways in 19th C Australian Society

Public utility / nation-building

Australia has played a dominant influence in shaping Papua New Guinea's development since the 1880s. Those Australians who came to Papua (and later New Guinea) brought with them development values shaped by the industrial revolution. As elsewhere, railways had provided Australians with the means to transform their relationship with nature and created the basis for an industrial society. But the relationship was more pronounced in Australia where the desire to conquer the *tyranny of distance* across a vast dry continent brought railways to a level of dominance in government, the economy and social relations unmatched elsewhere.

Given the low population and capital base, railway construction and operation became a government responsibility for *the public good.* When the NSW Government took over the bankrupt private company building the first railway in 1854 and the Victorian and South Australian Railways followed soon afterward, the first government railway enterprises in the British Empire had been founded. Through her railways, Australia created the modern public corporation, which came into existence not to control capitalism, but to provide the basic transport infrastructure necessary for more profitable forms of investment.[1] They helped create cultures in which the state was seen as a vast public utility whose duty was to provide the greatest happiness for the greatest number. The politics of the railway era were dominated by the demands of communities to gain a share of the *cargo*, which was mostly seen in terms of access to the railway network.

Australians built more railways per capita than any other country. Governments borrowed heavily from overseas for their railways and employed vast armies of workers to maintain and operate their systems. To meet the needs of the railways, foundries and the capacity to build locomotives and rolling stock were built up. Australian railways generated the engineering and operational skills necessary for a modern industrial society and developed an ethos among railway families as a way of life. By 1890, the NSW Railways employed 12,000 people and had become the largest industrial enterprise in the country.[2] Through strong railway unions, the *mateship* and solidarity of Australian nationhood was nurtured. Construction of the transcontinental railway from east to west was the essential platform for the federation of the colonies into a single nation

Railways shaped Australia's settlement patterns and helped create one of the world's most urbanised nations. They provided the efficient transport necessary to develop agricultural industries and exploit mineral fields. While railways provided isolated communities with a link to the outside world, they also served to funnel produce and wealth back to the capital cities and ports. Suburban railways and street tramways provided the base for rapid expansion of these cities.

Mining Railways

Bulky minerals required cheap and efficient transport. Private companies and individual entrepreneurs played a significant role in building the railways which enabled the exploitation of Australia's mineral resources. On the wet and rugged West Coast of Tasmania, for instance, 3 ft 6 in (1067 mm) gauge lines were built by private enterprise to the Mt Bischoff field in 1878, while the famous Mt Lyell mine attracted competing railways in the 1880s. Other mines in the Zeehan area were served by 2 ft (610 mm) gauge lines worked by small steam locomotives. Australia's railway entrepreneurs also built railways to open up the Broken Hill mineral field in New South Wales and mineral fields in North Queensland. The use of narrow-gauge railways in rugged terrain was to provide models and equipment for mining railways in Papua.

Agricultural Railways

In addition to the construction of government railways to serve agricultural areas, light railways played an important role within individual agricultural enterprises. The most important of these applications was in the sugar industry where large volumes of cane are transported from the field to central crushing mills. Since 1880, extensive networks of light railways, predominantly of 610 mm gauge, have played a central role in developing the Australian sugar industry into the world's most efficient.

Australian attitudes to tropical agriculture in Queensland and Papua were shaped in the sugar fields. In New South Wales, the sugar industry was established on a central milling system based on individual family farms linked to central crushing mills by extensive sugar railway networks. In Queensland, however, the plantation system was initially tried. The plantation regime was characterised by large farming units, vertical integration of the farming and milling process, and extensive human capital investment using low-cost indentured Melanesian labour. Opinion leaders in the north saw plantations worked by coloured labour as an essential element of their economic future, but it was a vision dependent on the continued supply of cheap labour.

The search for labourers by Queensland sugar plantations in the late 19th century impacted on Papua. In 1862 the new colony of Queensland passed a *Coolie Act* which provided conditions under which Asiatics could be indentured to work in the colony. Captain Robert Towns, a former Sydney merchant with far-ranging Pacific trading interests, was the first to take advantage of the new Act, when he proposed to employ Indians for growing cotton on the Logan River.

When Indians proved unavailable, Towns sent his schooner *Don Juan* to recruit labour in the New Hebrides in 1863. The labourers proved their worth and before long others recruited Pacific Islanders for cotton and sugar plantations at Cleveland, Caboolture and Maryborough.[3] Widespread recruiting of *kanaka* labour from the South Seas resulted. Most came from islands in Vanuatu and the Solomon Islands, but there was also some recruiting in south-east Papua, Bougainville and the islands of the Bismarck Archipelago. It was public concern over the activities of the more notorious of the recruiters, particularly the massacre of Buka Islanders on the *Carl,* which led to pressure in Queensland for a government presence in the islands to control the trade.

Most Melanesians came to the Queensland canefields out of a sense of adventure.[4] Although they played a key role as the founders of the Queensland sugar industry, public opinion in Australia was turning against the plantation system and its use of South Seas labour by the 1880s. The indentured labour system achieved low productivity, while technological advances meant that erection of sugar mills now required large-scale capital. Following a Royal Commission into the traffic in Pacific Islanders in 1885, legislation was introduced for cessation of the recruitment of Pacific Islanders after 1890. At the same time, the trend to central milling stepped up. By 1894 it was estimated that all but 110 of Queensland's 1,387 cane-growers were smallholders with less than 90 acres each.[5] Most of the remaining plantations were subdivided over the following decade. As the central mill system developed, farmers confined themselves to cane growing, sending their cane to a milling firm which dealt exclusively with crushing and refining.

With Federation, the Commonwealth Parliament became dominated by spokesmen for the *White Australia* policy. In October 1901, legislation was passed prohibiting the introduction of Pacific Islanders after 31 March 1904[6]. Attitudes against coloured labourers hardened in the white community and in the summer of 1906-07 the majority of Pacific Islanders were repatriated.

Efficient railway transport played a key role in the development of the central milling system. Although early locomotives and rolling stock for canefield use were imported from Great Britain and France, Australian industry was providing rails, rolling stock and locomotives from the 1920s.

Colonial Expansion

The expansion of German imperial power in the South Pacific in the later nineteenth century generated considerable concern within the Australian colonies, particularly Queensland which had become dependent on indentured labour from the region. John Robertson, Premier of New South Wales urged the British Colonial Secretary to take possession of New Guinea, New Britain, the Solomon Islands and the New Hebrides "in the highest interests of civilisation."[7] On 3 April, 1883, the Union Jack was raised in Port Moresby by a Queensland magistrate in an abortive attempt to annex New Guinea on behalf of Britain.[8].

In 1884, the German colonisation of New Guinea brought action by Britain to annex the southern part of the island as British New Guinea (BNG). The protectorate was primarily an Australian interest. The colonies contributed to the budget, the majority of officials came from the Australian colonies and the Administrator of Lieutenant-Governor reported to the Queensland Governor-in-Council.[9] Full responsibility for administration of the colony of BNG was transferred to Australia in 1902. However, implementation of the changes stagnated until September 1906, when the name was changed to Papua.

Colonial Development Policies

Development policy in British New Guinea was chiefly concerned with the protection of native society.[10] When gold mining attracted Australians to the new territory, officials attempted to restrict the employment of villagers by miners and planters. At the same time they sought to instil a work ethic on the local population using such measures as the forced planting of coconuts and head taxes.

A *Crown Lands Ordinance* was enacted in 1890 to make land available to potential investors.[11] The Hall Sound Company was floated by Australian investors, including Burns Philp & Company, with the intention of developing 80,000 hectares for agriculture, but only 2,025 ha was granted at Cloudy Bay.

Following a period of stagnation and conflict within the administration, a Royal Commission was established to enquire into the conditions in the territory. The Commission made optimistic recommendations for the rapid development of resources through the application of imported capital and the employment of native labour in agriculture.[12]

Australian attitudes to tropical agriculture and the role of coloured labour were shaped in the canefields of Queensland. The assumption was that agricultural development would be based on a plantation system with Papuans as the source of cheap labour. From 1907 to 1914, Papuan agricultural policy was dominated by E Staniforth-Smith, a former federal senator, who was appointed Director of Agriculture, Commissioner of Lands, Director of

Top- Burns Philp wharf at Port Moresby in 1897 with 1067 gauge railway.

PNG National Archives

Bottom - Unloading copra on the Port Moresby Government wharf tramway.

Camera Press

Mines and Director of Public Works.[13] Staniforth-Smith, who viewed himself as a specialist in tropical agriculture, sought to establish an Australian-dominated plantation economy in Papua. Although the area under lease rose to 364,088 acres by 1911, viable crops were not forthcoming. Only 15,880 acres of the leased land were planted. Between 1911 and 1914, 48 per cent of the leases were forfeited.

Coconuts provided the mainstay of the small plantation economy. The British connection provided the opportunity to import natural rubber planting material from Malaya, while sisal offered brief hope following the First World War. However, by 1922, Hubert Murray lamented the stagnation of Papuan agriculture due to low commodity prices and transport problems.[14] As the vision for plantation agriculture receded, the administration promoted a village-based agricultural system. There was a limited response from Papuan villagers.

Public Railways

Australians coming to the new colony brought with them cultural values regarding the role of the state and railways in the economy. It was therefore inevitable that they looked to the government to provide railway infrastructure to meet their transport needs. Despite the low level of economic activity, there was a surprisingly generous response by the colonial administration.

Port Moresby Wharf Tramways

Port Moresby attracted pioneer settlers on account of its fine harbour. An Australian trader, Andrew Goldie began operating at Port Moresby in 1875. Initially infrastructure was provided by the Australian trading firm, Burns Philp & Company (BP), which purchased Goldie's store in Port Moresby to gain a base in the new colony. BP were to play a dominant role in Papua New Guinea's economy over the next 100 years.

In 1891 BP were granted the right to construct a new jetty with a tramline running up to the store.[15] The wharf and railway were completed by 1895.[16] The gauge was 3 ft 6 in (1067 mm) and the gradient 1 in 6. The trucks had to be hand pushed over the 200 metres length of the line. While labour was cheap, pushing railway trucks did not have the status of a canoe voyager or even a carrier, and was heavy work. The line operated until 1910, when a new store was built.

Government involvement in the provision of public railway infrastructure was an early assumption. In 1891, Sir William MacGregor, Administrator of BNG, initiated the purchase of rails from Cooktown for use in construction of tramways at Samarai and Port Moresby. They arrived in 1894.[17]

Work commenced on a new government wharf near the Burns Philp jetty. Prisoners were employed on this project from 1896. In 1902 a temporary tramline was in use on the wharf for handling cargo and stores.[18] Three years later a new 2 ft (610 mm) gauge tramline, some 120 metres in length, connected the government store to the wharf.[19] Two trucks were constructed for the line and a derrick was erected on the wharf. Further improvements brought the length of the wharf to 638 ft (200 m), of which the first 138 ft was stone work.[20] This public work was undertaken by prison labour. The wharf tramway was double tracked by 1912.[21] This wharf suffered from the effects of marine worm (*Terrilis novelis*) and had to be replaced. A new wharf was built adjacent to the existing one in 1917.[22]. It was 777 feet (250 metres) long. A timber-framed receiving shed was constructed in 1923-24.

The wharf and railway were the scene of frenzied activity during the early stages of the World War II. In 1941 there were many complaints of congestion, including a claim that rail trucks were being used to store heavy materials and machinery because they were not being lifted off them by a crane.[23] It was proposed that a third set of rails be provided on the wharf to give two sets for full trucks and one set for returning empty trucks. Approval for extension of the wharf and a third rail line was given by Public Works in April 1941.[24]. Photographs dated June 1941 depict congested conditions. With the arrival of United States forces in January 1943, extensions to the wharf were constructed. The tramline was replaced by motor trucks and the tracks lifted by March 1943.[25]

Sapphire Creek Railway

The Astrolabe mineral field near Port Moresby, declared in 1906, brought fresh hopes of development for Papua. The first mine, the *Dubuna* was operational by 1910. However, ore had to be brought to the coast over an 18 mile track by mules at a prohibitive cost.[26] Construction of a railway to the area was seen as necessary precondition for exploitation of the field.

In 1910, The British New Guinea Development Company (BNGDC) was founded to establish plantations, undertake trading activities and to construct light railways.[27] The BNGDC entered into negotiations with the Government to construct a railway from Port Moresby to Sapphire Creek if it could also negotiate the rights to the hydro-electric potential of the Rona Falls on the Laloki River.

Construction of a public railway to stimulate the economy of the colony was soon being promoted by Administrator Murray, who claimed "the railway would justify its existence with sisal hemp and tobacco as well as copper."[28] The Australian Government did not require rigorous justification, and in July 1913 the following radio message was sent by Atlee Hunt to the Administrator:

> It is impossible to say definitely when money will be found for railway to Sapphire Creek before Parliament has considered estimates. The Treasurer has authorised survey of line and request made to Govt of Queensland land surveyor for that purpose ....[29]

By June 1914, the Engineer in Chief of the Commonwealth Railways was preparing a design for a railway from Port Moresby to Rona.[30] The administration estimated that 60,000 tons of ore would be transported over the railway annually. The engineer was apparently influenced by the light 2 ft 6 in (762 mm) gauge railways then being constructed by the Victorian Railways, the 2 ft gauge (610 mm gauge) Dundas Tramway on the West Coast of Tasmania and the Goondah-Burrunjuck railway in New South Wales which provided low-cost lines in rugged terrain. The survey was completed during 1913-14:

> The route adopted for this railway is practically that which the existing road now takes, with the exception of deviations in order to obtain a suitable grade. The maximum grade laid down is 1 in 40 and the minimum radius for curves is 2.5 chains. It is anticipated that under these conditions suitable engines will have no difficulty in drawing 80 to 100 ton loads at an average rate of 10 m.p.h.

> The starting point for the railway mentioned is on Ela Beach, and the terminus Sapphire Creek at a point contiguous to the surveyed township of Rona, the total distance is 19.25 miles. The object to the line being to facilitate the transport of ore and commercial products from the several mines and plantations in the vicinity and it is hoped that it will also be the means of further opening of the more outlying and remoter districts of Sogeri and Brown River.

Top - Typical departure scene at Samarai wharf in the 1940's. Railway tracks are clearly visible on the wharf, with the classic Customs House in the background.

Nelson, H. *Taim Bilong Masta*, ABC Books, p.58

Bottom - Samarai Railway : tracks leading to Burns Philp warehouses, c. 1930.

Courtesy - Burns Philip

It is proposed that a branch line be extended from the Ela Beach terminus on to the proposed new jetty to enable all exports to be shipped directly into the various steamers trading to the port.[31]

Construction of the line was authorised in July 1913, when the Australian Government made a 50,000 pounds loan available for the project. Advertisements were placed in Queensland for a suitable eight-coupled 2 ft gauge locomotive, either new or second-hand, with a maximum axle load of 6 tons.[32]. The *Port Moresby to Rona Railway Ordinance 1914* was passed on 19 August 1914. Construction work commenced in 1914 at Ela Beach. A contract was let to Elder Smith & Company and George Wills & Company for the delivery of 1200 tons of 35 lb rails, and fish plates on 16 February 1915[33]/. However, with the outbreak of War, work on the line was suspended indefinitely.[34] The huge cost of the war effort in Australia meant that this project in far off Papua was not resumed. The Laloki Copper Mine was soon to construct its own railway to develop the mines, thus bringing to an end the prospects of a government public railway in Papua.

Samarai Island

The small island of Samarai, in today's Milne Bay Province, was an early focus for the establishment of a colonial station. An initial task was to fill a swamp area, a project which was to extend over several years. Prisoners were employed on the project using a light railway to transport fill. Some 75,000 cubic yards were moved in 1893-94 and completed in 1898.[35] By this time, Burns Philp had constructed a slipway and a local trader, Whitlen, a wharf and store on the island. Work on reclaiming Samarai swamp was reported completed in February 1895.[36] The report of completion was somewhat premature. In 1899, Samarai residents petitioned for completion of the swamp reclamation project. [37] Work continued for a number of years. By 1905, prisoners were employed in the construction of a new jetty at Samarai. This involved the establishment of tramlines to assist the easy loading of steamers.

During and after the First World War there were several public meetings called by the Europeans of Samarai to protest over the state of the wharf, the tobacco duty and the need for a local railway.[38] Their pressure brought results. A new wharf opened in 1923 served by a 610 mm gauge railway.[39] The railway was gradually extended. Burns Philp, in conjunction with GA Loudon & Company, relaid the tramway from King's warehouse to their bulk stores in 1925.[40] They installed a turntable which proved satisfactory and the Collector of Customs requested similar facilities for the wharf tramway in 1925. This was installed in 1928, when the Steamships Trading Company (STC) laid portable track from this point to their copra store. Other lines were also laid, although problems were reported in obtaining rail lines for the tramline from the Quarry to Dart Street in 1929.[41] All wharves and facilities were destroyed by bombing early in 1942.[42] However, some lines survived or were reconstructed, as tramways were still in existence on Samarai in 1962. [43]

Daru Island

In the far west of the infant colony the administration established a station on the island of Daru, about 60 km south-west of the mouth of the Fly River, as one of the earliest European settlements. However, the shallow sea around the island made the transfer of cargo to and from ships difficult. Whaleboats were used for lightering cargo to ships. By 1896, construction of a jetty had commenced using prison labour.[44] It was to be an extended public works project which continued over the next 20 years to provide a stone causeway 174 metres long and a wooden pier, 143 metres in length, enabling ships to be unloaded safely at high tide.

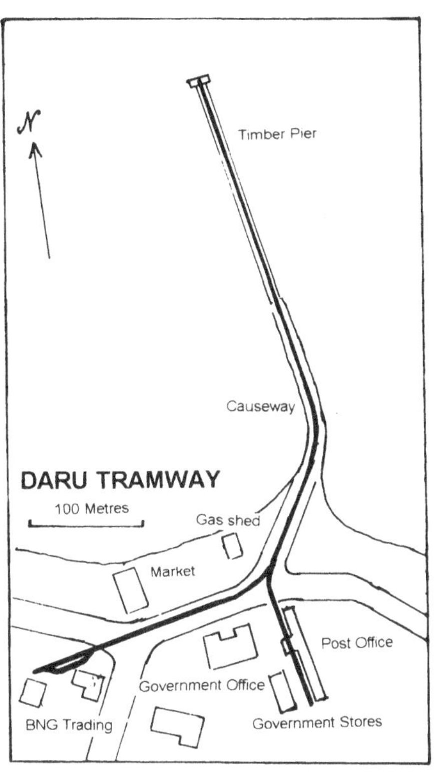

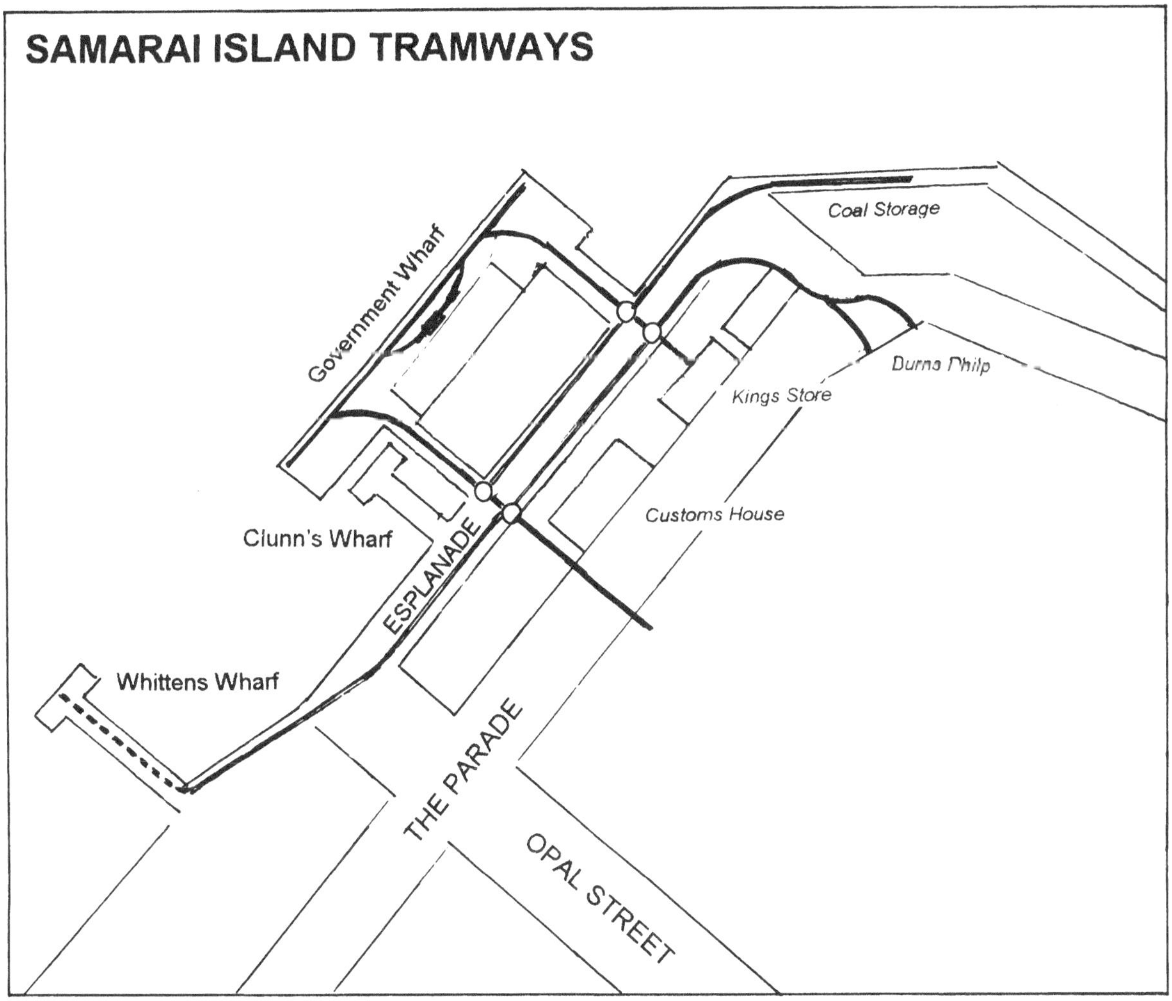

SAMARAI ISLAND TRAMWAYS

Above - maps of Samarai and Daru tramways

Top - Aerial view of Daru and old wharf, c. 1958. Railway trucks are visible in the street in front of the of the Government offices.

PNG National Archives

Bottom - View of Daru from wharf showing railway, c. 1958.

PNG National Archives

Top - Sisal drying operations, Fairfax Plantation with railway and trucks in foreground, c. 1915.
PNG National Archives

Bottom left - IC powered locomotive and wagons at Fairfax Plantation, c. 1918.
PNG National Archives

Bottom right - Loading sisal onto railway truck, Bomana Plantation.
Staniforth Smith, *Handbook of Papua*, 1912

In 1917, rail was purchased for a railway on the wharf. [45] The rails were 18 pounds/yard and were laid out as 2 ft (610 mm) gauge. Mangrove sleepers were used. A single line was laid over 500 metres from the end of the wharf to the government store wharf without any passing loop.

About 1945, Mr George Tabua was asked to repair and extend the wharf, which had fallen into disrepair. Using 300 labourers, the height of the wharf was raised and it was extended by another 50 metres. At this time the line branched on reaching the island at Wyborn's gas shed. The "main" line ran past the post office to the government stores, while the other branch served the Burns Philp store. [46]

A dozen 4-wheel flat trucks, each with a capacity of one ton, operated on the railway. They were hand-pushed by two labourers. Mail was unloaded from steamers and railed direct to the post office, where it was unloaded under the shelter of the verandah. Unusual cargo included an extra large crocodile, caught by Mr Craig, which required four trucks to carry it, and new generators for the Daru powerhouse. On the latter occasion, a tractor was used to pull the trucks.

In 1963 it was decided to build a new wharf. In the process the railway was dismantled in favour of motor lorries. Despite the poor condition of the railway track, the new arrangement offered few advantages. Only one lorry could negotiate the wharf at a time and the poor condition of the roadway meant that they were slower than the hand-pushed rail trucks. Breakages were common, while the local employment generated by the railway was no longer available.

Plantation Railways

The Sisal Ventures

Efforts to develop agriculture in the Australian colony fared badly in comparison to the more dynamic ventures to the north. Sisal growing offered hope for a period. In 1908 it was reported that over 20,000 acres had been leased for the growing of sisal in the Port Moresby area. [47].

The British New Guinea Development Company (BNGDC) established a sisal plantation at Bomana outside Port Moresby and Messrs Clark and Whitting also grew sisal on Fairfax Plantation to the north of the harbour. It was expected that 500 to 1000 tons would be exported in 1913. In fact, exports peaked at only 343 tons in 1918, then declined. By 1922, it was reported that:

> The low price ruling for this fibre and the high freights (charged by measurement, and not weight) have rendered this industry unpayable for the present, and these plantations have, generally speaking, a very neglected appearance. Very little hemp has consequently been made, the total exports for the year under review being 145 tons. [48]

Light railways were laid to transport the sisal from the fields. Photographic records suggest trucks were hand-pushed in the field, but a light IC-powered locomotive and a tractor converted to rail operation served as motive power on Fairfax plantation. The industry was abandoned during the 1920s. The Commonwealth Hemp Corporation made an attempt to revive the industry in the early 1930s at Tavai and Kiana plantations. [49]

Sugar Milling Proposals

Among the many development proposals which brought occasional hopes of prosperity for the struggling Papuan economy were several for the establishment of sugar milling ventures. In 1901, a float of 60,000 one pound shares in the Hall Sound Company, which planned a sugar mill on the Veimauri River, was reported.[50] The Company proposed to buy 13 miles of permanent tramline, 6 miles of portable tramline, two 12 ton locomotives and 150 trucks. Nothing more was heard of the venture.

In the Northern District, several attempts to establish a sugar industry were made during the 1930s. The most ambitious was at Sangara, where trial plantings were made and plans were drawn up for a sugar estate, mill, railway lines, rolling stock and a wharf, but the scheme failed to materialise.[51]

Other Plantation Lines

The operation of light railways are reported on a number of coconut and rubber plantations. The most significant railway was that at Robinson River, east of Abau. A Burns Philp inspector visited the plantation in 1932 and recommended a light railway, rather than a road, to serve the new wharf site.[52] In 1936, Robinson River was described as one of the biggest Papuan plantations, producing 1000 tons of copra annually and employing 150 labourers.[53] There were 20 miles (31 km) of railway lines. Railway trucks loaded with coconuts were pulled by tractor to the copra driers.

Several rubber plantations on the Sogeri Plateau behind Port Moresby used light railways in their processing factories. The rubber was cured in smoke houses which had a high fire risk, necessitating that these houses be located some distance from other buildings. Itikinumu Plantation operated about 400 metres of 900 mm railway and 100 metres of 4 ft 4 in (1275 mm) gauge line for drying trolleys.[54] The system was constructed in 1950, but is believed to have replaced an existing system. Eilogo plantation had a 2 ft 6 in (762 mm) gauge system with lines into the plantation.[55] It was later cut back to serve the factory operations. Trolleys of wet rubber were pushed to the smoke house for drying, then back to the main shed for packing.

Mining Railways

While the German colony to the north was building a strong foundation for agricultural and forest industries, the struggling colony of Papua was reduced to a gamble on mineral strikes. Papua New Guinea's most significant railways were built to meet the transport needs of these fields.

Woodlark Goldfield Railways

Gold finds on Woodlark Island in the far east of the colony brought early demands for improved transport. The Murua field was proclaimed on 6 November 1895. The testing of the Ivanhoe reefs brought investment in the field by Australian capitalists.

By 1903 there were three companies operating on the field - the Woodlark Island Gold Mining Proprietary Company of Sydney, the Kulumadau Woodlark Island Gold Mining Company Ltd, Charters Towers, and the Woodlark Ivanhoe Gold Mining Company, Adelaide - and about 120 Europeans were working the field.[56]. A township was established at Kulumadau. The field was not sufficiently rich to support three companies and the Ivanhoe abandoned its leases in 1903.

The Proprietary Company constructed a light railway from the landing place at Bunkanai to Kulumadau township, a distance of 2.5 km to enable processing equipment to be imported from Sydney.[57] The survey was undertaken by Mr GM Monk who made the trial survey for the Cairns to Herberton railway in North Queensland.[58] The line was built in two stages of equal length, the first in 1900 from Bunkanai to Kwaipan Creek and the second, in 1902, to Kulumadau. The company charged 5/- per ton for the transport of goods over its tramline.[59] The Proprietary Company closed in 1905 and its assets were taken over by the Kulumadau-Woodlark Island Gold Mining Company. In 1911, it was reported that the Company was building a light railway from the field to Bunkanai, which appears to be an upgrading of the existing line.[60] The gauge was 2 ft 6 in (762 mm) and the line was hand-worked.

Ore was generally bagged at small mines and lumped to crushing mills on the shoulders of Papuan labourers until light tramlines were laid down at the most important mines from 1911. Of 20 inch or 2 ft (610 mm) gauge, such lines operated at the Kulumadau mine, Federation mine at Busai and the Woodlark King mine at Bonivai. Other lines were laid down in the adjoining forests to transport timber and firewood. In 1913-14, a runaway ore skip at Kulumadau mine fell down the shaft killing six mine labourers.[61]

Miners actively lobbied the administration to build a locomotive-worked railway from Kavavakum through Busai and Kulumadau to the deep water anchorage at Boi-boi. Mr Amos, of the Queensland Railway Service, visited Woodlark Island in May 1912, and inspected possible routes for the line.[62] The following year, the Resident Magistrate reported:

> I am not personally aware of whether the proposition of a railway for Woodlark Island is likely to bear fruit. Certainly present indications are not sufficiently good to warrant a large expenditure in this regard.[63]

Although details are sketchy, it appears that a 5 mile (7.5 km) extension was built south to Busai by the Public Works Department in 1915 using rails supplied by the mining companies.[64] In 1915, the Kulumadau Company employed 28 Europeans and 253 Papuans. However, the mine closed in 1918 and the light railway fell into disuse. A wireless station had been constructed some 600 metres to the north of the Bunkanai-Kulumadau railway. In March, 1917, the OIC of the station sought permission to construct a light railway crossing the existing company line, over which the government had no running rights.[65] By 1921, activities on the Murua field were practically at a standstill. There was a short revival in 1924 when a new mine, *The Woodlark King* was floated, a mill erected and a long tunnel for draining the mine driven.[66] A 2 ft gauge tramline was constructed from the mine to the mill. The field continued on a small scale until the Pacific War.

Following closure of the Kulumadau mine, the railway continued to be used to service the Kwaipan Bay Plantation and Kulumadau town. In 1937, an advertisement for the sale of Kwaipan Bay Plantation, East Papua noted it was conveniently connected by light railway and punt over short distance of two miles to Kwaipan Harbour at which port BP steamers call at regular intervals. [67]

Goods for the Kulumadau store, located in the old wireless building and operated by the Hon. JG Nelson, were brought up the creek at Bunkanai by punts from the *Montoro* and loaded onto railway trucks which were hand-pushed to the store.[68] This line was still in existence in 1960. Some 4 miles of the railway formation from Kwaiapan Plantation to the mining settlement at Busai was converted to a motor road prior to 1942.[69]

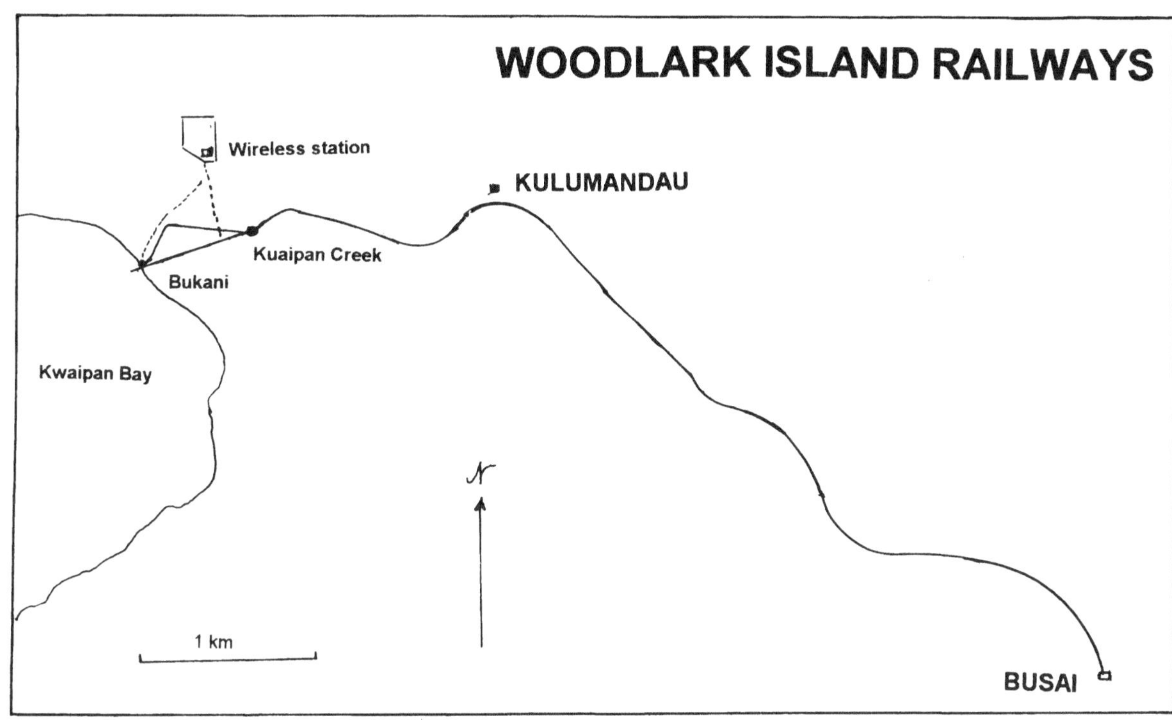

Top - Plan of Woodlark Island Railways

Bottom - Kulumadau Gold Mine, c. 1911.

Staniforth Smith, Handbook of Papua, 3rd. ed. 1912. p. 88A

Misima Island Railway

Alluvial gold miners arrived on Misima Island in 1898. Both Papuans and European alluvial miners worked the field with variable returns until 1914, when the "mother lode" was located. Miners pegged leases at Mount Sisa, Umuna and Quartz Mountain and tried to raise capital.

Following the First World War interest was revived in the Misima goldfields. The Block 10 Misima Gold Mines Company, a subsidiary of Block 10 Broken Hill and Block 14 Broken Hill[70], began extensive development on the field in 1914 and eventually took over all the leases on the Massive Lode at Umuna. The company invested heavily, tunnelling for several thousand feet, constructing a 7.2 mile (11.5 km) railway to the port at Bwagaoia, installing crushing mills, cyanide vats, a sawmill, carpenters shops, a power station and electric reticulation, staff accommodation and port facilities.[71] Power for the mine machinery was generated by a Babcock & Wilcox water-tube boiler, which fed steam to a fast-running Kelly & Lewis 450 hp engine, directly coupled to a large electricity generator.

In 1917-18 the company had 481 employees and treated 14,618 tons of ore. This increased to 45,045 tons in 1921-22 when there were 575 employees - 63 Europeans and 512 Papuans, mainly from coastal areas.

The mine location at Umuna, was about 6 km inland by walking track and some 125 m above sea level.[72] Initially, pack horses and mules were used to transport goods to and from the mines, but the Block 10 Company began construction of a light 2 ft (610 mm) gauge railway from Umuna to the port at Bwagaoia in 1919. It was operational by June 1920. Construction was under the supervision of the mine manager, RB Williamson, who came from Bullfinch in Western Australia.[73]

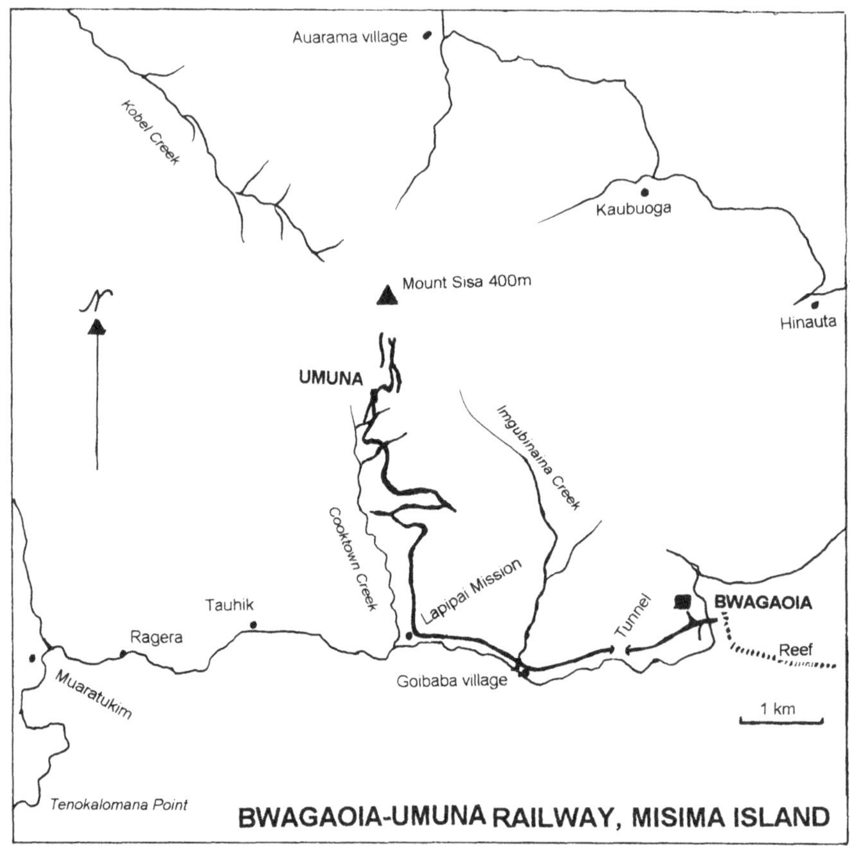

Above - Map of Misima Island Railway

At Bwagaoia two rail lines were laid on the wharf, spanned by a 22 ft travelling crane. From Bwagaoia the line followed the coast for about 4 miles (6 km), passing through the village of Gaibobo. A short 50 yard tunnel was constructed through a coral cliff after Mamata Creek. From the village of Lapapai, the line then climbed 410 feet to Umuna in only 3.5 miles (5.3 km). This scenic section included sharp curves, most of the 27 bridges on the line and a three stage "zig-zag". This provided a spectacular climb on three, parallel levels soon after Lapapai, although the ends of each section were connected by loops, around which the train ran, rather than the dead-ends of a true zig-zag. The line cost the company 30,000 pounds to build, a capital outlay which was to prove a significant factor in the short life of the operation.

To operate the line, a Kerr Stuart 0-4-2T locomotive (B/N 743/1901) was imported from Australia. It had been used on the Iron Blow to Mt Ellison railway in the Northern Territory. Sold to Cameron & Sutherland in 1906, it is thought the locomotive was reconditioned by Walkers Limited at Maryborough, Queensland, before shipment to Misima in 1920. The railway carried coal from the coast for the boiler furnaces at Umuna, together with food and general stores for the miners. The railway also served the transport needs of the human population. Initially, riding on the buffer beam of the locomotive offered a cool but risky ride, for the locomotive was notorious for its propensity to jump the rails.[74]

The company responded to the demand for passenger travel by converting a flat truck to a "passenger car". The facility was very basic. Seven uprights supported a curved roof and there was a rail running round the uprights at waist level. No seats were provided. At one stage the company provided a guard on the train, mainly to check on the delays from scheduled times which, it was suspected, were due to poker games.

Others chose a more exciting means of travel over the line. Dr Brown recalled that:

> The ride on one [a flat truck] from Umuna on the four mile downhill run to the coast was a greater thrill than Luna Park could provide. With a flat stick through the trolley platform as a brake,you endeavoured to slow it down before it was too late.
> 75

Apart from the passenger car, rolling stock comprised simple 4-wheel open trucks and at least one flat car. It appears that the bodies of the wagons were assembled at the mine.[76]

In 1975, elderly people from Gulewa village provided recollections of the railway in operation.[77] The mining era brought many outsiders to Misima, which provided market outlets for garden produce, but the influx of foreigners generated fear among the villagers. The steam train was a bewildering phenomenon for the locals, who described it as "a man smoking pipe and pulling many small children behind him". The machine is remembered for its large appetite of special black food. For children attending school at the Methodist mission beside the line, the train posed a serious disruption to learning routine as they always ran outside to watch the train passing. The train whistle, however, engendered fear among the children, who believed the engine was angry as it let off more smoke when it made this noise.

One weekend a group of village youths went to the sheds at Umuna where the train was kept. They began playing on some trucks outside the shed, and when someone pulled out the blocks holding the train, the group found themselves on a nightmare run down the mountain. Fortunately, the trucks remained on the rails and came to a halt safely. A very frightened group of youths ran off into the bush, leaving mine officials to puzzle over the whereabouts of their train next morning.

The Block 10 operation was short lived. By 1921, establishment costs placed the company in financial difficulty and, in November of that year, they turned to the Australian Government for assistance. A formal request was made for loan guarantees of 60,000

Misima Island Railway

Top - Kerr Stewart 0-4-2T locomotive at Bwagaoia terminus, c. 1920.

Photo - H. Gilbee Brown

Bottom - Passenger train on the Block 10 Company railway.

Photo - H. Gilbee Brown

Top - View of zig-zag on the Block 10 Company railway, Misma Island, c. 1920.

Photo - H. Gilbee Brown

Bottom - Heavy passenger loading on the Block 10 Company train, c. 1919.

PNG National Archives

pounds to complete equipment purchases and further mine development, and to repay a 25,000 pounds mortgage.[78] The Australian Government, already subject to requests for financial assistance from the Papuan copper mining industry, found the Misima mines were not commercially viable and rejected the request in August 1922. The following month a number of mine tunnels collapsed and the Block 10 company closed its operation.

The company's plant and equipment, including railway items, was sold to Miller & Company, machinery merchants of South Melbourne. The locomotive was subsequently regauged to 3 ft (914 mm) by Day's Engineering Works for EAC Russell's timber tramway at Gembrook, Victoria. There the locomotive had a short, but turbulent career:

> Due to the conversion not being carried out properly the loco was useless. The axles were too snug a fit, and the loco could not corner smoothly, and it would jump off the outside of the curves in the most unexpected manner, with disastrous effect on Mr Russell who was the driver. As most of the trestle bridges were curved, it can be appreciated that this was most unsettling to the peace of mind.[79]

A short section of tramline was retained in Bwagaoia from the wharf to the BPs store. In 1952, Mr ED Ryan extended this line to his copra store.[80] At Umuna, a local company worked the lease until 1928, when Freddie Cuthbert floated New Misima Gold Mines to reintroduce larger-scale workings. The route of the old railway was reformed to take motor trucks and a new treatment plant was installed.[81] The mine remained Papua's most profitable until the commencement of WW II.

Bootless Bay-Dubuna Railway

The outbreak of war had caused abandonment of the Sapphire Creek railway in 1914. Once the War was over, interest was again aroused in the Astrolabe mineral field. Papua's most ambitious mining and railway venture got under way in 1918 with construction of a 3 ft 6 in (1067 mm) gauge railway from a port on Bootless Bay, 10 km south of Port Moresby, to the Dubuna mine by the Laloki Copper Company.[82] Three Europeans and 30 labourers were employed in the construction task. The line ran through the sisal plantations of the BNG Development Company which anticipated reduced transport costs for its sisal hemp from running rights over the line.[83] As an interim measure, two steam traction engines were imported in July 1918 to haul ore by road from Sapphire Creek to Port Moresby and the administration was requested to assist with upgrading of the road.[84]

In 1920, the New Guinea Copper Company was formed to take over the venture. The 6 mile 38 chain (10.4 km) railway connecting the Dubuna mine with smelters and a wharf at Tahira on Bootless Bay was completed in 1920. The line cost 50,000 pounds and the jetty a further 10,000 pounds. The *Private Railway Ordinance* was passed by the Legislative Council on 13 November 1920 to cover the railway's operation, together with the Block 10 line on Misima. [85]

The railway extended the full length of the 140 metre jetty, with a siding extending for most of its length.[86] Leaving the wharf, a small timber locomotive shed and ash pit were located at the quarter mile post. The railway then passed through a short, deep cutting, before passing the extensive smelting works at Tahira. These were served by a spur line, 1.6 km in length and at a higher elevation than the wharf line. For the next 3 km the line passed low lying country, skirting mangrove swamps. The railway climbed steadily to Dubuna mine. The ruling grade was 1 in 40 against the load, with 3 chain curves uncompensated, and 1 in 22 in the reverse direction. For the first 3.5 miles to Wai Wai Junction the line was constructed with 60 lb rails and ballasted.

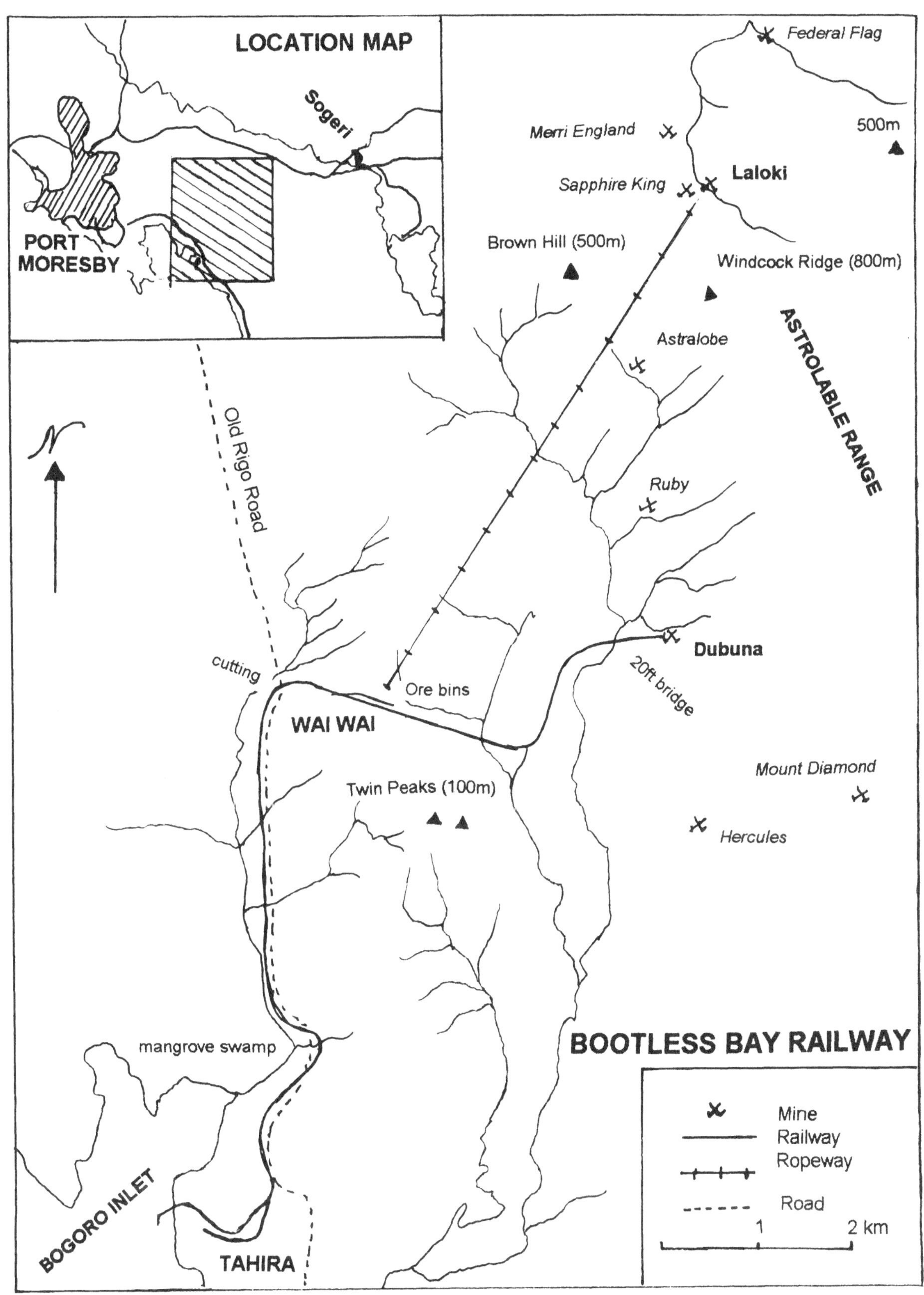

Above - Map of Bootless Bay Railway

Top - Locomotive Polygon hauls an ore train to Tahira with Papuan passengers.

PNG National Archives

Bottom - The Australian Minister for Territories, Mr Ponyton, rides the official train in 1921.

Winter's Studio, Burnie

The plan was to construct a branch line from here to the Laloki mine, but the rugged terrain would have required 17 km of railway to bridge the 4.5 km direct line distance.[87] Accordingly, a 6 km aerial ropeway supported by 31 steel towers was constructed to transport Laloki ore to Wai Wai. It opened in 1923 and could transport 25 tons of ore per hour. Ore transfer bins with a capacity of 3000 tons were constructed at Wai Wai Junction. Their foundations are still in place. From Wai Wai Junction, the line was constructed to pioneer standards using light 30 lb rail and unballasted track. Steep grades were encountered, rising to a maximum elevation of 175 feet, before the line descended into an attractive valley where the present Mount Diamond School is located. A bridge with a 6 yard span was crossed before reaching the mine.

The railway was worked by a steam locomotive from the outset. An 18.75 ton Andrew Barclay 0-6-0T locomotive (B/N 1544/1918) named *POLYGON* was purchased from Broken Hill Associated Smelters, Port Pirie and arrived in early 1921 to assist with construction duties. The light, unballasted track beyond Wai Wai Junction proved to be unsuitable for *POLYGON* and the long wheel-base rolling stock. Accordingly, a 14 ton, A-class Shay geared locomotive (Lima 2478/1911) was imported from the Hampton-Cloncurry Mines in Queensland in 1924. This locomotive was on loan to the New Guinea Copper Mines at 50 pounds per annum.[88]

Rolling stock comprised 12, 6.3 cubic metre hopper wagons built by Kelly & Lewis of Melbourne, two flat-top timber trucks and 20 small 0.75 cubic metre V-hopper wagons for transhipping ore at the wharf. It has been reported that flat-top wagons were created by placing timber planks on the underframe of hopper wagons [89]. Maintenance of the railway line was the responsibility of the engineer, Mr T Dwyer, and a staff of 40 gangers. There were two hand-pump trolleys and two petrol-powered trolleys for use by gangers.

The venture was by far the largest industrial enterprise in the colony and the company town of Tahira promised to outstrip Port Moresby as the major settlement. The Compound Manager at Tahira, Robert Hayes, reports that he was responsible for servicing the needs of 116 European and 2,300 Papuan employees. Robert and his wife Elsie recalled that the locals referred to the locomotive in terms of "*Polygon* he come" (etc) and that they were required to ride on freight cars, there being no passenger cars on the line.[90] Photographs show Papuans riding on top of loaded ore cars. More salubrious accommodation was provided in 1921 when the Minister for Territories, Mr Ponyton, rode on the line. A flat top wagon was equipped with empty boxes and cushions for the passengers and the locomotive was coupled behind so that the Minister would not be troubled by smoke.[91] It is reported that Mr Ponyton produced his gold pass for the journey.

Most Papuans employed by the company were restricted to low level labouring tasks. They acquired no useable skills and accumulated few savings.[92] Those who did serve in skilled positions, such as engine drivers or clerks, found their specialities were not required in the plantation and peasant-based economy.

The company turned to the Australian Government for financial assistance from an early date. In April, 1921, a request was made for an advance of 90,000 pounds in cash or bonds to cover the company's development expenses. It was claimed that the state of the base metal market and general financial stringency would force the company to close if such aid was not forthcoming. Although local administration officials supported the claim, it was rejected by the Board of Trade in August 1921. The company responded with a proposal for the Government to take over the jetty and railway for 45,000 pounds. This time, argument from Murray that the venture was vital to the Papuan economy and the company's own political lobby in Canberra gained the support of the Prime Minister. The Dubuna railway was acquired by the Commonwealth Government on 15 June, 1922.[93]

Top - B-class Shay geared locomotive (Lima 2478/1911) used on Wai Wai- Dubuna section of the railway.

RF McKillop collection

Bottom -Papuan labourers pushing ore trucks to ship at Tahira jetty, c. 1921.

Photo: C T Wurth, RF McKillop collection

Top - Papua's largest industrial enterprise, New Guinea Copper Mines smelters at Tahira, c. 1925.

RF McKillop collection

Bottom - The driver of locomotive POLYGON with Papuan assistants, c. 1921.

PNG National Archives.

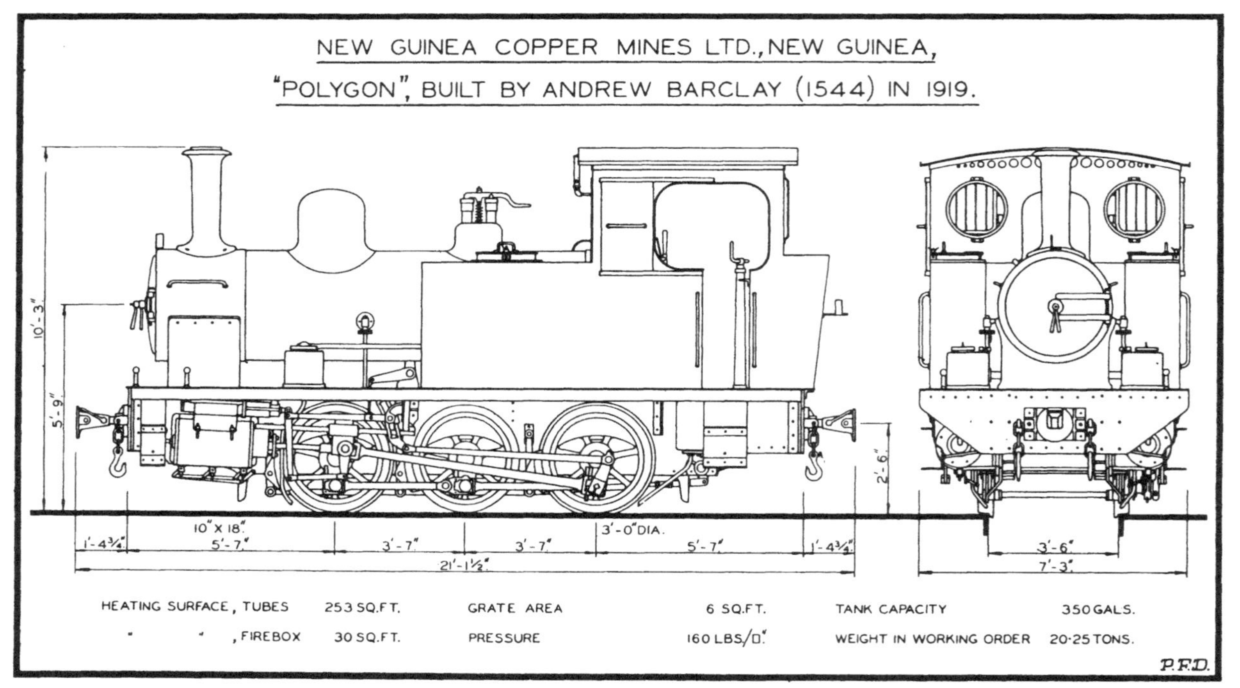

NEW GUINEA COPPER MINES LTD., NEW GUINEA,
"POLYGON", BUILT BY ANDREW BARCLAY (1544) IN 1919.
10'-3"
5'-9"
1'-4¾"
10" X 18"
5'-7"
3'-7"
3'-7"
3'-0"DIA.
5'-7"
1'-4¾"
21'-1½"
2'-6"
3'-6"
7'-3"
HEATING SURFACE, TUBES   253 SQ.FT.
"   "   , FIREBOX   30 SQ.FT.
GRATE AREA   6 SQ.FT.
PRESSURE   160 LBS/□"
TANK CAPACITY   350 GALS.
WEIGHT IN WORKING ORDER   20·25 TONS.
P.F.D.

Despite the Government assistance, technical problems kept the company in serious financial difficulties. The large copper smelters at Tahira were completed in 1924, but proved incapable of processing the ore. This was reported to be "due to relying on catalogue figures and installing inadequate blowing machinery."[94] Additional equipment was purchased and installed, but this resulted an 18 month delay. When the smelters finally did commence production in late 1925, continued difficulties were encountered. At the time of closure a year later, only 261 tons of blister copper had been produced.[95] The majority of copper had to be exported as low grade matte. Fires also hindered production. A serious fire at the Laloki mine in November, 1924, resulted in the mine being closed off and converted to open cut operation. A fire then broke out at the Dubuna, which was also converted to open cut.

With these problems, traffic on the railway did not meet expectations. From 1921 to 1924-25, ore was hauled over the line and stockpiled for the new smelters. Based on *Territory of Papua Annual Reports*, it is estimated that 23,000 tons of ore was transported in 1924-25, 34,170 tons in 1925-26 and only 2,700 tons in 1926-27.

The venture failed and went into receivership in September 1926. The last regular train operations were in early 1927, although maintenance work continued on the line for several years. As soon as maintenance work ceased, dry season fires burned out many culverts, bridges and sleepers.[96] Several inspections of the facilities were made by Commonwealth Railways officials after closure. The locomotives were stored at Tahira and were last in steam for an inspection in August 1931. At this time, the line was passable only for about 2 km. Railway equipment, including the Andrew Barclay locomotive, 9 large hopper trucks, 20 small hopper trucks, trolleys, 470 tons of 60 lb. rails and 120 tons of 30 lb rails, was advertised for tender by the Commonwealth in 1932.[97] No sale eventuated and the equipment, including both locomotives, was still stored at Bootless Bay in 1945.[98] However, Catholic missionaries lifted rails from the line for use on the wharf at Yule Island and the sawmill railway at Arokopina.[99]

Buna-Yodda Goldfield

An alluvial gold field was discovered at Yodda, some 130 km inland from Buna in the Northern District around 1910. A number of miners were working the field by 1909, taking five days to walk there from Buna.[100] By 1914, it was reported that an ambitious mining company had imported a dredge for the field.[101] The intention was to transport it from Buna to Yodda by means of portable railway line, about a mile in length, which were to be picked up and laid down ahead of the equipment as it moved inland.[102]. News of the outbreak of war was received when the strange caravan had proceeded about 10 km and the venture was abandoned.

The equipment included sawmilling equipment. Papuan Timber Industries Limited applied for registration in May 1914 to establish a sawmill at Buna and construct a tramline.[103] A small sawmill was operating by 1915 and approval to construct the tramway was given under Executive Council Order 14 the following year.[104] No further official reports of this railway have been located. However, it is reported that a Mr Evans used the Yodda goldfield sawmill machinery for a sawmill at Buna.

Oil Exploration

Oil exploration also fuelled the hopes of the Papuan administration and stimulated several minor railway lines. In 1911, Towards the end of August 1911 Messrs Letts and Thomas reported to the Warden of the Gulf Division that they had discovered what they believed to

Top - Sacred Heart Mission jetty and railway, Yule Island, dating from 1891.

PNG Collection, UPNG Library. Photo L148-36.

Bottom - Waterfront at Arokopina Catholic Mission, Central Province, with 1067 mm. gauge railway in foreground.

Fryer Collection, UPNG Library, Photo 494.

be petroleum near the Vailala River in the Gulf district.[105] A light railway to service a drilling rig was under construction on the Vailala field by 1915.[106] The line was located in difficult broken country, although the initial sections were over level land with only two culverts. The Anglo-Persia Oil Company took over the field in 1920 and undertook extensive exploration work over the next decade. Railways were used in several locations. In 1921-22, the company moved its operations from Upoia to Popo.[107] A haulage railway (funicular) was laid up the flank of a hill to transport the rig and equipment to the drilling site.

Mission Railways

The Society of Mary (Marist) sent its first missionaries in Papua to Woodlark Island, where they arrived in 1847. Protestant missions followed, each working within a "sphere of influence". The London Missionary Society concentrated on the southern coast, the Methodists on the eastern islands and the Anglicans on the mainland from Cape Ducie west to the northern boundary.[108] Papuan missionaries were less concerned with trade and commerce than their counterparts in New Guinea. Nevertheless, there were a number of applications of light railway technology to pursue mission endeavour.

The Most Sacred Heart Mission established their first permanent mission station on Yule Island in 1885. In 1891 the mission sent out post cards of their new mission station at Port Leon on the opposite end of the island to the latter Government station at Kairuku. The cards depicted the pier and station buildings. A tramline for transporting cargo is clearly evident on the pier. In 1936, Brother Delabarre helped dismantle rails from the Bootless Bay railway for use on the Yule Island wharf.[109] The line was described as being 100 metres in length.

Charles Abel of the LMS moved his mission station from Samarai to Kwato in August 1891. He received backing from a South Australian philanthropist, JH Angas, for an industrial mission at Kwato based on saw-milling and boat building.[110] Abel used a tramline to carry out swamp reclamation and to build a cricket field between 1892 and 1894.[111] Trucks were hand-pushed on the line.[112] Abel was a pioneer in introducing cricket to Papua. From 1913, he began the establishment of coconut plantations with Papuan managers. The success of the Kwato plantations aroused the wrath of European planters, who complained of unfair competition from "cheap nigger labour". Abel's efforts were confined to a small area of Milne Bay.

The Anglican Mission established their head station at Dogura in Northern Province in 1930. Dogura station stood on a hill, 160 metres above the beach at Wedau. To bring stores up to the station, a light railway line, probably of 2 ft 6 in (762 mm) gauge, was constructed.[113] In 1935, the mission commenced construction of a large cathedral to seat 1000 people.[114] The railway was kept busy over the next four years transporting hundreds of tons of stone, sand and cement for the project.

Timber Tramways

Missions operated logging and sawmilling ventures which employed light railways. The Catholic Mission at Ononghe in Central Province had a railway, about 1.5 km in length, to haul logs to their sawmill.[115] At Arokopina, the Catholic Mission used a line, 200-300 metres in length, from its sawmill to a store and jetty.[116] Rails and hand-pushed trolleys were obtained from the Bootless Bay railway in 1936. A line from the wharf to the Catholic Mission sawmill in Sideia Island, Milne Bay, is reported to have been "quite long". On Normandy Island, a sawmill at Sewa Bay had a short line, about 400 metres in length, laid with wooden rails. It ran from the wharf in a loop to the sawmill and back again.[117].

Notes on Chapter 3

1   McKillop, RF, "Railways in Australian history: a preliminary reconnaissance", *ARHS Bulletin*, No. 558, April 1984, p. 89-95.

2   *Ibid.,* p. 84.

3   Nolan, Janette, *Bundaberg: history and people*, Univ. Qld. Press, 1978, p. 124.

4   Moore, CR, *Kanaka: a history of Melanesian Mackay*, Uni PNG Press, 1986.

5   *Ibid.,* p. 239.

6   *Ibid.,* p. 249.

7   McIntyre, WD, *The Imperial frontier in the tropics, 1865-1975*, London, 1967, p. 348.

8   McKillop, RF and Firth, S, "Foreign intrusion and the establishment of agricultural institutions" in D Denoon and C Snowden (eds), *A time to plant and a time to uproot: a history of agriculture in Papua New Guinea*, Port Moresby, Univ. of PNG, nd, p. 87.

9   *Ibid.,* p. 95.

10   *Ibid.,* p. 95.

11   MacGregor, W, *Handbook of information for intending settlers in British New Guinea*, 1892, quoted by N Jinks, P Biskup and H Nelson (eds), *Readings in New Guinea history*, Sydney, Angus & Robertson, 1973.

12   Report of the Royal Commission, 1907, quoted by Jinks *et. al, op. cit.,* p. 92-6.

13   McKillop and Firth, *op. cit.,* p. 97.

14   Territory of Papua Annual Report, 1921-22, p. 6.

15   National Archives Box 6592 Correspondence (G120) 1888 to 1906,

16   British New Guinea Annual Report 1895-96. p. xxix.

17   Kerr, J&R, "Cooktown Quarantine Railway", *Light Railways,* No, 85, July 1984, p. 13-17.

18   British New Guinea Annual Report 1902-1903, p. 36-37, 44

19   British New Guinea Annual Report, 1905-1906, p. 80, 82

20   Territory of Papua Annual Report 1907-1908, p. 95 &108.

21   Gash and Whittaker, *Pictorial History of New Guinea* p.99 plate 200.

22   Territory of Papuan Annual Report, 1916-17, p. 18.

23   National Archives - Box 6441 Series G69 File 31/5 f /1-40. 26/2/41 Dept of Public Works.

24   National Archives - Box 6441 Series G69 File 31/4 f 41-134

25   Cornfield, RS, *Hold hands cobbers, Vol II, 1930-1990*, Melbourne, Brown Prior Anderson, photo p. 69.

26   Territory of Papua Annual Report 1910-1911, p. 35

27   Cleland, D, General Manager, The British New Guinea Development Co Ltd, 28 November 1978.

28   Francis West, *Hubert Murray - The Australia Pro-Consul*, Oxford 1968, Oxford University Press, p137 footnote a 45

29   National Archives. G72 External Affairs Despatches Received by Administrator Vol 1 7-5-13 > 23-7-13/ 25-4-14 > 26-7-14.

30   *Ibid.,* Radio Message June 4 1914 A Hunt to Murray. Note, spelling was Rona at this time.

31   Territory of Papua Annual Report 1913-1914, p. 6, 137

32   *North Queensland Register,* 20 July 1914

33   Australian Parliamentary Papers, 1914-1917, Volume 4.

34   Territory of Papua Annual Report 1914-1915 p 7 & 139

35   British New Guinea Annual Report 1893-94. pxxiii, 1897-98, p. 113.

36   British New Guinea Annual Report 1894-95.

37   British New Guinea Annual Report 1899-1900, p. 56

38   West, F, *op. cit.*, p. 190.

39   Territory of Papua Annual Report 1923-1924 p. 45.

40   PNG National Archives, letter from N Imlay, Collector of Customs to Treasurer, 5 May 1925.

41   National Archives - Box 1024 Out Stations N8/2 Samarai Wharf & Jetty Tramline.

42   Geographical Handbook, Naval Intelligence Pacific Islands, Vol. IV, 1945, p. 236.

43   *Pacific Islands Monthly* March 1962 p 34.

44   British New Guinea Annual Report 1895-96. p. 69

45   Territory of Papua Annual Report 1916-1917, p. 32

46   George Tabua, personal communication, Daru 1978

47   Territory of Papua Annual Report 1907-1908, p. 118.

48   Territory of Papua Annual Report 1921-1922 p. 80

49   *Pacific Islands Monthly*, September 1931, p. 9.

50   National Archives Box 6592 Correspondence, extract from *Melbourne Age* 20th Sept 1901 and *Bulletin* 5/10/01: T. F. Bevan "New Guinea Development Scheme".

51   *Pacific Islands Monthly*, Oct. 1931, p.4

52   Horne, JS, "Diary of visit to inspect Robinson River Plantation, 30/11/1932 to 22/1/1933", UPNG Library, PNG Miscellaneous Documents, 1885-1964, PMB627.

53   *Papuan Villager*, Vol. 8:4, April, 1936, p. 25-27.

54   Letter from ML Wundke, manager, Itikinumu Estate, March 1984.

55   A Bovelt, letter, 11 May 1978.

56   Nelson, H, *Black and Gold*, Canberra, ANU Press, p. 58.

57   British New Guinea Annual Report 1899-1900, p. 7; *Queensland Mining Journal*, 15th June 1900. A survey of the line, comprising leases GML 115 and GML 81 dated 8 June 1916 is held in National Archives.

58   Collinson, JW, *Tropic coast and tablelands*, 1941, p. 49.

59   British New Guinea Annual Report 1902-1903, p. 38-39

60   Territory of Papua Annual Report 1910-1911, p 28, 29 & 30

61   Territory of Papua Annual Report, 1913-14, p. 155.

62   Territory of Papua Annual Report 1912-1913, p. 58, 112 & 113

63   Territory of Papua Annual Report 1913-1914, p. 42 & 155

64   Memorandum by CEH of Lands, Survey & Mines Department of 26 July 1917, plus map supplied by RF Ellis.

65   National Archives G97 Series Box 2407 File 11.

66   Territory of Papua Annual Report 1923-1924 p. 30

67   *Pacific Islands Monthly*, 23 May, p 49 & 23 June, 1937, p. 29

68   ED Ryan, letter, 30 October, 1978, describing operations in 1936.

69   Allied Geographical Section, South West Pacific Area, Terrain Study No. 35, 23 rd Nov 1942. Area Study - Woodlark Island p. 9

70   Head office at 31 Queen Street, Melbourne.

71 A history of the railway was published by RF McKillop, "The Misima Island railway" in *Light Railways*, No. 51, Autumn 1975, pp. 4-7. The following is an updated version of this article using additional material, including original correspondence by H Gilbee Brown, the doctor at Umuna during the railway operation.

72 H Gilbee Brown, letter 21 Aug 1962

73 H Gilbee Brown, letter 26 September 1962

74 H Gilbee Brown, letter 13 April 1964. Dr Brown reported that "those in the know said it was the games of poker which caused the delays [not derailments]."

75 "Mountains, gold and railways", *Pacific Islands Monthly*, July 1962, article based on H Gilbee Brown notes.

76 RB Williamson (mine manager 1919-21), letter to H Gilbee Brown.

77 Field interviews by Michael Sakiasi, November 1975, reported in McKillop, RF, *op cit.*, p. 5-6.

78 PNG National Archives, Lieutenant-Governor's Office, file 15/8.

79 A correspondent to Mr Gilbee Brown signing himself "Phil", 7 June 1964.

80 ED Ryan, letter, 30 October 1978.

81 Nelson, H, *op. cit.*, p. 41-42.

82 McKillop, RF, "Papua New Guinea's Bootless Bay railway", *Light Railways* No. 47, 1974, p. 3-16, provides a detailed history of the railway and mining operations. Additional research has been incorporated into this book.

83 *The Financial Times*, October 20, 1920.

84 National Archives G74 Dispatch Schedules, Dispatch 18/7832 of 6 July 1918 and radio of 18 September 1918.

85 Territory of Papua Annual Report 1920-1921 p 19.

86 The map and description of the line are based on a map provided by the Australian Army in August 1950 (Dispatch 15293 to AD Lockyer, South Australia), field surveys by the authors and contemporary photographs.

87 *Queensland Mining Journal*, December 1921.

88 ES&A Bank, Melbourne, letter SW:JET of 11 May 1950 to AD Lockyer.

89 SA Lonergan, a/Government Secretary, Territory of PNG, letter CA 25/3/54 to AD Lockyer, 22 March 1950.

90 Letter from Robert Hayes, Newcastle of 23 May 1945 and Elsie Hayes of 4 August 1950 to AD Lockyer.

91 Stewart, I, *Port Moresby: yesterday and today*, Sydney, Pacific Publications, 1973, p. 109.

92 Denoon, D and Snowden, C, "Bootless Bay revisited", *Light Railways*, No. 74, 1981.

93 *Queensland Mining Journal*, 15 June, 1922.

94 *Papuan Courier*, 11 July 1924, p. 5.

95 Papuan Annual Report, 1924-25 and 1925-26.

96 SA Lonergan, *op. cit.*

97 *Territory of Papua Government Gazette*, Vol. XXVII, 6 January 1932.

98 Pearson, R, "A railway in Papua", *Light Railways*, No. 20, 1967, p. 21-23.

99 Br J Delabarre, letter, 21 October, 1979 detailing his participation in the dismantling task in 1936.

100 SMR Gill, letter, 14 April, 1923, Pacific Manuscripts Bureau microfilm PMB40.

101 Territory of Papua Annual Report 1913 -1914, p 156

102 Letter, *Pacific Islands Monthly*, April 1947.

103 *Territory of Papua Government Gazette*, Vol. IX, No. 8, 6 May 1914, p. 2. Also PPAR, 1914-15, p. 54.

104 National Archives Dispatch Schedules G72, Radio July 4, 1916, A Hunt to Murray

105 Territory of Papua Annual Report, 1911-1912, p. 33.

106 Territory of Papua Annual Report, 1914-1915, p. 137

107 Territory of Papua Annual Report, 1921-1922, p. 46

108 British New Guinea Annual Report, 1889-90, p. 19.

109 Delabarre, J, letter, 21 October, 1979

110 McKillop and Firth, *op. cit*, p. 99.

111 British New Guinea Annual Report 1891-92, p. 88

112 Photo in Air Niugini *Paradise* magazine, No. 42, July-September, 1983.

113 *Australian Board of Missions Review*, 17:8, 15 November, 1930.

114 *Pacific Islands Monthly*, September 1939, p. 6; *Papuan Villager*, 11:11, November 1939, p. 21-33.

115 Andrew Ikupa, interview, UPNG, 1993.

116 Delabarre, J, *op. cit.*

117 Simon Gina, interview, Tiop, 1983.

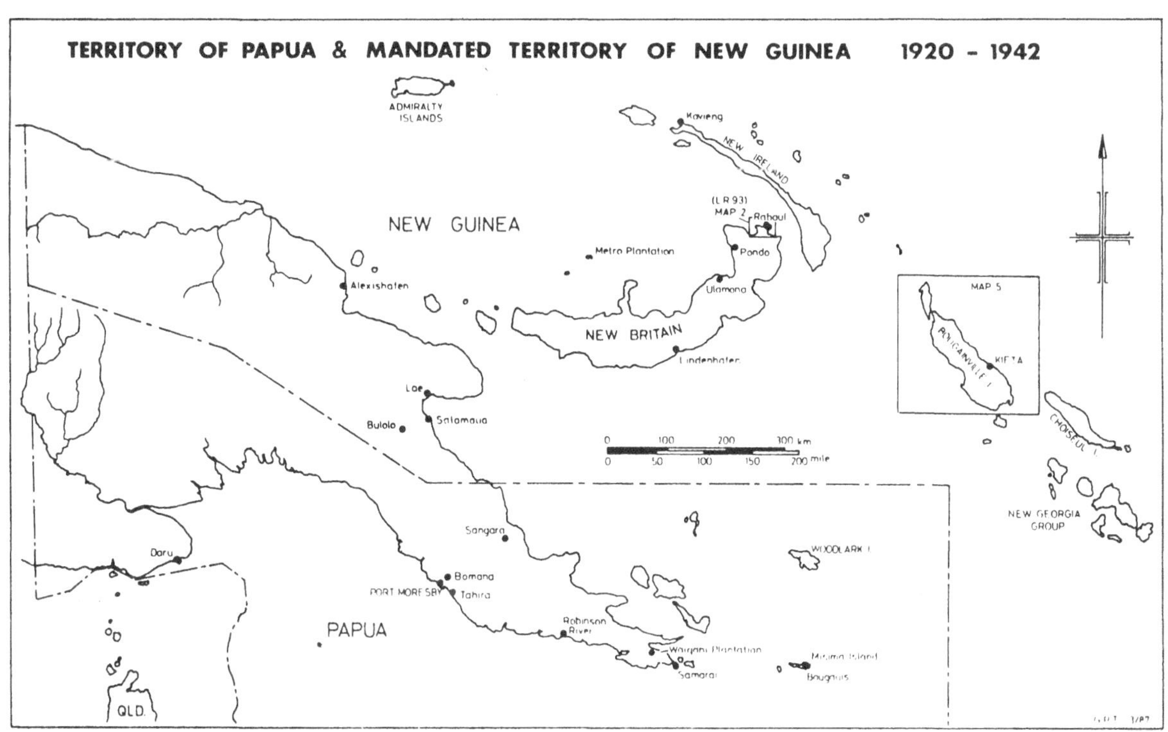

Above - Map of Territory of Papua and Mandated Territory of New Guinea

CHAPTER 4. MANDATED TERRITORY OF NEW GUINEA

Australian Administration

In September 1914, an Australian Expeditionary Force captured Rabaul and German New Guinea became an occupied territory. At the post-war Paris Conference, the Australian Prime Minister put forward an argument for the annexation of the German colony on strategic grounds. It was agreed under the League of Nations Covenant that that Australia would administer the territory as a "C" class Mandate. This provided Australia with responsibility to take charge of the "spiritual interests [of the natives] and their development to a higher development of culture."[1] However, Australia had its own internal problems to address and the new external responsibility was seen as a burden on the available resources for development at home. The administration for the Mandated Territory of New Guinea, established in May 1921, was expected to operate without external subsidies from the colonial power, in marked contrast to Papua and the former German administration.[2]

German plantations and trading stations were expropriated and war reparations paid to Australia to help pay for the cost of the war. As a consequence, expansion and maintenance of plantations was stifled until the long process of registering assets, tendering and transferring ownership was sorted out. The dynamic economic expansion which characterised the latter period of German colonial administration stagnated as a result of this expropriation process.

An Expropriation Board was established to administer the disposed German properties and their transfer to Australian owners. Some 268 plantations, 20 large stores, workshops, shipping facilities and other facilities were subjected to the expropriation process.[3] Plantations were sold to Australian soldier settlers, most of whom had little knowledge of or aptitude for agriculture in the tropics. WR Carpenters, an offshoot of the NGK from Western Samoa and Fiji which established an Australian base, bought out most of the NGK holdings.

The Australian trading company Burns Philp (BP) had established a subsidiary, Choisel Plantations, to establish plantations on Bougainville because the German administration had opposed their entry. BP took over many former German trading businesses. The other main trading firm in Papua, the BNG Development Company, was precluded by its charter from taking advantage of expropriation to expand into the Mandated Territory. Soldier settlers who had taken up plantation properties soon faced declining commodity prices as the world economy slid into the depression and became indebted to their suppliers. Burns Philp took over many of these plantations at this time.

In 1922 a solitary prospector *Sharkeye* Park found gold on Koringa Creek in the Bulolo area. The field was a rich one and attracted miners, but the journey into the remote location through inhospitable country was a major problem. By the 1930s, the Mandated Territory had a foreign population of 4500, four times that of Papua, of whom 1000 were Chinese and 400 German. Some 26,000 New Guineas were indentured labourers, two and a half times that of the southern colony. It was still a frontier territory, where men were driven by a quest for gold and spirit of adventure. Among the foreign population, men outnumbered women by three to one. A vast, unknown inland was still being explored, with the administration opening its first Highland patrol post at Upper Ramu (later Kainantu) in 1932.

As in Papua, the administration oscillated between competing extremes for development policies. The planters argued that the policy of "providing a book education" was a waste of money and:

> the only real education available to the native at present is provided in the homes of the colonists, in the workshops, on the ships, in the Christian Missions, and particularly on the plantations and trading concerns of the planting community. [4]

Others argued that the "native" must be compelled to work and grow crops for their advancement. From this perspective, recruitment of male villagers for plantation labour was seen as an anachronistic policy to maintain "plantation fodder"[5]. The outcome was conflicting policies which sought to keep the mass of people alive in their villages with as little interference as possible, while at the same time supporting labour recruitment to keep plantations operating. In practice, the need of plantations for labour dominated over support for *peasant proprietorship.*

There was also inherent contradiction over policy toward Asiatic immigration. Under the German administration, Chinese, Javanese and Japanese labourers had been introduced. The Australian military administration treated all Asiatics with similar status to Europeans, but under the Mandated administration, the Australian Government applied their White Australia policy.[6] Further Asiatic immigration was restricted, thereby making plantation development dependant on local indentured labour.

Rabaul Tramways

Rabaul, the main town and administrative centre, was served by the 750 mm gauge tramway system developed by the German trading companies (Chapter 2). These properties, including tramlines, were included in the sale of expropriated properties in 1922.[7] The new owners continued to use the tramlines for the transport of goods to and from their warehouses.

The Australian administration commenced construction of a new tramline, 2.14 km (1.5 miles) in length from Rabaul to Rapindik near Matupit, the site chosen for the new Native Hospital and police and native compounds, in 1922.[8] For this line, they selected the closest Imperial equivalent of the German street tramway gauge, 2 ft 6 in (or 762 mm) gauge. It was proposed to extend it through the town to link up with a new wharf site.

Tenders for the supply of petrol locomotives and rolling stock for the new line were called in Australia in late 1923.[9] A small Muir Hill locomotive was obtained for the line, probably in 1924. Few details of the locomotive have been located. However, the English firm Muir Hill built small narrow-gauge contractor's type locomotives.[10] Their 4-ton, 2-axle locomotive was powered by a Fordson four cylinder engine running on paraffin (kerosene). It had a patent two speed gearbox (2.5 and 7 mph), with reverse and synchromesh.

The initial line construction was apparently unsatisfactory, for the tramline was rebuilt and extended to serve the new "native hospital" under construction at Rapindik in 1927.[11] The hospital was finally transferred to the new site on 21 November, 1928. With this transfer, the administration commenced regular passenger services over the railway.[12]. Papua New Guinea's only public railway passenger service ran to the following timetable:

	Leave Old Hospital	Return Rabaul
1	0700	0755
2	0930	1025
3	1115	1200
4	1600	1655

The locomotive was under the care of a Chinese engineer. There was a passenger carriage and at least one bogie flat truck for freight.

In January, 1923 the former NDL wharf at Rabaul and its tramline was damaged by fire.[13] As a temporary measure, Malaguna coaling wharf was upgraded by the Administration with a 2 ft gauge tramline. Plans were announced to construct a new wharf midway between the former wharf and the coal wharf. This was built in the 1930's.

Tenders for the NGK wharf in 1926 list two tracks of 762 mm gauge tramline.[14] The wharf was purchased by WR Carpenters, while Burns Philp purchased the Malaguna wharf. The old NGK wharf was partially repaired by 1931.[15]

Another line was built from Ah Tams Wharf at the north of the harbour to a copra store. In December, 1929, a major fire destroyed this wharf and copra store then leased to WR Carpenters.[16] Following this fire, Carpenters established a new facility at Toboi, some 1.5 km west of Ah Tams. A tramline was built to carry copra from the wharf to the new storage sheds.[17] Bogie wagons were hand-pushed on the tramway and from 800 to 900 tonnes of copra could be handled per day. Field observations indicate that the tramway was constructed to 2 ft (610 mm) gauge with double track on the wharf.

Although serving an important role in trade and commerce and providing transport for New Guineans, Rabaul's tramways were given little status by the European elite. Their mouthpiece, the *Rabaul Times,* inevitably referred to the system with sarcasm. In 1928 it boasted that Rabaul had "more cars per head of population here than any where else in the world."[18] Presumably only Europeans were counted in the *Times'* version of civilisation. Their authority was challenged on the 2 January, 1929 when Europeans awoke to find all workers on a well organised strike. The event provoked outrage in the columns of the *Times* which described the strike as a mutiny and called for tough action against the ring leaders.[19]

Tolais remember the tramway system more positively. Haileen recollects:

> The tramline at Rabaul extended from Rapindik to Malaguna following the present roads - Sulphur Creek Road, Mango Avenue, Malaguna Road and some of the roads that do not follow the checker board pattern. The line along Namanula road proceeded to the Government houses at the top of Namanula Hill and also to the Police Barracks. [20]

On 29 May, 1937 Vulcan and Matupit, two small volcanoes, one each side of Rabaul Harbour, erupted showering ash over the town. Most of the population was excavated by ship, but some 500 people perished. There was extensive damage to property, particularly in the Rapindik area. Although roads were quickly cleared, most of the tramway was abandoned and only the wharf lines remained in use. It was decided to move the capital to Lae.

The Rapindik locomotive and rolling stock were put up for sale in October, 1937, while tenders were invited for the purchase of 10 light railway trucks in November.[21] Mr FV

Saunders of Kavieng purchased seven of the latter trucks and a quantity of rail. The Rapindik locomotive and rolling stock failed to find a buyer and were readvertised in 1940. By 1942 the move to Lae was almost complete.

Planters

The German regime had established a strong plantation base by 1914. Transport was provided by 600 mm gauge *Feldbahn* or light railways. Those which were clearly established in German times are covered in Chapter 2. With expropriation and the further development of plantations by Australian companies, additional light railway systems were established on a number of plantations.

Australian plantation railways were built to 2 ft (610 mm) gauge. Tramway materials were imported from the English firm of Robert Hudson for the Choisel-operated plantations in the 1920s. There are references to the use of small internal combustion (IC) engined locomotives on several of the lines during the 1930s. These were small 2-ton locomotives with 7 hp petrol engines built by RA Lister and Company of England, for whom Burns Philp were the South Pacific agents.[22]

During the Mandated Territory era, most operations appear to have had a single railway line running through the plantation. Ox-drawn carts hauled green copra from the field to the railway, over which it was then transported to the copra driers. Dried copra was usually transported from a central storage shed to the wharf for shipment.

NW Bougainville Plantations

Soraken plantation, established by Choisel Plantations in 1913, was using a light railway by the 1920s. There was a double tramline on the wharf by 1925.[23] Reports of the railway operation before World War II are sketchy. Railway lines were removed or destroyed during the Japanese occupation.

The Choisel Plantations holding at Kunua, also on the north-west Bougainville coast, was established in 1925.[24] It appears that 2 ft gauge tramlines were established from this date using equipment supplied by Robert Hudson. Railway lines were removed by the Japanese during the war.

NE Bougainville Plantations

Baniu plantation, owned by Choisel, had a light railway system, at least 9-10 km in length, through the coconut plots. It was built pre-war, although the establishment date has not been identified. The terrain was rugged for rail operations. Although one section of the railway operated on a relatively flat plateau, another section ran down from here into the rougher area of the plantation. The line wound around and down a ridge from the plateau into a valley where it branched several times and crossed the creek in at least 3 different places. Grades of up to 1 in 20 with considerable earthworks were necessary to negotiate these ridges. Embankments about a metre high took the line to bridges over the creek. Part of this line ran down to a landing on Baniu Bay.

A small Lister locomotive hauled trucks of green copra from the field to the driers, then the dried copra onto the store. Father McConvil travelled on a hand-pushed trolley on the tramline during his escape from the Japanese about Christmas 1942.[25] A feature of the railway was the use of concrete sleepers. Although the lines were removed in the 1960s, many concrete sleepers and a large iron bridge (damaged) remained when the site was inspected in 1982.

The Choisel-operated Teopasino Plantation 15 km south of Tinputz had a light plantation railway, 4.1 km in length. It was established pre-war.[26]. Oral history recollections indicate that the railway operated in conjunction with ox-drawn carts to haul green copra to the driers. [27] Rail trucks were fitted with high sides for the green copra and were hauled by a small petrol locomotive, probably a Lister. A substantial bridge was built to cross the river. The system was pulled up in the 1960s and the rails are reported to have gone to Soraken. [28] The extensive earthworks remain through the plantation.

Buoi Plantation came into BP ownership in 1928 when it was auctioned.[29] Some 4 km of 2 ft gauge tramway are reported on the plantation. Wagons were hand-pushed and the line was still in use up to the Bougainville crisis.

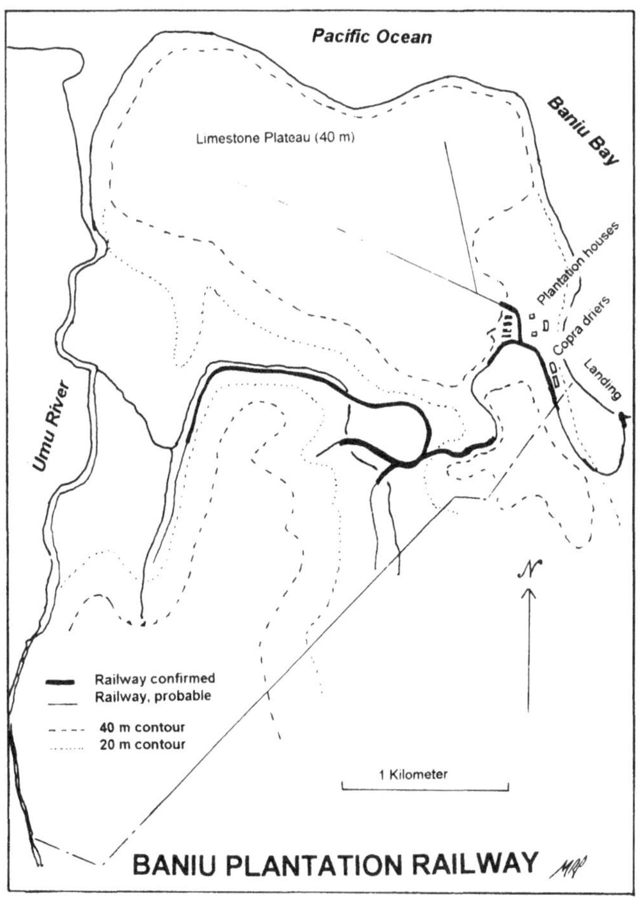

Above - Map of Bainu Plantation Railways

Central Bougainville

Arigua plantation managed by Choisel Plantations and Kuwina plantation managed by Burns Philp were linked by a common light railway line. The line, served Arigua with a branch line to the Kuwina bungalow and labour complex.[30] One view of the operations on this railway during the 1930's is recorded in the writing of the then manager, Robert Stewart:

> We had a small diesel engine which pulled flat-top cars on rails which were used for transporting green copra from the fields to the driers. All copra cut in the field was collected by bullock drays or the truck and then transported to the diesel train... A train load of copra was usually accompanied by boys who had finished their tasks for the day which, on account of the transport available, was four bags a day instead of three at Tenakau.
>
> As the return journey by train to the driers was all down hill, it was not an uncommon occurrence for the train to be derailed when negotiating the curves. Sometimes the brakes failed and when this happened, the train would career down at a great speed, and if not derailed would eventually be stopped and derailed by buffers, installed near the driers. When this occurred there would be utter chaos, bags of copra and boys would be thrown in all directions but curiously enough, no one was ever seriously injured.[31]

The locomotive was one of the early Lister units imported by Choisel Plantations.[32] It could haul nine trucks on the line. There are no reports of post-war operations.

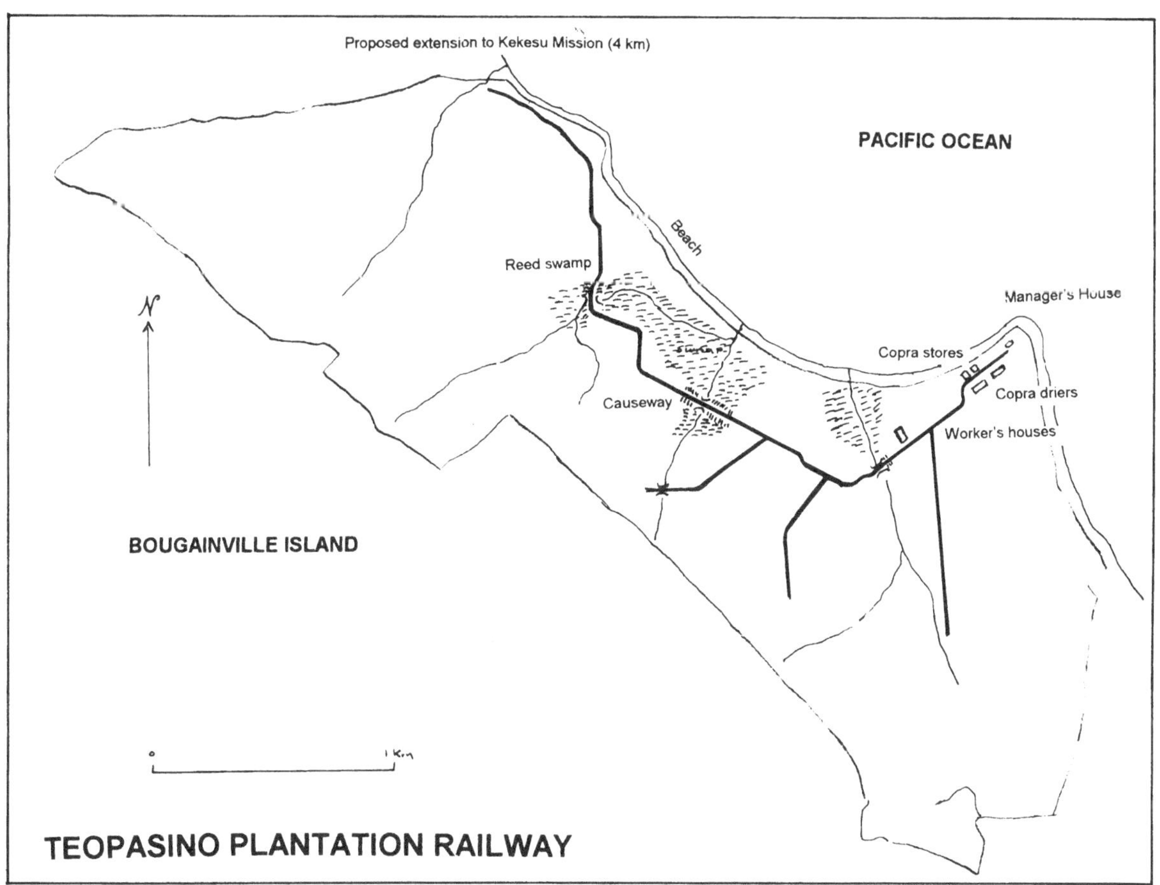

Above - Map of Teopasino Plantation Railway

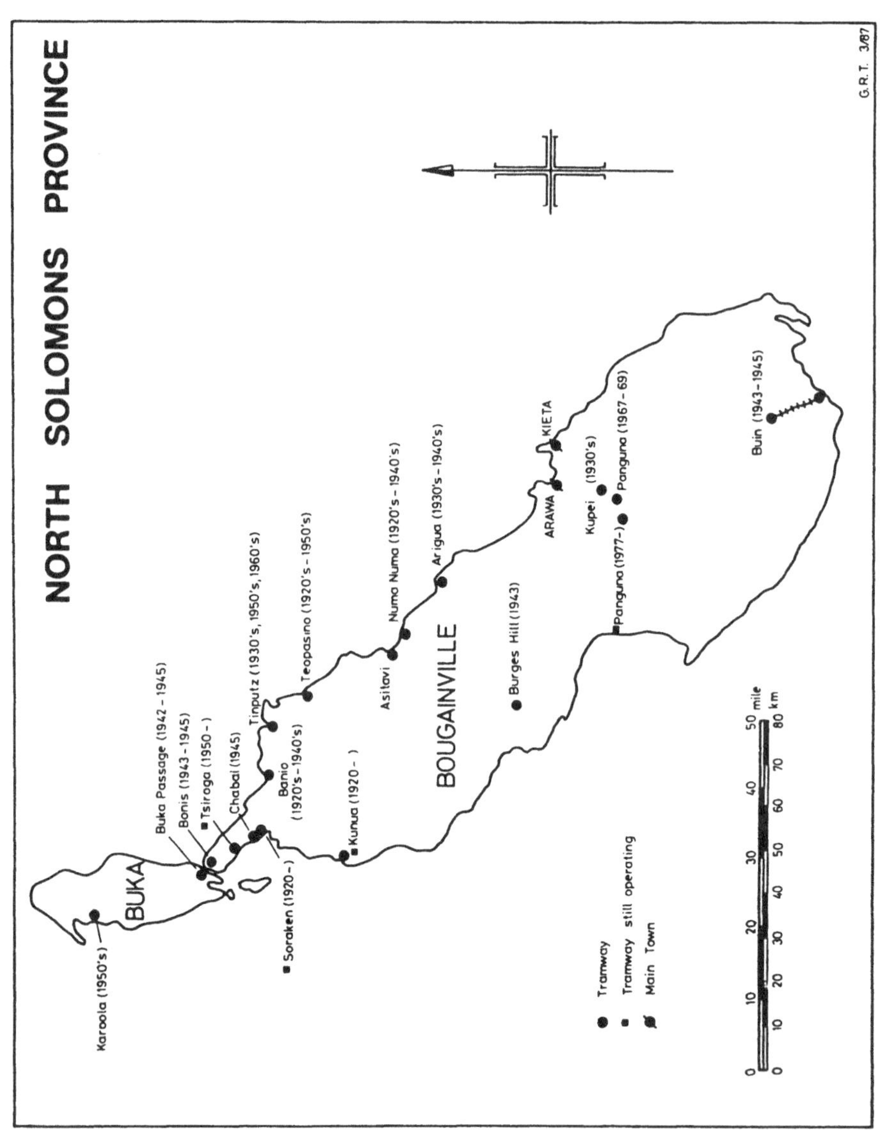

Above - Map of North Solomons Province

West New Britain Railways

Lindenhafen plantation on the isolated Kandrian coast of West New Britain came under BP ownership. In 1932, 8 km of light railway was in operation. The railway extend from the factory and kilns at the beach right through the middle of the estate to near section 11, where it branched to serve sections 10 and 12.[33] Another branch line served No. 6 block, thence into the bush to transport firewood for the factory and driers. These lines required major overhaul in 1932, suggesting they had been in operation for some time. A further branch had recently been constructed parallel to the beach to transport shingle for ballasting the main line. The seven trucks on the railway were pushed by hand.

In 1943, Allied intelligence reported 11 trucks on the plantation, each with a capacity of 1 ton of green copra.[34] A *kiap* who visited Lindenhafen in 1955 reported seeing a steam locomotive housed in a shed, while the railway was operated by a home-built locomotive based on a Ferguson tractor.[35] One manager is reported to have named"stations" after railway stations on the Sydney suburban railway system.

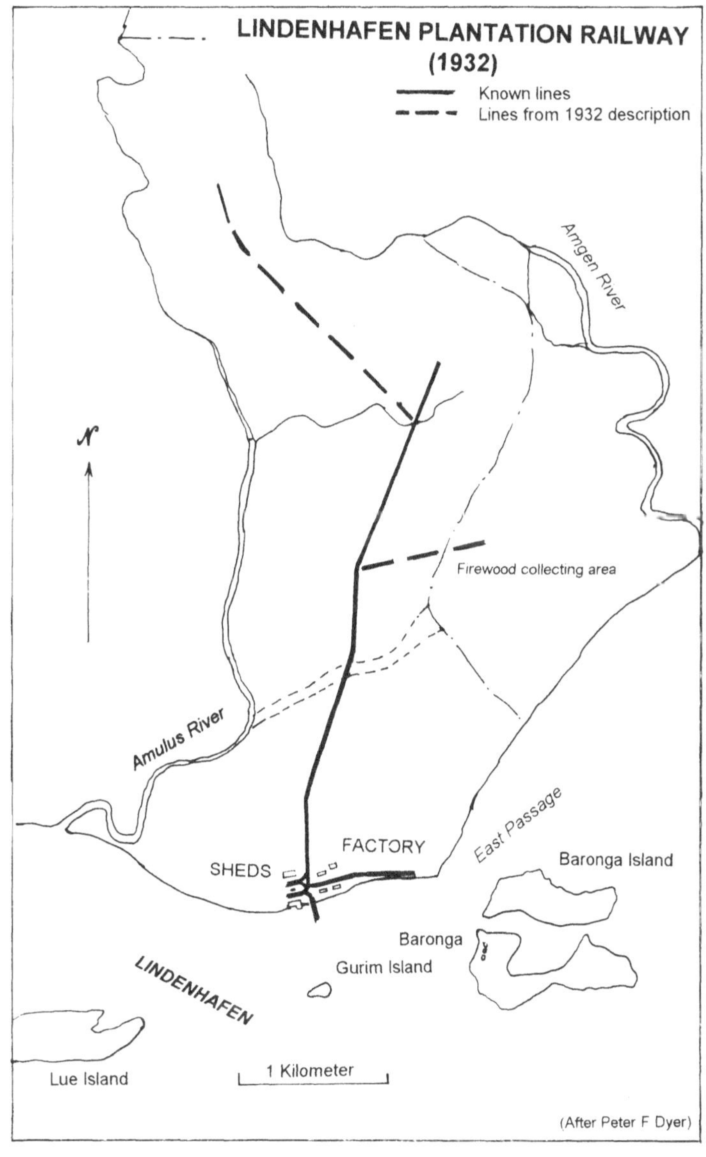

Above - Map of Lindenhafen

The track was in bad condition in 1978 and was lifted the following year. A small Lister-powered locomotive was transferred from Lindenhafen to Soraken at this time.

Bali Plantation on Unea Island in the Witu Group of today's West New Britain Province had a railway from the copra driers through the plantation to Bali Harbour. The gauge was 2 ft 6 in (762 mm). No other details are known.

At some time following the First World War, the tramline on Meto Plantation on Garove Island, also in the Witu Group (see Chapter 2), was extended to the adjoining Ilia Plantation owned by the Catholic Mission, a distance of 1 km. The line served the factory and copra sheds at Ilia.[36]

Other Plantation Railways

Neinduk plantation on the Gazelle Peninsula had a timber-railed line which ran through the plantation to haul raw copra to the smoke house on the beach.[37] There was a branch, running 4.5 km inland to a small sawmill owned by Bolton Brothers at Namburg.[38] This led down to a wharf on the adjoining plantation to Neinduk. There were four flat-trucks which were loaded with timber and hand-pushed to the loading point on the beach.[39] The grade allowed the workers to ride on the trucks as they free-wheeled for much of the journey.

Several plantation lines on New Ireland date from the Mandated Territory era. At Kalili Plantation a line ran through coconut groves to the copra drier, then down to a jetty. Trucks were hand-pushed on the line.[40] In the post-war period, rails from the line were used for various applications on the plantation. A 610 mm gauge wheel set located in 1995 is said to come from this railway. At Lossu plantation on the east coast, a buffalo-worked railway carried coconuts from the field to driers. Other lines are reported on Kimadon plantation on the east coast and Waramung plantation on Anir Island.

Forestry Railways

As described in chapter 2, German mission sawmills employed rail technology in their forestry operations. They were low impact operations which were able to sustain their venture over the long-term. By the 1930's, however, the availability of crawler tractors and motor trucks were bringing about basic change in forest logging operations. Contractors could now fell large numbers of trees quickly and move on to exploit new areas. This technology came to New Guinea, notably in the Bulolo area. Few new logging or timber tramways were constructed in the Mandated Territory.

A small sawmill operation was established by the New Britain Timber and Mercantile Company Ltd in 1926.[41] A steel-railed line, half-a-mile in length, was constructed to serve the mill. The venture was unsuccessful and the receiver called tenders for the sawmill and railway in 1931.[42]

On Bougainville the Marist Brothers' Catholic Mission established a sawmill at Tinputz. A narrow gauge railway was constructed for the transport of logs and timber in 1930. The line extended into the forest where the lumber was cut and placed on trucks and pushed to the sawmill.[43] It is reported that about 50 tons of rail for this sawmill (equivalent to 4 km of line) was lost at sea. Rails which went down with the MV *Raphael* off Teop Island 1934 were raised and used at Tearouki mission.[44] The line later served as transport from the wharf to store. A stationary steam engine was noted at the former sawmill site during a field inspection in 1975.

Mining Railways

The gold finds of Edie Creek and the Bulolo area in the 1920's brought a rush of prospectors to the field. However, the fields were inland and supplies had to be transported over inhospitable country.

Carrier lines of up to 200 men were hired for the task. Carriers were able to handle only 20 kg apiece. It took two weeks for the journey, so half the load of each carrier consisted of food for the journey. Conditions were wet and slippery, while disease and accidents, as well as attacks by hostile natives took their toll on the carriers. Soon there was pressure for a railway to solve the transport task.

Bulolo Railway Proposals

CJ Levien, the main driving force on the field, was the first to push for a narrow-gauge railway to Bulolo.[45] He saw that such a railway would not only bring in the equipment needed by the miners, but that back-loading of timber from the fine stands of klinki pine in the area would meet the costs of the investment. Levien also looked at road and air transport options from an early stage.[46]

A government engineer, Wisdom, inspected the terrain in April 1928, and selected the Markham-Wampit-Bulolo route for a light railway or road.[47] However, the Administration ran out of funds before a survey could commence. Recognising that the government was unlikely to provide the necessary transport infrastructure, the mining companies began their own search for a solution. The Ellyou Corporation, backed by the massive Mining Trust of London, commissioned Broughton Jensen, a former railway draftsman, to prepare a plan for a railway to link the Bulolo goldfield to the coast.[48] Jensen's initial proposal was for a 90 mile line down the Buang route at an estimated cost of 250,000 pounds.

The Ellyou Corporation entered into negotiations with the Administration for the rights to construct the railway, rights to timber and water, rights to minerals in the right-of-way (1000 m wide) and the right to set freight rates.[49] Negotiations continued over the next 12 months with little progress, until the Administration rejected rights to minerals and to set freight rates.

By 1929, the gold beds at Bulolo were assessed to be suitable for profitable dredging. The Ellyou Board put pressure on local managers to undertake a survey for a light railway to establish the most favourable route from the coast to the field.[50] This was completed in November, 1929 based on a route from Salamaua, along the Markham, then to Bulolo and Wau via Wampit. The proposed 2 ft gauge line was 166 miles (266 km) in length with many bridges and tunnels. However, the cost was prohibitive. Several alternatives were examined, including an aerial ropeway from the goldfields to link with a 45 km narrow-gauge railway to Salamaua.[51]

With escalating costs and unsatisfactory negotiations with the government, the railway proposal spluttered to a halt. Levien looked to a quick fix solution which would by-pass the need to provide expensive transport infrastructure.

Lae Railway

Mr Levien backed aircraft to handle the transport task. He formed the Bulolo Gold Dredging Company (BGD), ordered a new all metal Junkers G-31, the largest transport plane of the times for Guinea Airways. He had a dredge prefabricated into parts of not more than 3-tons, the G-31 payload.

Top - Lae Railway, The second steam crane operating at Voco point in 1937. The Burns Philp steamer *Bulolo* is in the background.

Fryer Collection, UPNG Library (AH 224, photo 472)

Bottom - Newspaper photograph of destruction at Lae airstrip from Japanese bombing in 1942. A bogie flatcar is in the foreground.

Courier, 27 February 1942

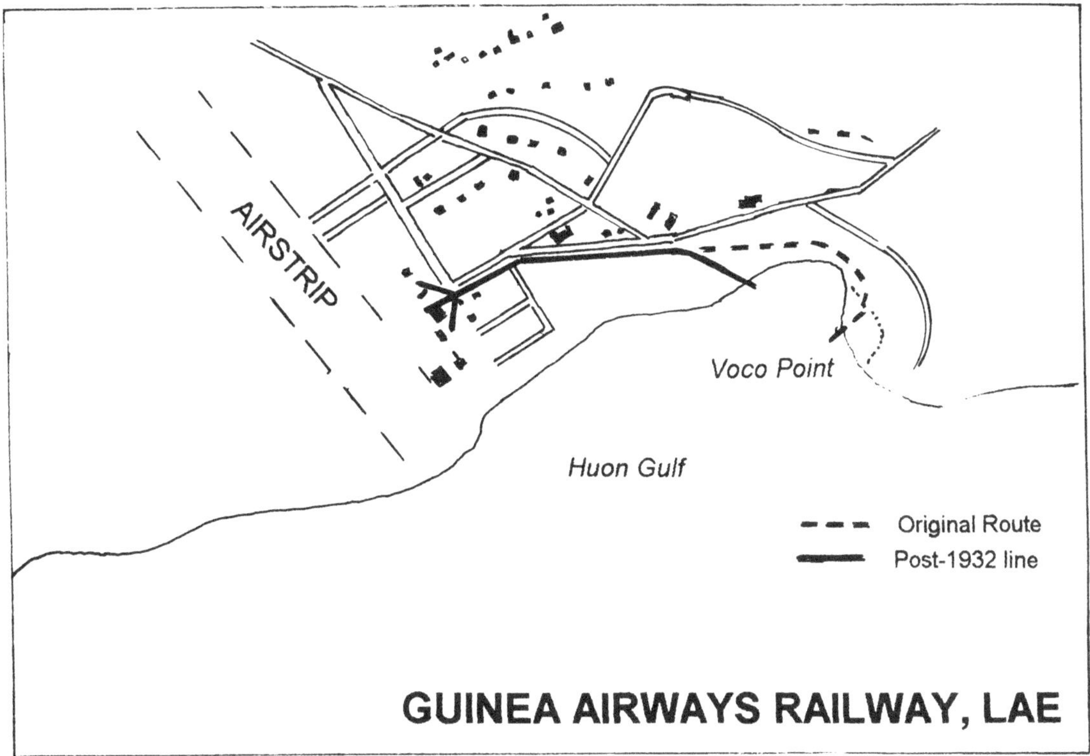

Above - Map of Lae

For the BGD operation, a 1200 metre standard gauge (1435 mm) railway was constructed from the wharf at Voco Point to the Lae airstrip in 5 weeks during 1931.[52] Dredge components and other equipment were transported along the line for freighting to Bulolo in the Junkers G-31 aircraft. The railway was operated by a 10-ton self-propelled steam crane and the rolling stock consisted of a number of flat cars. The crane arrived in mid-1931 and was operational by August.[53]

The airlift was the largest in the world to this time. By November the G-31s were lifting over 500 short tons a month and some 40,000 tons of material were carried between 1931 and 1942. In total, eight large dredges weighing 1500 to 2500 tons each were airlifted to Bulolo and assembled there for operation on the field. Lighters carried the goods from steamers to the Voco Point jetty.[54] The locomotive crane lifted the item from the lighters and swivelled it around to the flat trucks behind. Lloyd Rhys described the scene in 1932:

> Two steel barges and a hundred tons capacity steam lighter bring the cargo to the wharf. Here the chattering natives saunter, bustle when bustled, and with never-ceasing interest, watch the steam-engine which has been installed for landing machinery. Then comes into fussy action New Guinea's novelty - a broad-gauged railroad running from the wharf to the aerodrome.[55]

The self-propelled steam crane was a fascinating technology to European and New Guinean alike. Ian Grabowsky recalled:

The loco crane was a perfect example of mechanical Heath Robinson oddity. When working, either lifting, lowering or swinging into place various cargoes, it belched steam from everywhere, but its glory was most apparent as it towed a dozen six-foot long trucks along a perfectly level railway. Lucas, the licensed qualified operator, was always amazed how pilots were able to judge distances so accurately when landing, whilst the pilots always marvelled how Lucas managed in later months to load 3-ton hunks of machinery into the frail aircraft without doing any damage to them.[56]

In August 1932, an earthquake and subsidence occurred at Voco Point without warning as the crane was unloading cargo from the *Macdhui*.[57] The wharf, steam crane and trucks collapsed into the water, taking the driver, *Trousers* Jim Lucas with it.[58] Lucas got free within seconds and escaped, but his beloved steam crane, some 200 yards of railway line and 3 acres of foreshore were lost.

The wharf and the railway line were rebuilt closer to the airstrip, opposite the Cecil Hotel, and a 7-ton steam crane replaced the lost unit. The crane and new rolling stock arrived on the *Macdhui* on 6 October, 1932.[59] The pace of operations picked up and crews worked double shifts moving the cargo from the wharf and fitting items into the confined space of the G-31's. Three rail branches were established at the aerodrome: one to the loading tarmac, one to the BGD freight shed and a third to a stiff-legged electrically-operated crane which handled heavy lifts onto aircraft.[60]

A small petrol mechanical locomotive was imported from the US builder Brookville in 1932 (B/N 1704/1932) to assist with haulage of wagons from the wharf to the aerodrome, thus releasing the crane for lifting duties at the wharf.[61] The 4-wheel, 2-ton, standard gauge locomotive was classified by Brookfield as their Model BFA.

Operations on the Lae railway came to a sudden halt in February, 1942 when Japanese bombing destroyed the Guinea Airways operational base and the railway. Photographs of the damage depict bogie flat wagons on the railway.[62]

Salamaua Railway

Salamaua, 28 km south of Lae, was an early base for the Bulolo goldfields as it had a safe anchorage compared with Lae. Diggers set out from here with their carriers for the new goldfields in the 1920s. An airstrip was constructed at Salamaua to service the field, but it had restricted approaches and was subject to flooding.[63] A light railway connecting the wharf with the airstrip, a distance of 2.5 km, was reported in early 1929.[64]. This line apparently fell into disuse. In 1933 it was proposed to relay the railway in association with a project to construct a new jetty[65] and the line is clearly depicted in a 1938 photograph of the jetty.[66]

In September, 1936, a contract was given to Mr BE Watson for maintenance of the Salamaua runway.[67] A narrow-gauge light railway, some 2 km in length, was established to transport stone from a quarry to the airstrip. It ran parallel with and close to the runway for a distance of 700-800 metres and was used solely for airport maintenance.[68] A number of tip trucks were hauled by a small petrol or diesel locomotive.

Wau-Bulolo Railways

The inland towns of Wau and Bulolo grew rapidly as miners were attracted to the goldfields. In addition to the huge dredges introduced by the Bulolo Gold Dredging Company to work the alluvial field, New Guinea Goldfields operated a number of mines. Their Upper Ridges and Golden Ridges Mines had light railways hauling ore from adits to crushing mills by 1938.[69]

Kupei Goldmine

A goldfield was proclaimed at Kupei, behind Kieta on Bougainville Island in 1930.[70] The Roman Catholic Bishop of Brisbane, Dr Duhig, established the Kupei Gold mine which had a narrow-gauge railway to haul ore from the adit to crushers.[71] The site was to be later developed as the giant Bougainville copper mine which became pivotal to the development of the post-war economy and its subsequent decline (see chapters 6 and 7).

Top - Salamaua jetty with tramway, c. 1937.

Taim Bipo, p.38

Bottom - Miners pushing an ore truck from a gold mine adit at Bulolo, c. 1960.

PNG National Archives

Notes on Chapter 4

1   Eggleston, FW, "The Mandate and the Australian People" in FW Eggleston (ed), *The Australian Mandate for New Guinea*, Melbourne University Press, 1928, p. 7.

2   Piesse, EL, "Financial relations of the Territory of New Guinea with the Common wealth", in FW Eggleston, *Ibid.*, p. 43.

3   Spicer, JA, "The expropriation and sale of German plantations", in FW Eggleston, *Ibid.*, p. 37.

4   "Statement by New Guinea Planters' and Traders' Association to the Common wealth Government", in FW Eggleston, *Ibid.*, p. 60.

5   Roberts, SH, "Racial and labour problems", in FW Eggleston, *Ibid.*, p. 78.

6   *Ibid.*, p. 83.

7   *New Guinea Gazette* No. 33, 30 May 1922, p. 159.

8   *New Guinea Gazette* No. 40, 15 September, 1922, p. 194; No. 65, 15 August, 1923, p. 357; *Mandated Territory of New Guinea Annual Report* (MTNGAR), 1923-1924, p.45.

9   *Sydney Morning Herald*, 1 December 1923, p. 3.

10   *The British internal-combustion locomotive, 1894-1940.* Dimensions of the Muir Hill locomotive were length 9 ft, height 5 ft, or 7 ft 6 ins with cab, width 3 ft 6 ins, wheel base 3 ft 2 ins wheel diameter 20 ins.

11   *Rabaul Times*, 5 August, 1927.

12   *Rabaul Times*, 23 November, 1928.

13   MTNGAR 1922-1923, p. 47.

14   *Rabaul Times*, 22 October, 1926.

15   *Pacific Islands Monthly*, December 1931. Photo on p. 2 shows rebuilding.

16   *Rabaul Times*, 20 December, 1929.

17   Gash, N, and Whittaker, J, *Pictorial History of New Guinea.*

18   *Rabaul Times*, 30 November, 1928.

19   *Rabaul Times*, 4 January 1929.

20   Haileen, interview Rawa Plantation, Bougainville, 1980.

21   *New Guinea Gazette* No. 504, 15 October, 1937 p 38; *Rabaul Times*, 5 November, 1937.

22   Letter, RA Lister Australia, 21 March 1984.

23   From 1925 photograph in UPNG New Guinea Collection depicting the line with labourers unloading copra from a rail truck into a boat.

24   *Rabaul Times*, 3 July, 1925.

25   Fr McConvil, personal communication, Chabai, 1983.

26   Allied Geographical Section, South West Pacific Area (AGS SWPA), Terrain Study No. 41, Updated 24/5/1943. Area Study of The Mandated Solomon and The Shortland Islands p 25, 26, 35.

27   Interviews with local villagers, particularly Mr Hoagae of Yokomore village, 1983.

28   One 2 ft gauge wheel and axle set was found with markings "Hadfields Best Toughened Cast Steel H.C.M."

29   *New Guinea Gazette* No. 195, 29 February, 1928, p.1390.

30   AGS SWPA, Terrain Study No. 41, Mandated Solomons and the Shortland Islands, revised 20/12/1942; Updated 24/5/1943, p. 24.

31   Stewart. Robert, *Nuts to You,* Sydney, Wentworth Books, p. 133.

32   AGS SWPA, Terrain Study No. 41 p 24

33   Extract from letter addressed to the Secretary, Lindenhafen Estates Ltd. Sydney from A.H. Gauld, District Plantation Manager, Lindenhafen, New Britain dated 17th December 1932.

34 Allied Geographical Section, South West Pacific Area, Terrain Study No. 60, 19/7/1943. Area Study of Gasmata p 16, 23.

35 Interview D Moorehouse, July, 1987.

36 Allied Geographic Section, South West Pacific Area, Terrain Study No. 67, 1943, pp. 43, 52 and map 11.

37 Letter M A Ferguson, 8 Aug 1979.

38 Mandated Territory of New Guinea Annual Report, 1921-1922, p. 69-70.

39 Interview with Maria Bonnet's father at Hanahan, 1982.

40 Interview with two old men in Mesu village, September 1995.

41 *Rabaul Times*, 11 June, 1926.

42 *Rabaul Times*, 30 October, 1931.

43 Mario Tobasi, interview at Tinputz, 1983.

44 Rev A H Voyce, letter, 2 September, 1981.

45 CJ Levien, letter to director Wells, 6 April, 1925.

46 Sinclair, J, *Wings of Gold*, Sydney, Pacific Publications, p. 44.

47 Healy, AM, *Bulolo: a history of the development of the Bulolo region, New Guinea*, NG Research Bulletin No. 15, 196-, p. 34.

48 *Ibid*, p. 35.

49 Grabowsky, I, AMF 70, UPNG Library NG Collection, p. 246-248, conditions of Ellyou railway proposal.

50 Sinclair, *op. cit.*, p. 55.

51 *Rabaul Times,* 14 March 1930

52 *Ibid*, p. 73; *Pacific Islands Monthly*, February, 1931, p.3; interview with Adolf Batze who supervised construction of the line, Cairns, December 1978.

53 *Pacific Islands Monthly*, September, 1931, p. 2.

54 Idress, IL, *Gold dust and ashes*, Sydney, Angus & Robertson, 1934, p. 244.

55 Rhys, L, *High lights and flights in New Guinea*, UPNG Library A919.546, R479, p. 158.

56 Grabowsky, *op. cit.*, Part 2, p. 46.

57 Rabaul *Times*, 16 September, 1932.

58 Weston, AE, "Pre-War shipping, Huon Gulf, New Guinea", *Journal of the Morobe District Historical Society*, 3:1, July 1975, p. 42-52.

59 *Ibid.*, p. 146.

60 Cooke, J, *Working in Papua-New Guinea, 1931-1946*, Lara Publications, 1983, p. 219.

61 details provided from Brookfield builders list by Ray Graf.

62 *Courier* newspaper, 27 February, 1942.

63 Grabowsky, *op. cit.*, 1929, p. 12.

64 *Rabaul Times,* 18 January, 1929.

65 Grabowsky, *op. cit.*, p. 130.

66 Coutts, M, *Taim Bipo: a selection of photographs from PNG*, Port Moresby, South Pacific Magazine, 1990, p.38.

67 *Pacific Island Monthly*, September 1936, p. 75.

68 Allied Geographic Section, SW Pacific Area Terrain Study, No. 33, Salamaua, November 1942.

69 P. L. Lowenstein, *Economic Geology of the Morobe Goldfield Papua New Guinea*, Volume 1, PNG Dept. Mines, 1982.

70 MTNGAR, 1929-30, p. 92, p. 262; *Rabaul Times,* 10 January, 1930.

71 Rev A H Voyce, *Peacemakers*, p. 49; Nelson, H. *Black, White and Gold*, p. 264.

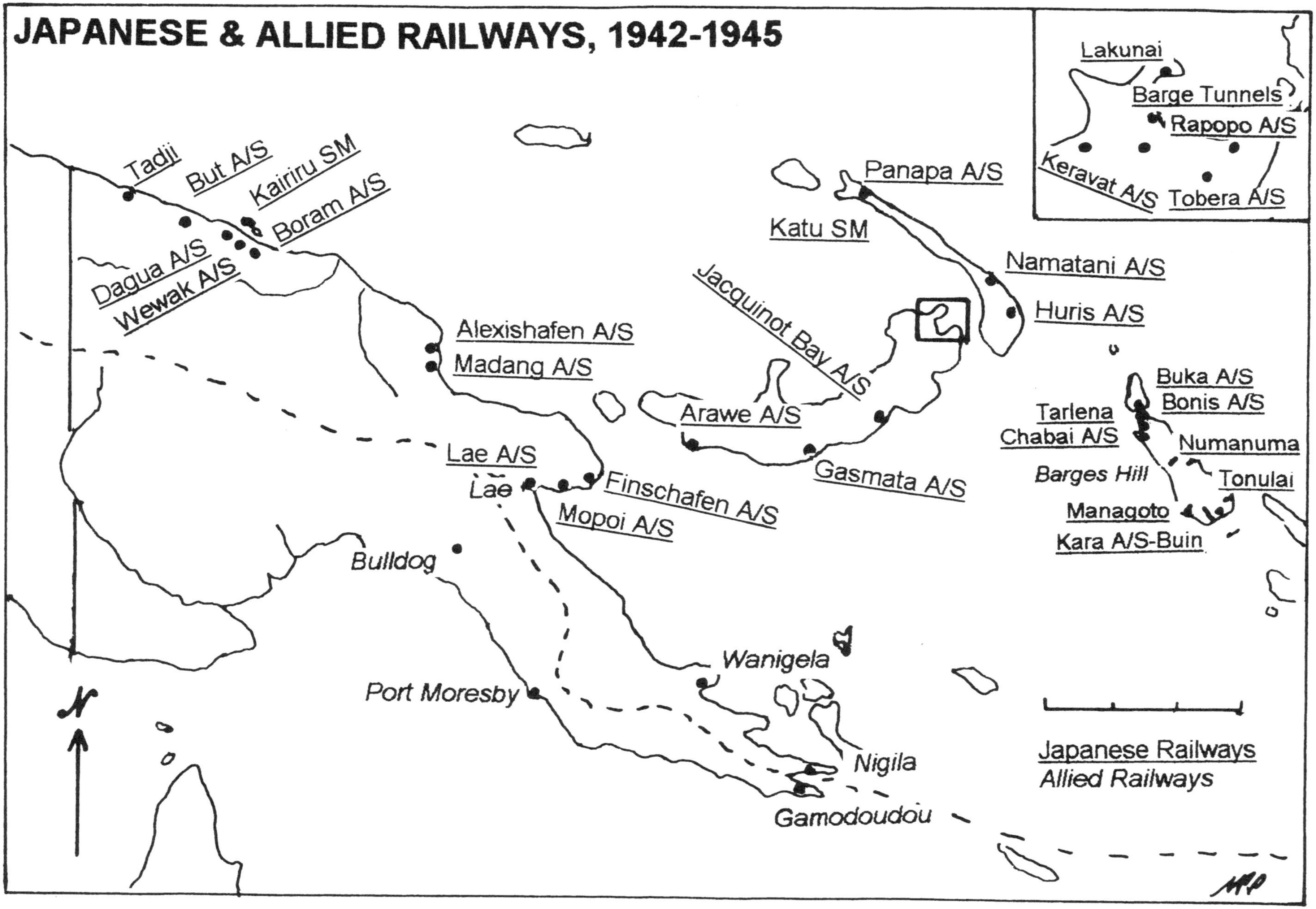
JAPANESE & ALLIED RAILWAYS, 1942-1945
Lakunai
Barge Tunnels
Rapopo A/S
Keravat A/S
Tobera A/S
Tadji
But A/S
Kairiru SM
Boram A/S
Dagua A/S
Wewak A/S
Panapa A/S
Katu SM
Namatani A/S
Huris A/S
Jacquinot Bay A/S
Alexishafen A/S
Madang A/S
Arawe A/S
Buka A/S
Bonis A/S
Tarlena
Chabai A/S
Numanuma
Barges Hill
Tonulai
Managoto
Kara A/S-Buin
Lae A/S
Lae
Finschafen A/S
Mopoi A/S
Gasmata A/S
Bulldog
Wanigela
Port Moresby
Nigila
Gamodoudou
N
Japanese Railways
Allied Railways

CHAPTER 5. TURMOIL OF WAR

The early vision for railways was of a progressive, democratic force for the betterment of mankind. The reality was a new force for governments to tighten their grip over dissident forces, both domestic and foreign; for it was through railways that the power of industrial capital could be mobilised for concentrated effort. This chapter covers the Pacific War in Papua New Guinea and assesses the role of railways in that conflict. The war brought the might of industrial capital to the former isolated colonial outposts and demonstrated its superior power over indigenous culture.

The war was a watershed in PNG's development process. And amid the destruction of war, railways played a significant role in building new infrastructure. Although the war experience was only of three and a half years duration, the authors have identified 26 railways constructed in PNG during this period, several of them being significant operations.

War Machines

As discussed in Chapter 2, railways were to play a central role in building the war capability of the Prussian, then the German army. Through the 20th century, railways continued to provide the essential sinews of war efforts, mobilising men, weapons and machines for the front. By the 1914-18 War, the use of railways to transport troops and supplies had become an intricate planning process to ensure that the vast quantities of food and ammunition required at the front was brought to its point of use. In Europe, both sides used mainline railways to bring troops, tanks, artillery and supplies to the front. From marshalling yards about 12 km behind the front line, 600 mm gauge light railways carried troops, ammunition and supplies to within 3 to 5 km of the front.[1] Here the goods were stored in corps dumps and thence to divisional dumps. Light railways operated by petrol tractors or mules to carry supplies forward to brigade dumps and field artillery batteries lines.

Paradoxically, it was the Germans who lost the fundamentals of the supply equation in World War II, lured to destruction by their miscalculated belief in the superiority of their Panzer divisions and the perceived ability of *Autobahns* to provide supply routes. The lesson was not lost on the Russians in the Eastern front, who used the Trans-Siberian railway to move the whole of their heavy industry away from the invading Germans.[2] Strategically, the Russians were able to use their railways to bring their *Winter Army* from Manchuria to save Moscow in the winter of 1941, then to transport the ammunition for the 40,000 heavy guns with which they pounded the Germans.

The Pacific War brought a new imperial power to the shores of PNG. The Japanese had learnt their military strategies from the Japanese-Russian War of 1905. In this encounter, the emerging Asian power had humiliated a European nation. An important watershed in global power relations had been reached.

Military tendencies became a dominant force in Japan through the twenties. From 1931, Japan expanded its imperial power into Manchuria. The Japanese Army established a number of railway units covering field railways (*Yasen Tetsudo*), special railways (*Tokesetsu Tetsudo)* and railway transport (*Tetsudo Yuso*) in the major war theatres of Manchuria, Korea and Japan itself.

In the late 1920s Japan began to experiment with Special Naval Landing Forces (*Rikusentai*) which were first used against China. In planning for a Pacific War, ships and aircraft were the key to military thinking. But these machines of war needed bases and airstrips from which to operate and, therefore, the logistics to build these facilities were an important aspect of military planning.

As the Pacific War progressed, the Imperial Japanese Navy became heavily involved in the seizure and defence of Pacific Islands. For this role, a number of new naval organisations came into existence.[3] Of particular interest to this analysis were the Pioneers (*Setueitai*) and the Navy civil engineering and construction units (*Kaigun Kenchiku Shitetsu Butai*). The Pioneers were responsible for the construction of airfields, fortifications and barracks. Units, of 800 or 1300 men, comprised 25-33 percent Japanese with the balance made up of Koreans or Formosans. The civil engineering and construction units were mostly engaged in labouring tasks for the construction of airfields, fortifications and barracks. They primarily comprised Koreans with Japanese overseers.

Japanese engineers made extensive use of portable railways in their construction tasks. These included standardised prefabricated 2 ft gauge rail sections, 18 ft long and using light rails of 10 pounds per foot.[4] Switch sections were prefabricated. Large quantities of 13 kg/m rail were also imported. Light V-hoppers or flat cars, 4 feet wide and 6 feet long were used, being either pushed by man-power, or pulled by small, gasoline-powered locomotives.

Between 1941 and 1943, the Kato Works Company Ltd, Shinagawa, Tokyo constructed a total of 729 2 ft (610 mm) gauge, 4-wheel locomotives for the Japanese Imperial Navy.[5] Comprising 3-ton, 4-ton and 5-ton units, it was the largest standardised group of 2 ft gauge locomotives ever built. Records suggest that most were fitted with 6-cylinder in-line petrol engines. However, other Japanese war-time prime movers also had diesel-powered models and locomotives found in PNG include diesels.

Australia also had experience in the use of railways in war. The Australian Imperial Force had gained extensive experience of war-time railway operations during the First World War. Six railway units, each comprising some 260 men, were formed by volunteers from the state railway systems to serve in France and Belgium operating standard gauge and light railways to serve the Allied war machine.[6] The 15th Australian Light Rail Operating Company, for example, operated 137 locomotives and 112 petrol tractors and hauled 25,000 to 45,000 tons of goods per week.

At the outbreak of the Pacific War, Australia found its railway system, hindered by break of gauge and lack of investment through the 1930s, ill equipped to support the war effort. The Australian Army established its own Directorate of Railway Transportation and, in August 1941, it drew up War Railway Timetables for Strategic Concentration.[7] They covered movements on three general routes across continental Australia. In the Northern Territory, the toy railway operated by dilapidated locomotives and rolling stock under the grand title of North Australian Railway was taken over by the military. Traffic increased from several hundred tons a week to 24,000 tons as the nation rushed to defend its north.

Railway workshops made a major contribution to the war effort, building armoured vehicles and ammunition and commencing Australia's first national locomotive-building project, the ill-fated Australian Standard Garratt.

For construction purposes, the Australian Army used light 2 ft (610 mm) gauge railways. The Army obtained forty-five small 4-wheel petrol-mechanical locomotives built by the Melbourne engineering firm of Malcolm Moore between 1941 and 1944. Several of these saw service in New Guinea.

On 23 January 1942, Japanese forces landed at Rabaul and quickly extended their occupation to other islands and most of the New Guinea mainland. By August, 1942, the Japanese Empire stretched from Burma in the west across the Pacific to Alaska's Aleutian Islands.

In February 1942, Japanese bombing brought destruction to the railway and associated facilities at Lae. Many of the existing plantation railway lines were dismantled by the Japanese and the rails moved elsewhere for more pressing tasks. On landing at Tinputz, Bougainville, on 1 January, 1943, a Japanese reconnaissance party dismantled the sawmill, plant and railway and loaded it on vessels for shipment to construction sites.[8]

More widespread destruction occurred as Allied forces turned the tide on the Japanese advance. In July 1942, Australian troops halted the Japanese advance at Milne Bay and on 7 August Allied forces counter-attacked on Guadalcanal in the Solomon Islands. The Japanese, who had concentrated their forces at Buna for the Papua campaign, were caught by surprise.[9] After heavy fighting, the Americans gained control of the airfield at Henderson on Guadacanal, from where they launched attacks on Japanese forces in the New Guinea Islands.

Aerial bombing was heavy at many locations where railways were operating. Early in 1942 the Japanese bombed the Bootless Bay railway near Port Moresby, although the line had not been operational for over a decade.[10] The infrastructure at Alexishafen and Marienberg were among the sites levelled by heavy Allied bombing. When Allied planes bombed Lae, Australians were informed by their controlled media that "the railway marshalling yards at Lae had been bombed", a claim which was greeted with mirth by those with local knowledge of New Guinea.[11]

Coastal villagers suffered dislocation and damage from the heavy bombing. There was widespread, but unknown loss of life; much destruction of gardens, villages, livestock, crops, trees, canoes and various resources; and much deep-seated social dislodgment[12]. The war experience jolted villagers from their settled patterns of existence and subjected them to a degree of anxiety previously unknown.

Japanese Construction

The occupation brought a period of hectic construction of airstrips and exploitation of timber stands by the Imperial Navy. With the loss of Guadalcanal in September, 1942, the Japanese fortified their positions on Bougainville and New Britain with construction of a number of airstrips.

Official records obtained by Charles Small indicate that 93 of the standard Kato military locomotives were dispatched to "Big Harbour" (Rabaul). These comprised five 5-ton, 25 4-ton and 63 3-ton locomotives.[13] It is not known how many of these units arrived at Rabaul. At least seven locomotives were used on the Buin Naval railway, the builders numbers of which differ from those listed for "Big Harbour."[14]

Buin Railway

At Buin on the south of Bougainville Island the Japanese military constructed PNG's most extensive railway system. Its total length was in excess of 30 km. The railway was initially established for the construction of a fighter airstrip at Kara, near the present town of Buin, in November, 1942. Heavy fortifications were built up in this area. At Kangu Hill, overlooking the landing on Buin Beach, heavy naval guns and a radar station was established. Soldiers planted extensive gardens for food supplies and there were plans for Japanese settlers in the area to the north of Kangu Hill, which became known as *Little Tokyo*.

Japanese Navy Units constructed a 2 ft gauge light railway from Buin Port (Kangu Hill) to Kara airstrip, a distance of 15 km. The line was initially built with light 6 kg/m rails for hand-pushed trucks. As the tide of the war turned in 1943, Buin became an important holding base. The railway from Kangu Hill to Nakaro was upgraded with 12 kg rail for locomotive operation. A sawmill was established at Nakaro, together with workshops for vehicle maintenance.

Several branch lines were also constructed. The formation of one line, branching from the main line 3 km from Buin Port, was followed south for over a kilometre to the Little Siwi River in 1987. There are reports that this extended a further 5 km through swampland to Moila Point, possibly because this was a more favourable landing area. It is also reported that there was a branch line, running from the branch of Buin road at Nakaro, west toward the Siwai area for about 12 km, although this has not been confirmed.[15]

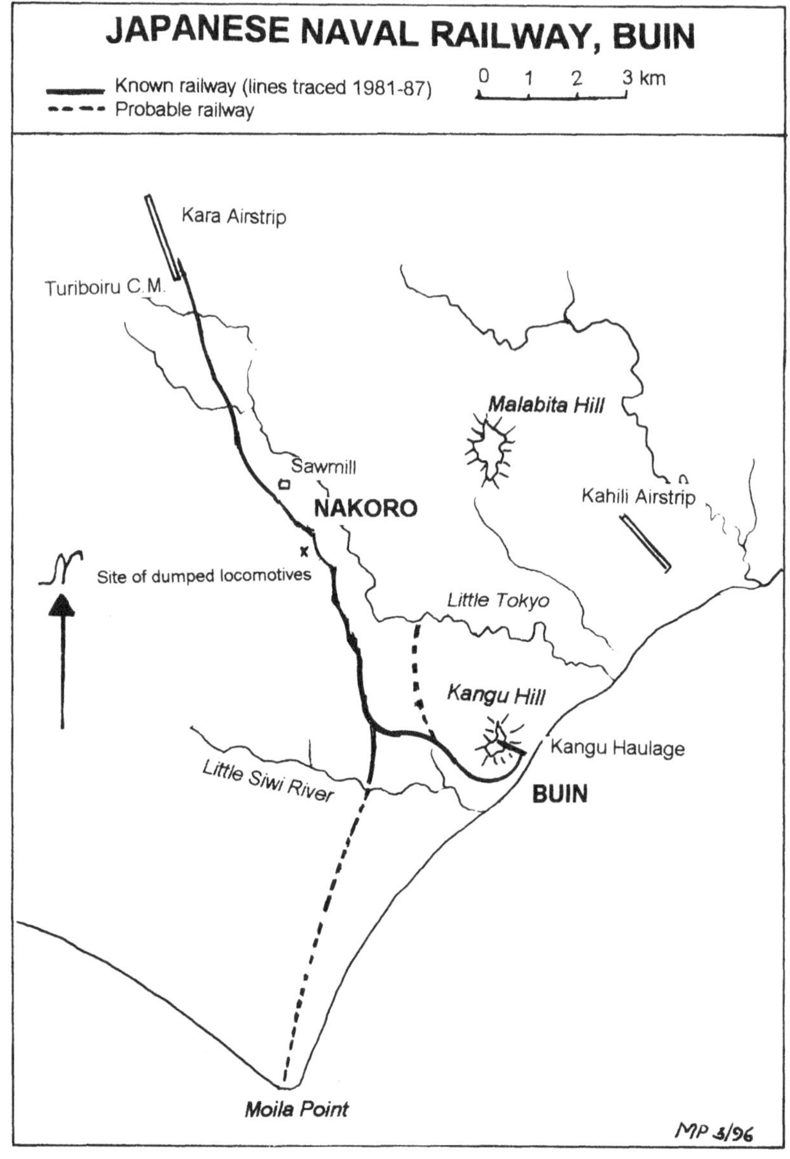

Above - Map of Japanese Naval Railway, Buin

The line initially carried basalt from Kangu Hill for the Kara airstrip, but later stone came from a quarry at Malabita Hill, some 3.5 km east of Nakaro, so a branch to the quarry is also a distinct possibility. Supply trains were mainly operated between Buin Port and Nakaro, although some trains continued to Kara over the light track. Munition trains ran from dump sites at Kangu, Nakaro or Moila Point as required.

Secrecy was an important element of the operation. Local villagers were kept away from the installation and all operations were strictly carried out by Japanese personnel. The narrow footprint of the railway assisted its camouflage under the forest trees. Only small sections of line were spotted by the Allied forces from the air. Unlike other locations, the Buin railway was not bombed and locomotives showed no signs of war damage.

At least seven locomotives were used on the line. In the 1960s, four Kato Works locomotives and two smaller units of unknown parentage were found dumped in the bush near Nakaro, while a seventh locomotive in good order was held at the PWD store in Buin.[16] The Kato locomotives were fitted with 6-cylinder engines, were 3 metres in length and weighed 4-5 tons. Kungka, a PWD mechanic at Buin, used the locomotive from the PWD store on the line well into the 1950s. When this unit was no longer operable, he poled trucks along the track to supply Turiboiru Mission.

At Buin port, a haulage line was established from the Block House near the beach at the port up Kangu Hill to gun emplacements. A Yanmar diesel Type H20 drove a winch which was located about three-quarters of the way up the hill. The line was 2 ft gauge with 10 kg/m rail.

The railway from Buin to Kara was still in place and serviceable in 1947.[17] In 1948, Parer Brother gained the salvage rights for the Buin area. The railway was used to transport scrap metal to Nakaro, where it was transhipped to motor lorries for transport to Lamuai. Here it was melted down into blocks of aluminium, brass, bronze and copper. The locomotives were stripped and the rails lifted for scrap or for use by plantations in building structures.

Post-war, Buin port was threatened by encroachment by the sea. The town was relocated inland. The former Japanese fighter airstrip at Buin was reopened for light planes by the Mission Aviation Fellowship. It was upgraded for DC3 aircraft in 1958.[18] In 1972, a road from Buin to Arawa via Panguna was opened. The old port site at Kangu fell into disuse.

Other Bougainville Railways

Extensive dumps of railway equipment have been found in the area of Bonis plantation on the south side of Buka Passage. Here the Japanese commenced construction of a 3,300 ft x 200 ft airstrip but were unable to complete it due to Allied bombing. In the area between Bonis and Tarlena village, 7 km to the south, the Japanese had extensive bivouac and supply areas in 1944. At Chabai, 3 km further east, a start was made on another airstrip. There were construction railways at all three sites and some reports suggest they were interconnected. By this time, the Japanese forces on Bougainville had been cut off from their supply routes, and there are reports that rails were pulled up from Kunua and Soraken plantations for the project. However, rails remaining during field inspections were the heavier 12 kg/m standard imported from Japan. Steel bridge connecting plates were used as sleepers.

Villagers state the line was initially constructed to carry planes from a workshop at Chabai to Bonis and to supply a munitions dump.[19] Railways were also used in the construction of the airstrips. Up to six Kato Works locomotives are reported to have been used on the Chabai line. The locomotives are remembered as being much heavier and more powerful than the small Listers then used on plantations in the area. At Bonis, trucks were hand-pushed during airstrip construction.

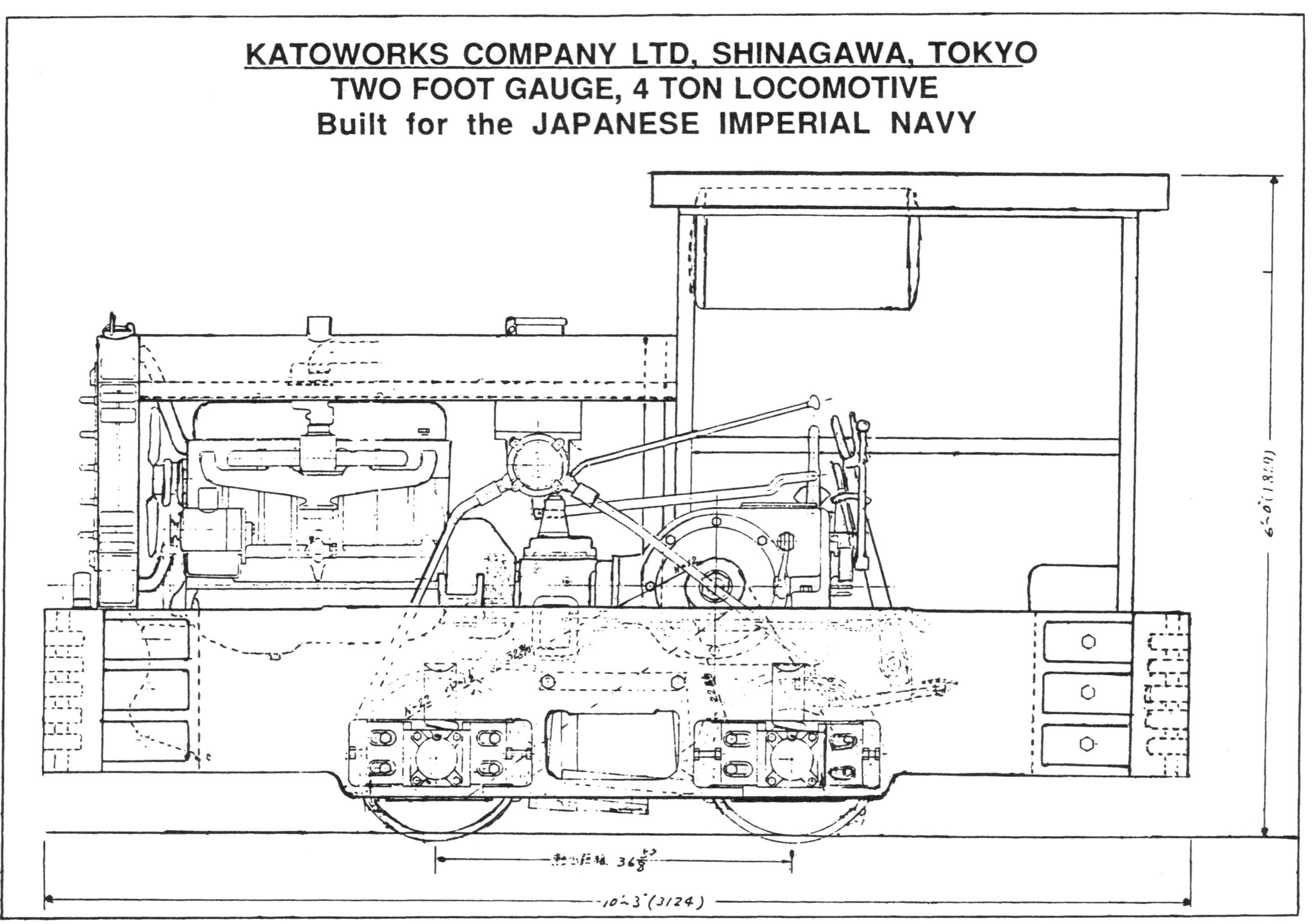

KATOWORKS COMPANY LTD, SHINAGAWA, TOKYO
TWO FOOT GAUGE, 4 TON LOCOMOTIVE
Built for the JAPANESE IMPERIAL NAVY
6'-0" (1829)
10'-3" (3124)

Top -Restored Japanese Imperial Navy Kato Works 4wDM locomotive and rolling stock at Buin High School, 1987.

M.Pearson

Bottom - Side view of Kato Works 4wDM locomotive (22086/1942)

M.Pearson

Tram tracks were also laid into gardens established at Tarlena and Chabai to grow food for the Japanese troops.[20] These lines were used by villagers after the war who pushed hopper trucks from the fields to transport their own garden produce. The Catholic Father at Chabai had a small trike built to haul the trucks. The length of the line used post-war was some 2 km from the wharf to the garden then extended to the junction of the Chabai-Tabut and Porton-Tabut roads.

Following the war, most of the railway equipment was swept up by scrap metal dealers. A number of field visits were made to these areas between 1973 and 1983. There were many railway relics, mainly light, prefabricate rail sections and wheels, at Bonis Plantation in 1973. By 1979 the rails had been used for posts, construction in buildings, fences and power lines. Only four sets of wheels remained by 1982.

At Tarlena, the remains of a 2 ft gauge line from a wharf to the bivouac area were visited in 1980. Three V-type hopper wagons and one hopper were located, one of which was removed for restoration. At Chabai, three hopper wagons were noted in the sea at the wharf, while eight war-damaged hopper wagons or frames were located at various locations along the railway route. Three hopper wagons were transferred to Buoi plantation for use of a short line there in 1984, while a frame from Chabai, the hopper from Tarlena and wheels from Bonis were used to reconstruct a Japanese wagon at Buin in 1985.

Further north, the narrow sea passage between Buka and Bougainville islands was of strategic importance and the Japanese built up a large base there in 1942. Airstrips were built on either side of the passage on Buka Island and on Bonis Plantation. Two thousand men were reported unloading large quantities of supplies and equipment from ships.[21] Large fuel and explosive dumps were built up and a number of heavy coastal defence guns were brought in. Light railways were constructed at both sides of the Buka airstrip and at least one locomotive was used to operate the lines.

The Buka railway ran past the post-war government office to the airstrip, then proceeded to Novah Road.[22] A branch line on the north-west side of the airport carried materials up Kubu hill where there was a Japanese encampment and, later, a shrine.[23] The memorial was used to cremate the bodies of soldiers so that their ashes could be sent to Japan. Reports indicate that trucks were hand-pushed, although a locomotive was still present on Buka in 1956.

Relic equipment found in 1982 included wheels, rails and a dump truck frame, although the latter appeared to be of German rather than Japanese origin.

Rabaul and New Ireland

Rabaul was the main Japanese base from January 1942 and the area remained under their control until the surrender in September 1945. The Japanese built numerous tramlines for the construction of airstrips and the exploitation of timber stands around Rabaul.

In the Rabaul Barge Tunnels broad gauge tramlines of between 500 and 1000 metres in length were laid into the tunnels constructed into the hills around Rabaul Harbour so that the barges could be stored well protected from enemy bombing. Some barge tunnels were 30 metres above water level and well in from the shore. Prisoners-of-war, including many Indians brought to Rabaul, worked on the wharves and the many tunnels dug into the mountain side.

At Tobera, Vunakanau and Lakunai on the Gazelle Peninsula, the Japanese used tramlines to transport the crushed coral to construct their airstrips. At Tobera, two tramlines and a string of hopper trucks are clearly visible in a US Airforce photo of the airstrip of January, 1944.

Some of the older Tolai population can still remember having to work on the construction of these airstrips. A Kato Works locomotive from Tobera was used on a Gazelle plantation after the War and is now on display at the Kokopo War Museum. To the west, the Japanese are believed to have used railways for airstrip construction at Jacquinot Bay, Gasmata and Arawe.

On New Ireland, the Japanese constructed a railway from Katu Plantation southward to serve a sawmill. The sawmill, powered by Isuzu diesel engines, was protected by AA-guns.[24] Rails from the line were salvaged by plantations around 1950 for use in copra driers and other construction work. A number of rail trucks were still there in the 1950s.

At Panapai, 8 km from Kavieng, the Japanese used a 610 mm gauge railway to clear a coconut plantation and to construct an airstrip on the site.[25] Railway trucks transported coconut logs to the shore for dumping in the sea. A railway was also used for airstrip construction at Huris, 90 km south of Namatanai. A number of Japanese rails are still to be found in this area.

New Guinea Mainland Railways

Although the Japanese occupied a vast area of the New Guinea mainland and constructed many airstrips, few details of construction railways have been located. A light railway had been constructed on the south side of Lae airstrip by mid-1943.[26] To the north, there was also airstrip construction activity at Alexishafen where the SVD mission had an extensive pre-war light railway system.

Boram airstrip, which now serves as the airport for Wewak, was constructed by the Japanese using a light railway operated by a locomotive and hopper wagons.[27] On Kairiru Island, just off the Sepik coast, a narrow gauge railway was constructed along the coast from a semaphore base at the former mission station to emplacements for large guns at the eastern end of the island. There are reports that line was lifted from St Anna plantation for this railway. A post-war report indicates that two branch lines were built up creek valleys to haul logs down to a sawmill established by the Japanese.[28] Other Japanese airstrip construction railways are believed to have operated at Mopoi, Finshhafen, Dagua, But and Tadji.

Allied Railways

In contrast to the Japanese, the Allied war machine had access to heavy construction equipment to build airstrips and bases. Nevertheless, large quantities of rails and railway equipment was brought into New Guinea to aid the war effort. This was used for the transport of munitions and supplies around the bases.

As part of the Bulldog to Bulolo road construction in 1943, the Australians built a 7 mile (11.2 km) section of 3 ft 6 in (1067 mm) gauge railway to bypass the heavily silted Tivari branch of the Lakekamu River.[29] By mid-1943, barges were no longer able to reach Bulldog and cargo had to be unloaded at the junction of the Tiveri and Lakekamu Rivers, thus delaying the important road construction task. The road, once completed, was only used for 16 days when the fall of Lae rendered the Bulldog trail no longer necessary.

For the Bougainville campaign, the Australian Army built a cable haulage to haul supplies up the escarpment at Barges Hill on the Numa Numa trail. The construction was commenced on 23 May, 1945 and completed by 9 June.[30] The track was 490 mm gauge and 760 metres in length.[31] The vertical climb was 290 metres, the average grade was 1 in 2, and the maximum 1 in 1. Three sets of trestles were required to maintain the grade over

Top - Barges Hill incline railway, Numa Numa Trail, Bougainville, September 1945. RAAF 5Tac/R Squadron personnel test the carriage at Harrisville, the bottom station.

JL Buckland, RF McKillop Collection

Bottom - View of the Barges Hill incline railway with sign "Riding on tramway strictly prohibited", September 1945.

JL Buckland, RF McKillop Collection

the gullies. and two Ford V8 driven, double drum power winches, were used for hauling the trucks. The tramway was intended to lift 10 tons per day, but a maximum of 25 tons per day was achieved.

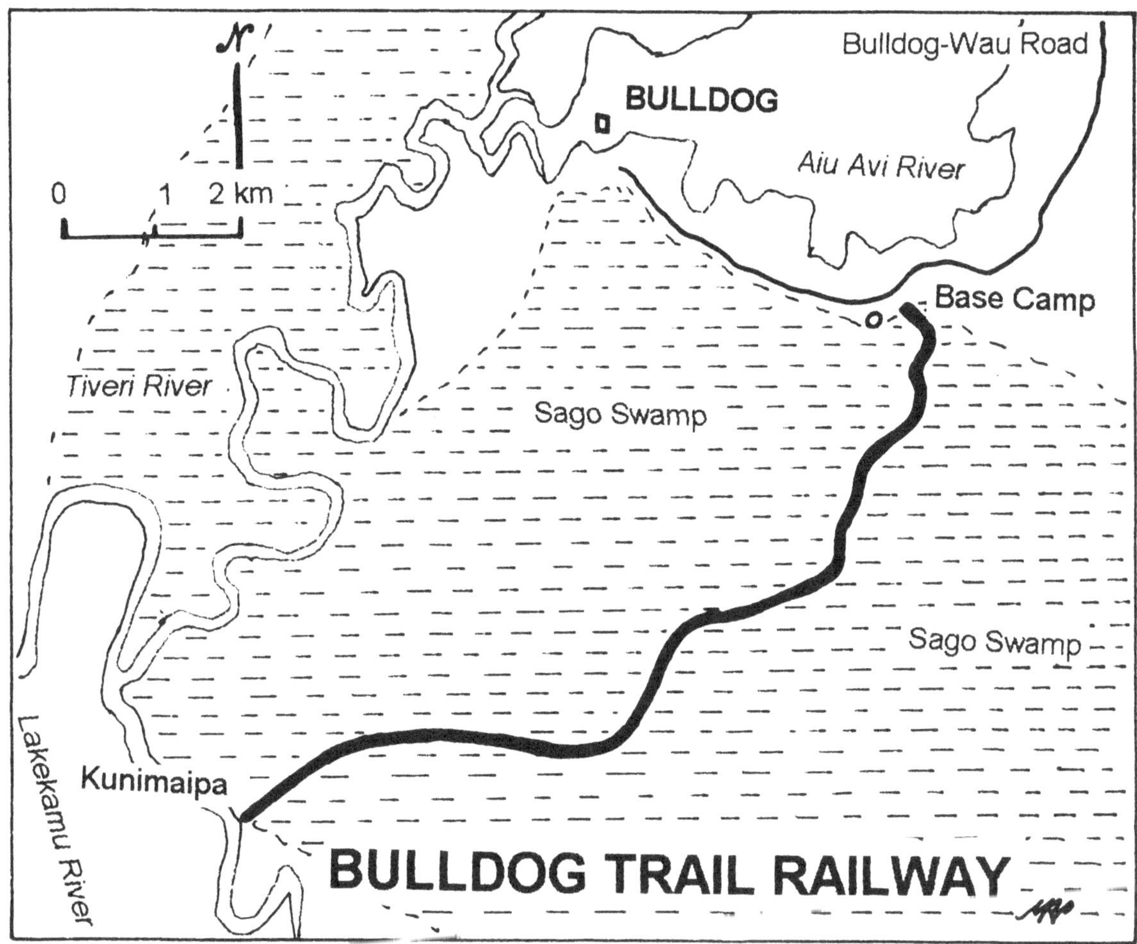

Above - Map of Bulldog Trail Railway

The operation had a short life with the Japanese surrender in September. Australian railway enthusiast John Buckland came across the line in late 1945 and reported:

> After the Japs had surrendered finally about ten days after the cease-fire, we had plenty of time to explore parts of the island formerly out of bounds and this included the Numa Numa Trail across the central part of the island to the East Coast. There was a very steep cable haulage ... worked by the Army, on which some mates and I rode up and down quite illegally and took some photos.[32]

Over Easter 1986, a patrol was made across Bougainville island from Torokina to Wakunai to inspect the remains of the Barges Hill incline railway. Most of the rail was still in place, but the steep climb took an hour's hard hiking. Only the bottom section of the rails and bridge across a small stream had gone. Two trestle bridges were noted on the line.

In Milne Bay, the US Navy established a large naval base at Gamodoudou (also referred to as Wagawaga), across the bay from Alatou, while the Australians built a base at Ladava on the shorefront of Giligili Plantation. The Americans constructed a 610 or 762 mm gauge tramway for the movement of naval supplies. The rail lines were overgrown after the war and were only discovered when the Ulabo Timber Company cleared the area for use as their logging yard.[33] US-rolled rails laid to 762 mm gauge were noted at Giligili Plantation post-war. The Allies also built airstrips at Vivigani on Goodenough Island, on Kiriwina Island and at Gurney which now serves as the airport for Alatou.

The Allied build up of troops and supplies for the New Guinea campaign was focused on Port Moresby. Airstrips were constructed at Wards, Jacksons Kila, Durano, Schwimmer and Berry. Extensive stores and munitions bases were constructed around the present city area, notably at Barune (site of the present University), Wards, Wallaby, Waigani (adjacent to the Waigani Swamp), Bomana and Schwimmer, while new wharves were built at Port Moresby and on the north of Tatana Island. Large quantities of rails were imported for the movement of ammunitions and supplies around these bases. There are also reports of rail operations at Rouna Quarry. It is believed that Malcolm Moore petrol locomotives were used on these lines. A photograph depicting the unloading of American P-41 fighter planes from a ship at a Papuan port depicts three railway tracks on the jetty.[34] This may be the wharf constructed by the Americans at Tatana Island in Fairfax Harbour. The gauge appears to be 3 ft (914 mm) or wider.

As the Allied forces drove the Japanese from the New Guinea mainland, they established a large number of airstrips and bases in the Morobe area. The Australian Army had bases at Lae and Finschhafen, the US airforce established bases at Lae, Nadzab and Gusap in the Markham Valley. There were some 700,000 US Marines in the Finschhafen area at one stage.[35] Several of the Malcolm Moore petrol mechanical locomotives built for the Australian Army were brought to New Guinea during the war. Few details of their use have survived. In December 1947, tenders were called for the purchase of Malcolm Moore locomotive No. 1005 and a Fordson 2 ft gauge locomotive at Lae.[36] It is thought that these units were used on light railways for the movement of munitions at Lae.

Post-war Exploitation

The brief moment of railway operations during the war faded as the technology of war gave way to the slumber of colonial outposts once more. However, the waste of war provided a field day for scrap metal merchants and rapid fortunes were made collecting material to feed the furnaces of post-War reconstruction in Japan. The remains of railways, locomotives and rolling stock were swept up by eager metal collectors or were used by all and sundry for copra driers, bridges, fence posts and numerous other construction tasks. Some were used to build short plantation lines from copra sheds to wharves. Railways with heritage value to Papua or New Guinea were not spared. Outside Port Moresby, the Bootless Bay railway and its locomotives were a prize booty. They were sent to Japan as scrap metal in the early 1960's.[37]

Top - US military personnel unloading P41 Lightning aircraft, probably at Tatana Island wharf, Fairfax Harbour, Port Moresby. Note the railway tracks on the wharf.
Bottom - 762 mm. gauge railway tracks uncovered in April 1982 at Gamodoudau, Milne Bay - the site of an American naval base during the Pacific War.

Photo: Al Bovelt

Notes on Chapter 5

1   Bullen, J, "Australian Railwaymen at War, 1916-1919", *ARHS Bulletin*, Vol. 46, No. 695, September 1995, p. 250.

2   Faith, N, *Locomotion: the railway revolution*, London, BBC Books, 1993, p. 90

3   *Handbook on Japanese Military Forces*, US War Department Technical Manual, 15 September 1944, TM - E.30-480 p. 76-80.

4   *Ibid.*, p. 330-331.

5   Information provided by Charles Small, Honolulu.

6   Bullen, J, *op. cit.*, pp. 243-256.

7   Harvey, JY, "War railway timetables", *ARHS Bulletin* No. 685, November, 1994, p. 291.

8   AD Fauer (ed), *Coastwatching in the Solomon Islands: the Bougainville reports, December 1941-July 1943*, New York, Praeger, 1992, p. 90.

9   Ballard, RD, *The lost ships of Guadalcanal*, London, Weidenfeld, 1993.

10   HE Prosser, ex-141 General Transport Company, letter to AD Lockyer, 22 May 1947.

11   Willis, Dr Ian, letter, 9 September, 1978.

12   Stanner, WEH, *The South Seas in transition*, Sydney, 1953, p. 87.

13   Records provided to RF McKillop by Charles Small, Honolulu, 9/1987. Builders Nos. were 21805/12, 22093/112, 22160/9, 22171/5, 22181/5, 22196/200, 22257/66, 22364/8, 22377/81 and 22402/21 of 1941 to 1943.

14   Numbers included 22086 of 1942 and 3130.

15   Interviews with local villagers, 1981. The formation was still discernible in 1987.

16   Interview, Clement Koiri, PWD power operator, Buin, 1981. The dump is suggested as the location where locomotives were handed over to the Allies at war's end.

17   Reference Patrol No 3 of 1947, 15th March 1947, R. R. Cole A/Assistant District Officer. p 4.

18   *Rabaul Times*, 16 May, 1958, p. 4.

19   Report by Timothy Torova, Saposa Island, 1983.

20   Interviews with Leo Hannett, who grew up at Chabai to the age of 12, interviews of 1981 and 1995.

21   Jack Reed - Coastwatcher - Manuscript November 1942.

22   Interview Old Michael of Ieta Village

23   Interview John Hakena, Kubu

24   Lusack, W, verbal report, 1992.

25   Oliver Kanavi, sword-bearer for Japanese colonel who was OIC for the airstrip, interview September 1995.

26   *Impact*, Vol 1, No 5, August 1943, p. 4.

27   US Air Force Photo B 25456 A.C.

28   Report from Brother Pat Howley, headmaster, St Xaviers High School, Kairiru.

29   N Robinson, *Villagers at war*, p. 58

30   Report of the 23rd Brigade - Brigadier Potts

31   M Pearson, field observations, 1986.

32   Buckland, JL, letter, 29 May 1987.

33   Observations and report from A Bovelt, 25 June 1982.

34   Coutts, M, *op. cit*, p. 59.

35   Nihal, H, "The Second World War in Morobe District, *Journal of Morobe Historical Society*, 1:1, May 1972, p. 7.

36   *Papua-New Guinea Gazette*, 3 December, 1947, p. 214.

37   Peter Fox, personal communication on shipping, Goroka, 1968; Canon Ian Stuart, letter to M Pearson, 18 October 1978.

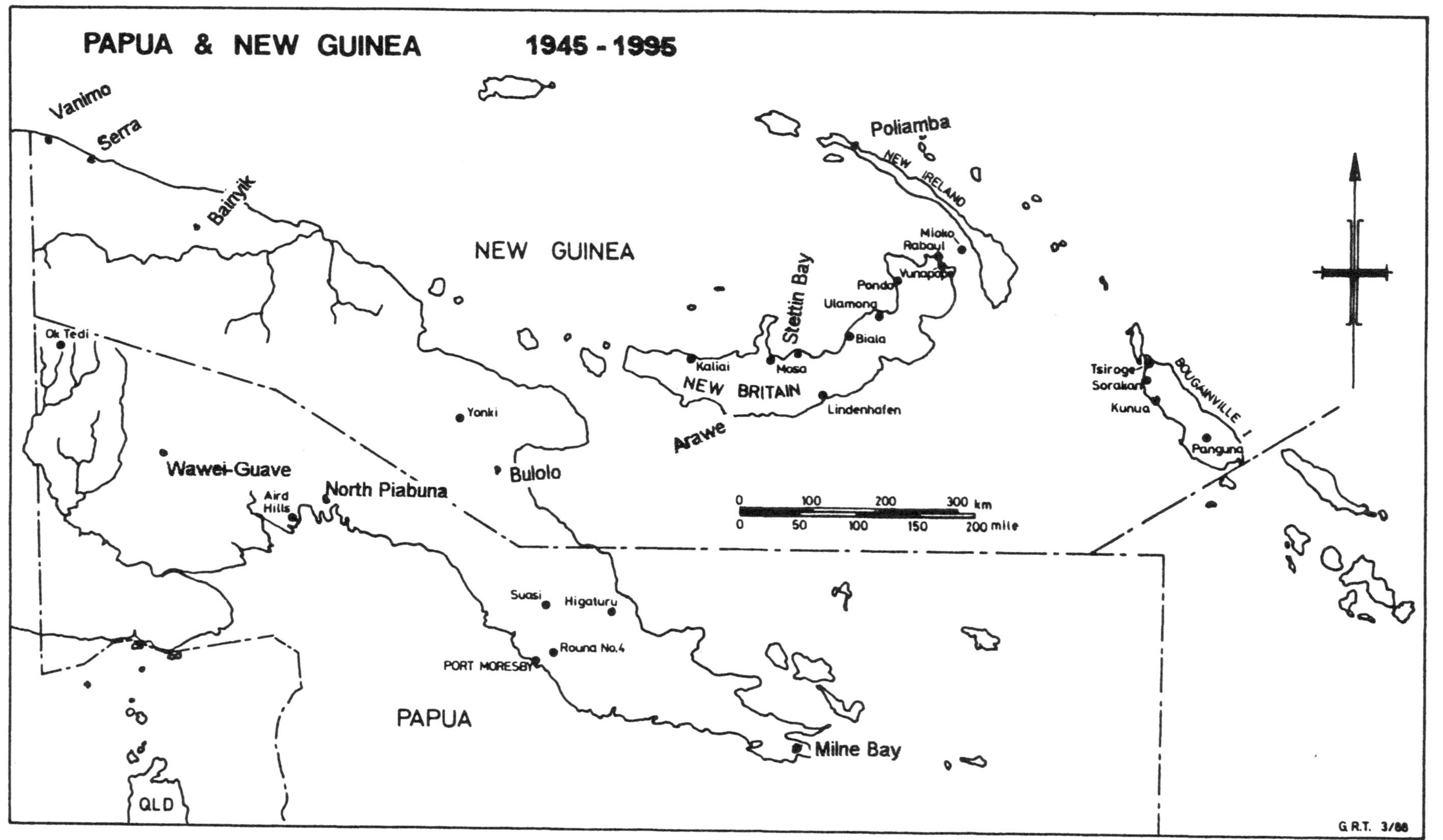

PAPUA & NEW GUINEA   1945 - 1995
Vanimo
Serra
Baiyik
NEW GUINEA
Ok Tedi
Yonki
Wawei-Guave
Aird Hills
North Piabuna
Bulolo
Poliamba
NEW IRELAND
Mioko
Rabaul
Vunapope
Pondo
Stettin Bay
Ulamong
Biala
Kaliai
Moso
NEW BRITAIN
Lindenhafen
Arawe
Tsiroge
Sorakan
Kunua
BOUGAINVILLE
Panguna
Suasi
Higaturu
Rouna No.4
PORT MORESBY
PAPUA
Milne Bay
QLD
0   100   200   300 km
0   50   100   150   200 mile
G.R.T. 3/88

CHAPTER 6. POST WAR RECONSTRUCTION

International conflict during the War led to a new world order, divided between East and West, with the Western block dominated by the United States of America. The values which shaped policies in Australia were increasingly influenced by US trends. It was a world view dominated by automobile and aircraft manufacturers: railways were seen by many as a relic of the *steam age*. In Australia, and particularly in developing countries, railways failed to attract the necessary investment for reconstruction and modernisation following the war.

In PNG, there was a new urgency for reconstruction and development, but construction of railways to provide the basic infrastructure and institutional base for a modern society was given little attention. It was generally believed that roads and air transport would help propel the colony into the modern era. Nevertheless, railways continued to play a minor role in agricultural development and the establishment of large-scale mines. This chapter covers some 20 railways established in PNG in the period 1946 to 1975.

Decolonisation

The post-war era brought a new awareness that colonised peoples had a right to independence and self determination. In Papua and New Guinea, economic development was directed by the interaction between internal factors and the values and policies generated in the external political arena. The period saw the emergence of a new generation of Papua New Guineans less in awe of the Australians and eager to participate more equally in the post-war reconstruction.

Among many coastal groups, however, the influx of industrial wealth they had experienced during the war generated very different expectations of the development process. The anti-European resentment of the 1930s emerged as cargo cultism in a number of areas, including Manus, the Rai Coast and Bougainville. Cults, such as the Hahalis Welfare Society on Buka Island rejected the church and adopted pagan rituals in search of material wealth.

Australians came out of the war experience with closer ties to her northern neighbours. A new deal for Papua and New Guinea was proclaimed in a 1945 policy statement by the Minister for Territories, Mr EJ Ward, which has often been quoted as the Australian charter for post-war New Guinea.[1] The program for rehabilitation and development would have regard to "the moral and material welfare of the native inhabitants and the strategic importance of the area to Australia."

Administration in New Guinea and Papua had been amalgamated in 1942 under the Australian New Guinea Administrative Unit (ANGAU). With the Japanese surrender on 6 September, 1945, ANGAU became fully involved in repatriating prisoners-of-war and the local population. ANGAU continued its control until June 1946, when both territories were embodied in the *Papua-New Guinea Provisional Administration*. In December 1946 the United Nations granted a Trusteeship over the Territory of New Guinea to Australia.[2] A single administration for the Territory of Papua and New Guinea was established with its headquarters at Port Moresby. In contrast to the low levels of budget support provided between the Wars, Australian government grants increased markedly from 1946 to support development and public service expansion.

The Australian government prepared plans for massive budget increases to assist in education and health and to prepare the people of PNG for self-determination. Political development, based on Western-style democracy was encouraged, initially through the development of local government councils. They were intended to overcome the problem posed by absence of suitable indigenous authorities and to "serve as institutions suited to the needs of Papuan society in a period of change."[3] By 1969 there were some 142 councils in existence, representing almost 2 million people. There were also optimistic hopes for cooperative societies.

But first, both the Administration and the commercial sector were faced with a massive task of rehabilitating infrastructure and getting the economy back on its feet. During the 1950's the light aircraft fields of the country were improved as the basis of inland transport, while flying boat services existed in the island's regions. The air control centre at Madang became one of the busiest in the world handling air freighter flights to the newly opened Highland centres such as Goroka, Kundiawa, Banz and Mount Hagen where Australian settlers and village farmers were rapidly building up an important coffee industry. Air travel became an everyday mode of travel to "Territorians" and increasingly, to Papua New Guineans. In towns and isolated settlements throughout the country, the airport provided the medium of social exchange with the outside world, just as the railway station had done elsewhere in the world.

Coastal shipping, dominated by Burns Philp & Company and Steamships Trading Company, remained the basis of coastal and inter-island transport. For coastal villagers and those living along the major rivers, traditional canoes continued to provide the main means of transport. However, outboard motors from the United States and Japan made their transport task much easier and faster. Nevertheless, the lack of technical skills and service infrastructure in rural areas meant that outboard motors were frequently unserviceable after a short life. Efforts were made to promote less sophisticated types of motors which might be more suited to PNG conditions in the 1970s, but the marketing power of multinational manufacturers held sway.

On land, the motor car and truck came to be seen as the desired means of transport and the symbol of progress. Road construction was rapid as Administration officials mobilised thousands of Highlanders with picks and shovels to forge feeder links to main centres. By the end of 1953 there was an embryonic road from the Markham valley climbing into the Eastern Highlands and across the Ramu-Markham divide, through the Goroka valley and onto Mount Hagen.[4] Along the coast, feeder roads came to ports, while inland they connected plantations and villages to government centres and airstrips.

In 1962, a United Nations mission led by Sir Hugh Foot visited PNG. The Foot Report was critical of the gradualism of the colonial administration and recommended to the Australian Government that the pace of self-determination be hastened, that a national parliament be established, and that the existing Legislative Council should be expanded into a representative House of Assembly.[5] The recommendations were in accord with world-wide sentiment for decolonisation and independence.

In 1964 the first national election was held and, in 1968, the Administrator's Executive Council (AEC) was formed as the paramount decision-making body in PNG. Unlike a parliamentary cabinet however, the agenda of the AEC was limited: the Australian Minister for External Territories retained responsibility for decisions on some critical departments and functions.

In 1966 the World Bank sent its first mission to PNG. It urged a shift from the gradualist policies of the Australian administration to a focus on areas with a high potential for economic development.[6] The mission recommended large infrastructure and agricultural projects to establish the economic base for Independence. Oil palm development was planned for West New Britain and, in 1964, exploration commenced for a giant copper mine on Bougainville Island. The report was criticised for its over-emphasis on European capital and management for agricultural development, its failure to address the issue of industrialisation and the lack of analysis of the institutional requirements to handle development tasks.[7]

By the late 1960s there was in-principle bipartisan support in Australia for PNG to move to independence, though many people, especially in the Highlands, considered that the pace of change should be gradual. In 1969, Mr EG Whitlam, then Leader of the Australian Labor Party, visited PNG and proclaimed that self-government would be achieved in 1972 and independence in 1976. Whitlam became Prime Minister of Australia in 1972 and thus provided impetus towards self-government and independence. However, it was Michael Somare's leadership and drive which successfully held politicians together in a National Coalition and led them into self-government on 1 December 1972, much sooner than generally had been expected.

In 1965, PNG's most ambitious transport infrastructure project was commenced, an upgraded road from Lae and Madang up to the Highland centres of Goroka, Kundiawa, Mount Hagen and Mendi. Eventually it would become a sealed highway from Lae through to the highlands moving up to 500 tonnes of produce and materials each day. As the road construction proceeded, the need for air services to isolated settlements was diminished and many airstrips were either down graded to charter services or closed completely.

Railways as infrastructure were rarely envisaged. Indeed, official reports continually stated that there were no railways in PNG. Railed transport, however, continued to find a role in construction and industrial applications.

Agricultural Railways

The traditional railways which provided transport in coconut plantations provided the main focus for rail operations in the post-War era. Burns Philp decided to rebuild the Choisel Plantation tramways on Soraken, Lindenhafen, Tinputz, Boau and Kunua plantations after the War. Salvaged and second-hand railway materials imported from North Queensland sugar plantations were used in this reconstruction. The pre-war operating pattern of ox-drawn carts hauling green copra to a central rail line was no longer appropriate as most draft animals had been killed and animal transport was regarded as outdated in an era dominated by the internal combustion (IC) engine. Accordingly, the new systems were laid to a grid-iron pattern through the plantations to enable labourers to lump bags of copra to the nearest rail line.

The longest serving plantation railways were on Soraken and Kunua plantations in north-west Bougainville where swampy conditions and sandy soils meant that roads were difficult to construct. Consequently, these plantations were selected for railway reconstruction in 1951.

Railway lines were laid in a grid-pattern, 400 metres apart so that bags of green copra would be carried no more than 200 metres to the railway. The Soraken railway totaled 21 km in length, while the Kunua railway was 11.1 km. From 1957, at least three small Lister diescl-powered locomotives were imported from England to operate the railways.[8] The 7 hp 2-cylinder locomotives were expected to haul 2-ton loads up the 1 in 20 hill to Chula driers. Older Lister petrol locomotives were rebuilt with diesel engines in 1960, making two units available for each plantation. In 1962, 16 turnouts and 12 trucks were imported for extension of the systems. Additional 14 lb rail was imported in 1963 and 1964

By 1967 the Lister locomotives were experiencing maintenance problems and had long periods out of service. A major upgrading of the railways commenced in 1977 when two new Hunslet locomotives (B/N 7531-2/1977) were imported for the railways. These were standard Hunslet 43 hp, 3.5 ton diesel locomotives which were shipped on the *MV Olivebank* in March 1977. To upgrade the Soraken railway, 10,000 steel sleepers were imported, but the bolt spacing was incorrect and they were never laid. Consequently, the system deteriorated.

Top - Lister 4wDM locomotive frames ex. Lindenhafen Plantation stored at Soraken Plantation, Bougainville, 1982.

M. Pearson

Bottom left - Hunslett 4wDM 3.5 tonne locomotive hauls a load of green copra at Soraken Plantation, 1980

M. Pearson

Bottom right - Passing loop on Soraken wharf with storage shed at right, 1980. Track has been damaged by tractors.

M. Pearson

Top - Large bridge on Kunua Plantation tramway, September 1979. Note condition of track.

M. Pearson

Bottom left - Hunslett locomotive operating over deteriorating track at Soraken Plantation, 1981.

M. Pearson

Bottom right - Point set on concrete slab at Kunua Plantation.

M. Pearson

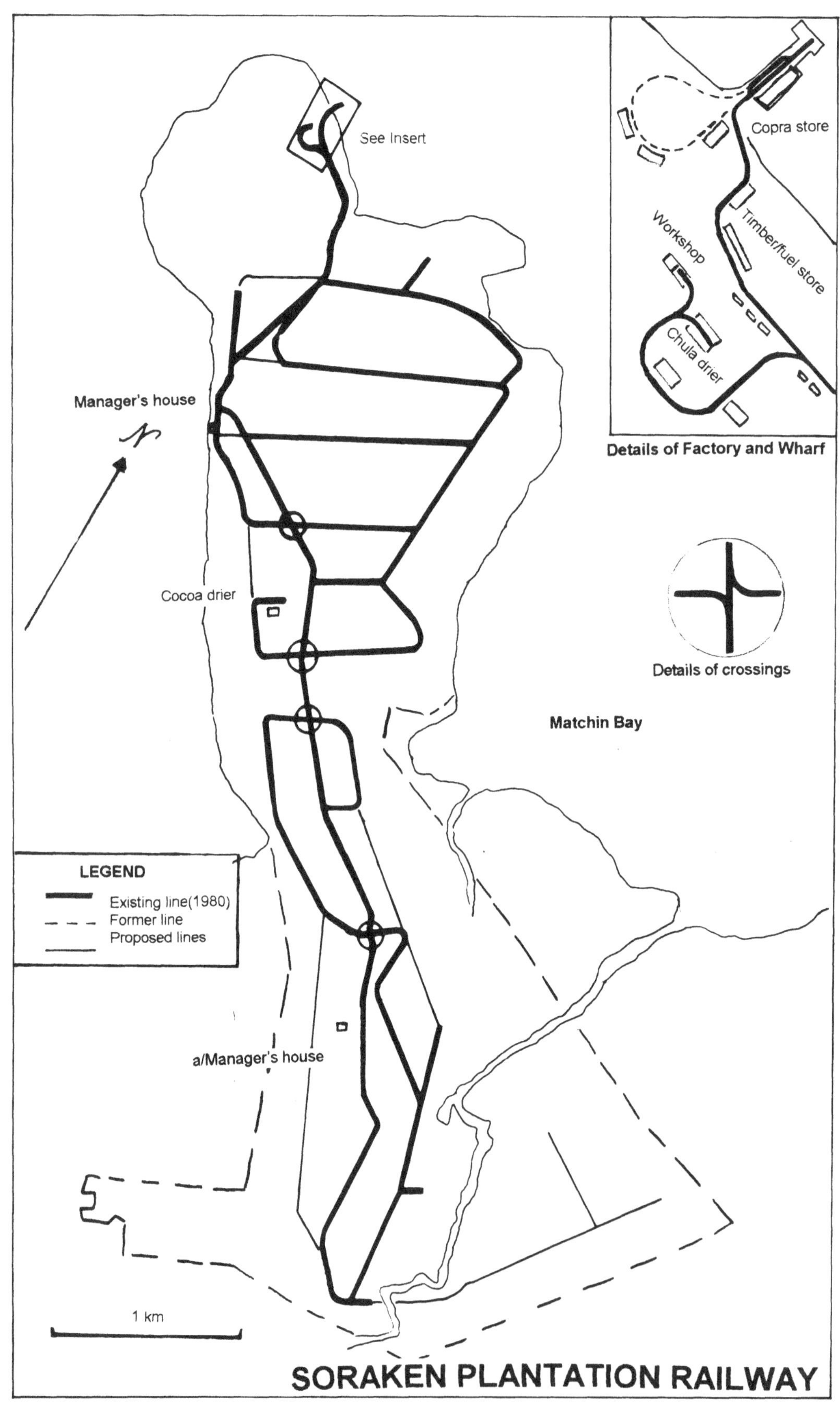

Above - Map of Soraken Plantation Railway

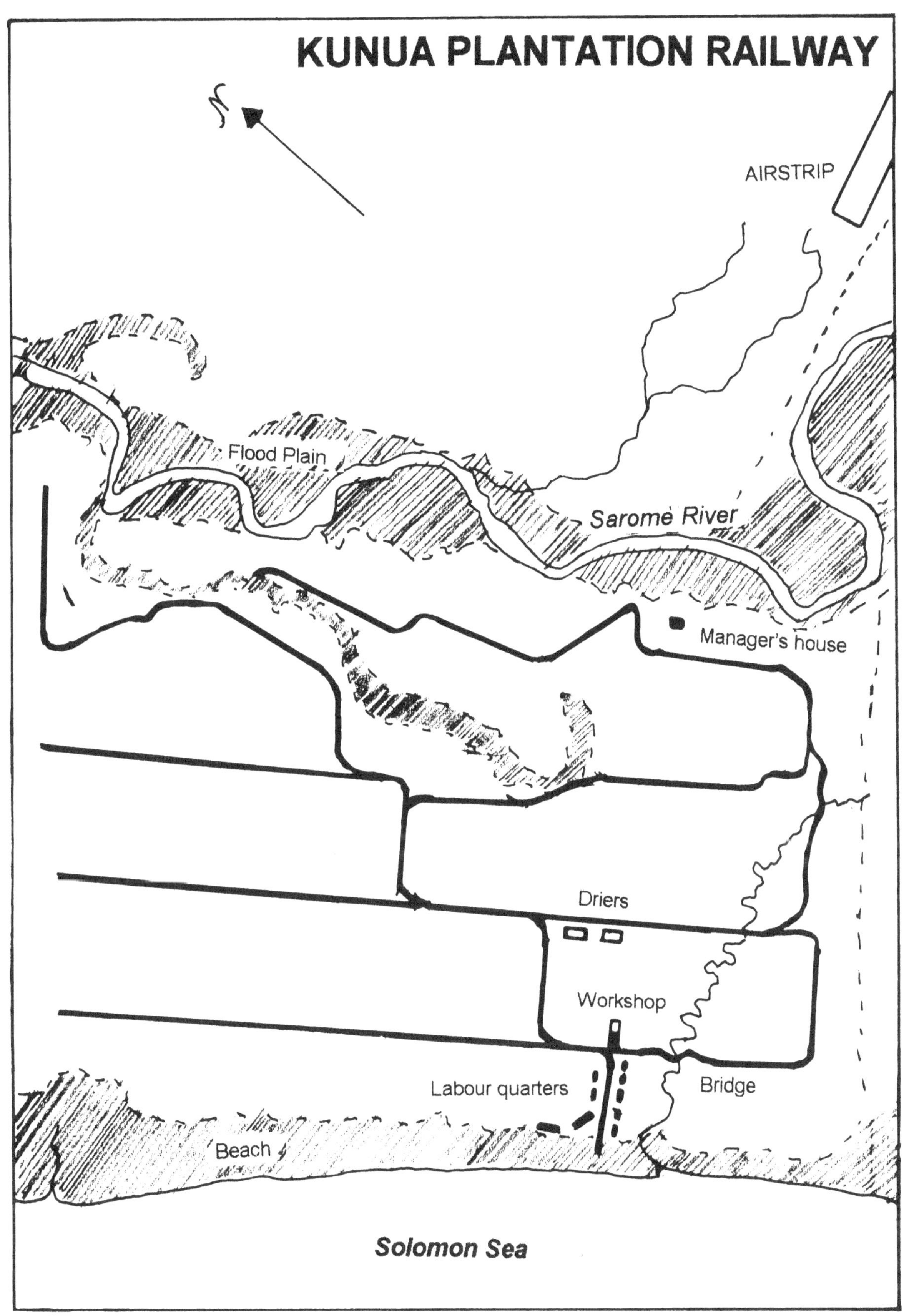

Above - Map of Kunua Plantation Railway

A 1978 report on the Soraken railway indicated the relationship between plantation labourers and the railway:

> The only stories I was able to get from the people who have been working on the tramline are that they really liked working on it and that it was exciting and enjoyable to work on. The workers on the tramline have been careful... [and] there have been no accidents recorded since the tramline was laid.[9]

By 1981, the railway systems, particularly on Soraken, were in poor condition.[10] The Hunslet locomotives were too heavy for the light lines and bridges in the sandy conditions and were a major factor in their deterioration. Another factor was the decision to use herbicides to keep the lines clear rather than labour-intensive hand-cutting of grass, as this resulted in washaways under the lines. As tractors were introduced, they too contributed to the demise of the railways as they created deep ruts into which the tramlines subsided or clipped the ends of sleepers, dislodging them from the ballast.

Support for the railways varied between managers. Colin Disley (1976-77) laid concrete slabs under the points during his term to improve operations. Tim Whale, Kunua manager during a visit in 1981, considered that the tramline was much easier to maintain than roads and he was rehabilitating the system after a period of neglect. Roads took more space and generated bogs which required large quantities of fill. The railway system was also more robust than tractor-hauled road trailers as trucks could still be hand-pushed if the loco was unserviceable, but tractor break-downs meant that the transport system stopped. However, Mr Whale noted that a brief period of neglect under an unsympathetic manager could undermine many years of effort to maintain the railway as an effective transport system.

The plantations were purchased by New Guinea Plantations in 1982. The Soraken railway was lifted in 1984, to be replaced by roads. The conditions required roads 7 metres wide for dual-wheel tractors, compared with 2 metres for the railway, resulting in the loss of significant areas of production land. The Kunua railway remained in service up to the Bougainville crisis of 1990.[11] The Soraken plantation buildings were destroyed during the crisis, but it is reported that railway equipment was still at Soraken in 1993.

Cutch and the Great Railway Robbery

The Borneo New Guinea Mangrove Company established a pioneer factory in the swamps of the Kikori River Delta at Aird Hills to extract *cutch* (a tanning fluid from mangrove bark).[12] A short tramline (about 1300 metres) was built from the wharf to the factory. It carried firewood and the bark inwards, and cutch out for shipment.[13] There was a small IC-engined locomotive which hauled flat trucks and hopper wagons over the line. By 1958 the venture had failed and the equipment was abandoned. Mr Keith Tetley, a local trader, collected rails to build a wharf and copra drier.

Steamships Trading Company (STC) eventually purchased the assets of the Borneo New Guinea Mangrove Company from receivers with the intention of using them at their Baimuru Sawmill. On arrival to collect their bounty, STC crews discovered its disappearance. Whereabouts of the railway equipment was soon discovered and the company took Mr Tetley to court, thus commencing the case of PNG's *Great Railway Robbery*.[14] Mr Tetley eventually won the case as there was no caretaker at the site and the rails were not on land belonging to the company, and therefore, they could be considered abandoned.[15] He is reported to have arrived at the Kerema Hall for the annual Christmas party pulling a toy train, much to the delight of those present. Steamships lost out, not only losing the rails and the money paid for them but also having to pay court costs.

COMPARISON OF LAND USE FOR LIGHT RAILWAY AND ROADS

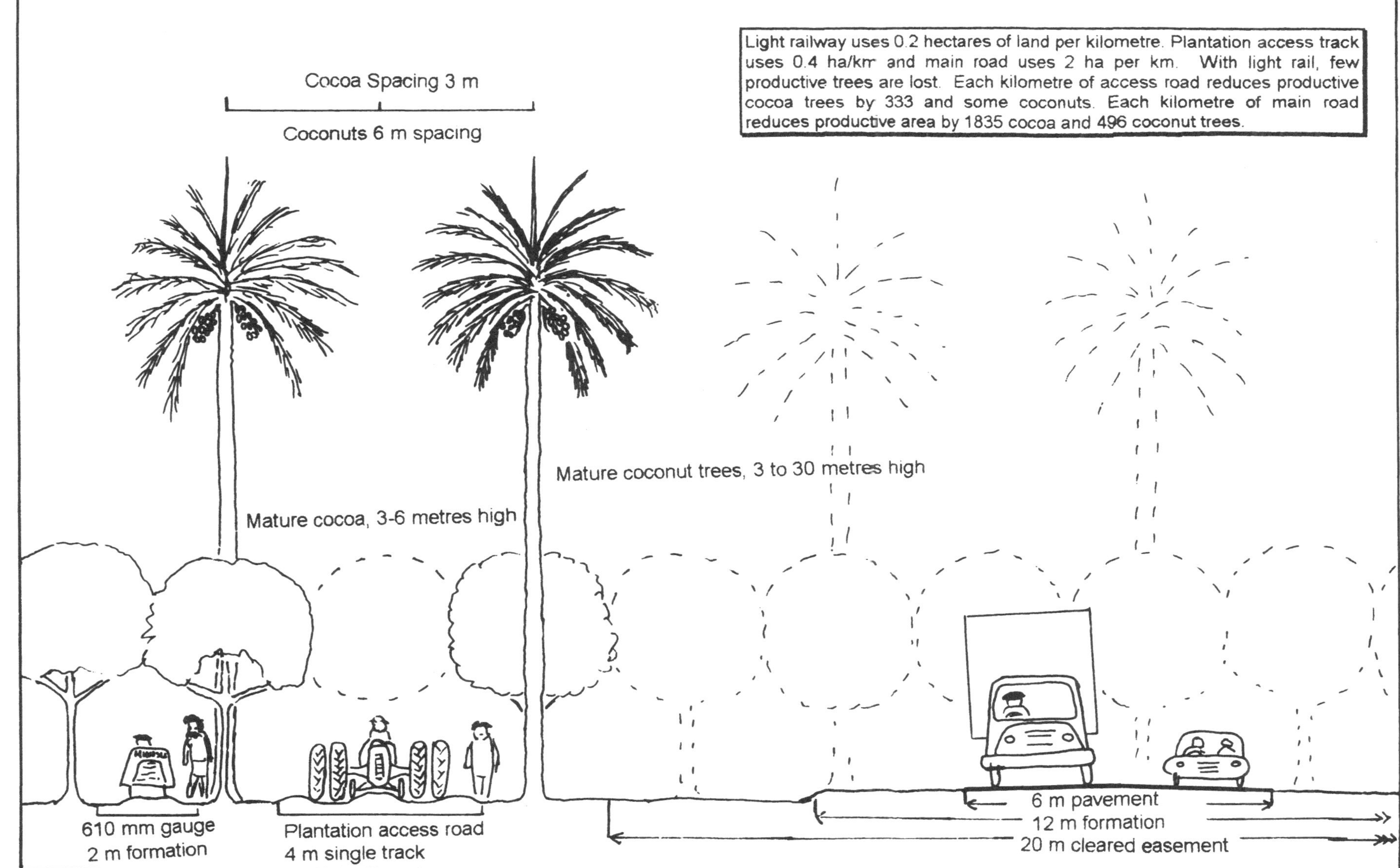

Top - Tractor shunting bins on 700mm gauge system at Mosa mill.

PNG National Archives

Bottom - Lister 4wDM locomotive shunts bins loaded with palm oil fresh fruit bunches on 600mm gauge rack at Mosa mill in 1972.

R. F. McKillop

Oil Palm Railways

With World Bank support, PNG's first oil palm project was initiated in the Talasea-Hoskins area of West New Britain in 1967. For the first time, PNG was growing a high volume plantation crop. In Malaysia and Indonesia the oil palm industry used railway transportation to haul the fresh fruit bunches (FFB) from the field. Oil palm also required a constant flow of raw material through the processing mill, including the sterilisation of fruit in pressure chambers, an application ideally suited to railed transport. Transport over rough roads and excessive handling of the fruit causes bruising.

The Mosa palm oil factory opened in July 1971. The company took the "quick fix" and chose road transport to haul oil palm bunches from the field. The bunches were transferred to rail at the factory. Initially 530 metres of 600 mm gauge railway track consisting of a balloon loop and three tracks through the factory were constructed to move oil palm bunches through the sterilisers at a constant rate.[16] This railway was operated by a 1.5 tonne, 12.5 hp, 4wDM Lister locomotive (B/No. 56115 of 1969) and there were 40 steel bins of 2.7 tonne capacity. The locomotive was unsuitable for the task due to oiled track and was set aside in 1974.

The oil palm project was highly successful, with yields well in excess of the planned capacity of the mill. A Kina 4.2 million expansion program to lift mill capacity to 10,000 tonnes of fruit per year was initiated in 1974. The original railway was replaced by a larger 700 mm gauge system with 1620 metres of track, including five sidings through the mill. Steel hopper wagons with a capacity of 2.5 tonnes of fruit are propelled through the mill by conventional wheeled tractors. With the successful establishment of an oil palm industry in the Mosa area, further mills have subsequently been established, each with a small rail system to transport fruit through the factory. These are described in the following chapter.

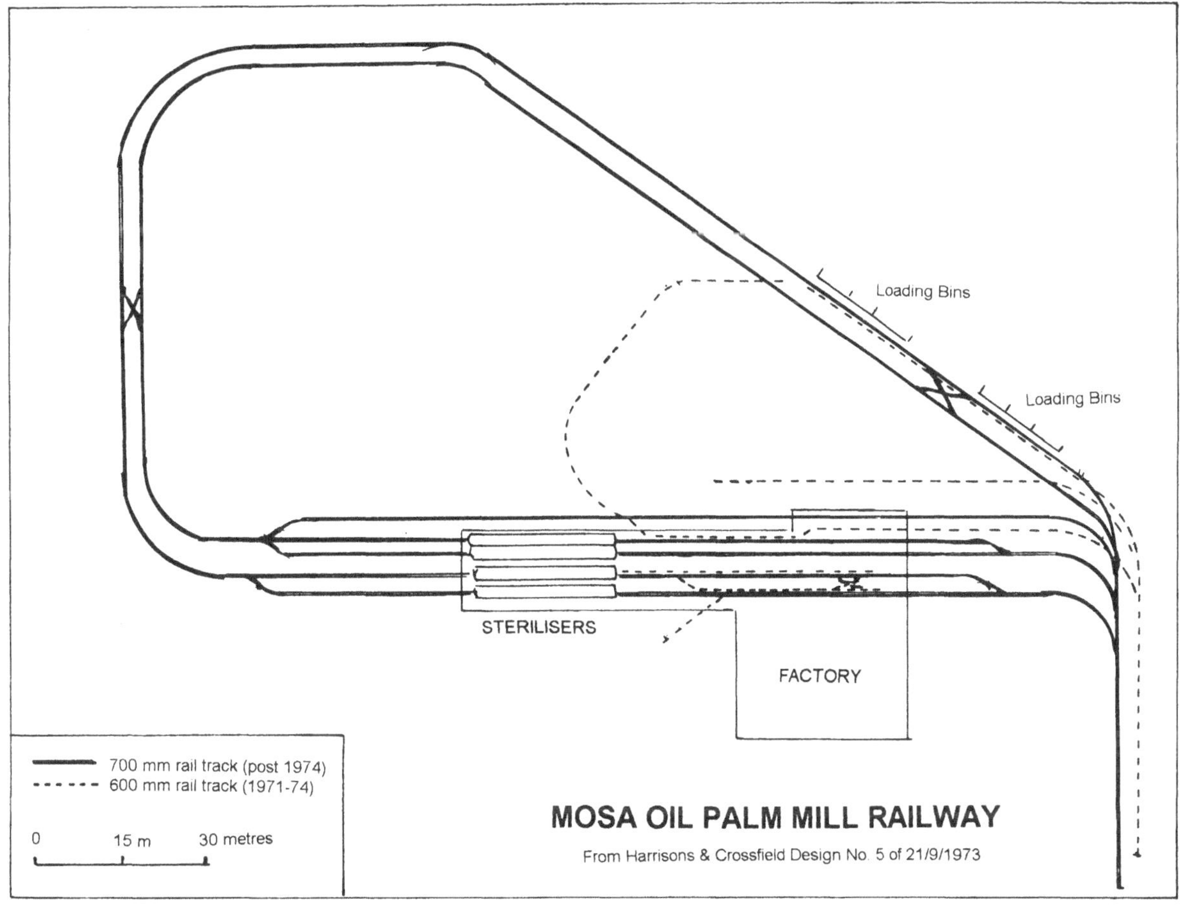

Above - Map of Mosa Oil Palm Mill Railway

Public Railways

The construction of railways by the government was not a priority in post-war Australia. Nevertheless, the PNG Administration operated a short railway at their Bulolo sawmill and gave consideration to construction of a public light railway in Sepik District. In the late 1950's, rice growing was promoted to village farmers in the densely populated Maprik area of Sepik District. A rice mill and base for agricultural staff was established at Bainyik. Transport to this isolated inland area was via the Sepik River to Pagwi, thence over a 56 km road which was difficult to maintain.

In December, 1959, the District Commissioner at Wewak proposed the construction of a 2 ft gauge light railway over the route using second-hand materials from Queensland canefields.[17] Field staff anticipated that such a line could be built for 50,000 pounds, but Public Works officials in Port Moresby estimated that the line would cost in excess of 200,000 pounds. Their report noted that a road would be no more costly than the railway and that Queensland canefield railways handled far greater tonnages than that offering to Bainyik. A request for second-hand rails was made to the Colonial Sugar Refining Company in April, 1960. When CSR responded in the negative, the Director of Public Works urged construction of a second-class road rather than a railway.

The administration was also involved in forestry at Bulolo where there were natural stands of klinki pine. Kilinki and hoop pine plantations were established post-war and a large government-owned sawmilling and plywood factory was opened in Bulolo town. Logging was undertaken by bulldozers and sniggers, with logs being brought to the mill by road transport. However, the first Bulolo sawmill established in 1946 had short railway lines running from the mill to the dressing and joiners shop building.[18] There were two parallel lines, about 150-200 metres in length, to bring timber to the planing machines. Light rails from war disposals were used with six hand-pushed trolleys. There was also a 200 metre line from the mill to the sawdust heap. These lines were taken up about 1966.

Mining and Construction Railways

Years of mineral exploration finally brought positive results in 1967 when work commenced on the giant Panguna Copper Mine in Bougainville Island. It was the largest enterprise in the country, employing 12,000 workers and contributing some 17 per cent of the PNG Government's internal revenue over the period 1972 to 1989. Establishment of the mine was opposed by missionaries fearful that its industrialism would bring forces to assault mission status and moral values. [19] The mine was developed as a large open-cut operation using heavy road trucks to move ore to the mill. There were, however, some rail operations. Some illustrations are to be found on the book cover.

In order to test the extent of the Panguna copper deposits, Dillingham Construction commenced drilling of mining adits in the hills behind Arawa Plantation in 1967.[20] Two 610 mm gauge lines ran into horizontal adits into the ore body: the Panguna Adit of 1600 metres which operated between August, 1967 and October, 1968, and the Western Adit of 2600 metres, between May, 1968 and October, 1969.[21] Three small *Gemco Traminer* battery-electric locomotives and Granby side-dump wagons were used on the Panguna Adit, while there were four locomotives used on the Western Adit line, including one of the former units.

Construction of the first phase of the giant Ramu Hydro-Electric Scheme to provide power to New Guinea mainland centres commenced in 1972 at Yonki in the Eastern Highlands District. Hyundai Construction was awarded the contract for the construction of a 2.4 km tail water tunnel and they used a 914 mm gauge railway and two underground diesel-hydraulic locomotives for this work.[22] The tunnel was completed in 1976.

Dillingham Construction Western Adit Railway, Bougainville, 1968-70.
Top - Mechanical repairs to a bogie dump truck outside the adit entrance.

Bottom - Gemco Traminer 0-4-0BE locomotive on the line into the 2.6km tunnel.

PNG National Archives

Top - Yonki Hydro Scheme: Hyundai Construction 4wDH underground locomotive hauls a train from the 2.4km tail water tunnel.

Post-Courier

Bottom - Korean and Australian engineers with 4wDH underground locomotive on the Yonki Hydro scheme tail water tunnel construction railway.

PNG National Archives

Missionaries

The European mission enclaves at Ulamona, Vunapope and Marienberg continued rail-based logging operations into the post-war era. These lines were covered in Chapter 2. Several mission-based entrepreneurs, particularly by Marist Brothers missionaries on Bougainville, established short railways post-war. At the Asitavi mission near Wakanai on Bougainville's east coast, a light rail line was built by Brother Ansgar to carry timber from the sawmill to the wharf.[23] There was also a line from the mill out into what is now the farm at Asitavi where the logs for the mill were cut. A little further south at Mabiri plantation, near Arigua, a narrow-gauge line was built by Br Ansgar from the wharf to a store shed and out into the plantation.[24] Br Ansgar tried, in conjunction with Mr Mack the manger at Kurwina, to link the two tramlines across the Mabiri River.

At Tubiana mission, near Kieta, a 2 ft gauge line, about 100 metres in length, ran from the wharf into the store shed. It originally ran through the store to a workshop. When visited in 1982, the tramline was no longer in use. Two rail trucks were purchased by the author and moved to Sunvahoara. One was restored and the other had the journal removed to restore a skip truck from Chabai. One had an Orenstein & Koppell wheelset of 600 mm gauge which is believed to have come from Numa Numa Plantation. The restored truck was taken to Buin and then to Toniva. Its present situation is unknown.

Yet another Marist Brothers' railway was at Tsiroge Mission north of Soraken, where Brother Pius constructed a 200 metre 610 mm gauge tramline from the wharf to his workshop in 1950. It used war surplus, ex-Japanese equipment and rails lifted from Soraken for use at Chabai.[25] The railway originally consisted of a mainline which ran from the wharf to the carpenters shop about 200 m directly inland, with a branch to the mechanics workshop. The points caused many problems with the wheels jumping the blades and frogs of the point and it was replaced with a 6-foot turntable constructed by Brother Pius from old Japanese material. There were two hand-pushed trucks used for carrying engines from the workboats to the workshop for maintenance and return. The line remained in use until the Bougainville crisis of 1990.

On the north coast of West New Britain, Father Birkmann built a light railway in 1966 from a copra shed at Kaliai mission, through Taveliai village, to a landing place at the far end of the village.[26] He used rails and a set of wheels from the Ulamona logging line. The wheels were used to build a trolley, which was poled along the line. The line operated in the north-west season when ships had to anchor some distance from the copra shed.

At Suassi in the Papuan Highlands, the London Missionary Society used a short tramway for construction of an airstrip. The local missionary, Bert Brown, arranged for carriers to bring in two sets of rail wheels, weighing 90 lbs each, and eight lengths of rail. A one-ton wooden truck was built by the station using fish tins as bearings. The wagon was pushed back and forth along 60 ft of track, which was moved as the airstrip was made.

Urban Development

Post-war development in PNG saw the establishment of the first significant towns at Port Moresby and Lae. Their planning was influenced by current trends in Australia. Australian cities had been shaped by the electric tram and suburban railway which provided efficient public transport services. Post-war urban development saw a dramatic swing away from public transport to the provision of infrastructure for private cars. The structure and character of cities was dramatically changed as the space requirements for cars generated urban sprawl.[27] As cities became more car-based and spread out, individuals needed to travel further to work and other exchange opportunities thereby requiring high levels of energy use.[28]

The shift from public to private transport also had important implications for the function of the city. Public open space for exchange became usurped by the private interest of the motorist for movement and storage of his vehicle.[29] Travel in private cars restricted the traditional social exchange of the city as motorists also assumed new power and aggression over pedestrians and other road users.

These trends were to impact on the fledgling PNG towns. These were designed by Australian planners eager to apply the latest car-orientated designs to the new frontier. Suburbs in Port Moresby and Lae followed similar patterns to those in Canberra, Darwin or Townsville. But car ownership was largely restricted to the privileged expatriate community. Papua New Guineans were left to fend for themselves as pedestrians or consumers of poorly conceived and supported public transport services. In Port Moresby a bus company provided non-timetabled services between the main residential areas and work places.

Counter views on the importance of rail-based public transport were put forward in the 1970s. The danger of road-based transport and the potential role of electric, light rail systems in Port Moresby emerged on the public agenda in 1974.[30] The following year, the Commission of Inquiry into the Rationalisation of Imports investigated the economics of an electric light rail public transport system for Port Moresby.[31] The concerns were also expressed by national politicians. In 1974, opposition leader Tim Ward claimed that PNG had become a road-oriented economy with unsustainable reliance on imported fuels.[32] He put forward a *Railway Plan,* with electrified lines from Port Moresby to Marshall Lagoon, Kapakapa, Kemp Welch, Hood Point and Cape Rodney, and from Ok Tedi to Port Moresby. Mr Ward claimed that railways would steer development away from existing   ports of Port Moresby, Milne Bay and Oro Bay. The Plan also sought to tap Papua New Guinea's hydro-electric potential.

Notes on Chapter 6

1   Jinks, B, Biskup, P and Nelson, H, *Readings in New Guinea history*, Sydney, Angus & Robertson, 1973, p. 324.

2   *Ibid.*, p. 322.

3   Legge, JD, *Australian colonial policy*, Sydney, 1956, p. 219.

4   Nelson, H, *Taim bilong masta: the Australian involvement with Papua New Guinea*, Sydney, ABC Books, 1982, p. 73.

5   Report of the 1962 United Nations Visiting Mission to the Trust Territory of New Guinea, New York, 1962, p. 24-6.

6   IBRD, *The economic development of the Territory of Papua and New Guinea*, Baltimore, 1965.

7   Schaffer, B, "Thoughts at Goroka", *New Guinea*, June/July 1965.

8   Choisel Company records. Locos imported in 1957, 1959 and 1962. Other reports indicate Lister locomotives were used pre-war.

9   Letter, Francis Bougin, clerk at Soraken, 28 November, 1978.

10 Pearson, M, field inspections, 1981

11 James Rira, locomotive driver at Kunua, interviewed at Kalili, September 1995.

12 *Pacific Islands Monthly*, November, 1950, p. 89.

13 N Nicklason, letter recalling visit to railway in 1954, 1 May 1978.

14 *Black and White*, December 1966, p. 10-11; *South Pacific Post*, October 1966.

15 *Post-Courier*, 16 April, 1993, K Tetley obituary.

16 McKillop, RF, "Mosa Oil Palm Mill, West New Britain, PNG", *Light Railways* No. 69, 1980.

17 PNG National Archives, Access 36 PWD Box 6211 File 60/3/8/2

18 Low, LJ of Bulolo, letter, April 1984.

19 Griffin, J, "Bougainville - a challenge for the churches", *The Independent*, 10 May 1996, p. 6

20 *Bougainville Copper Bulletin*, Oct. 1967, Vol 1 No. 1, p. 2

21 Douglas, B, "Mine tramways at Panguna", *Light Railways*, No. 64, p. 28.

22 *Post Courier*, 1 December, 1973, p. 111. *Highland News*, Vol. 3:2, 11/1/73, p. 1

23 Leo Hannett, interview, Port Moresby 1995.

24 Leo Hannett, interview, 1995.

25 Interview Brother Pias, 1983

26 Fr Birkmann, information provided via Sister Mary Ruth, letter, 7 August, 1981.

27 Newman, P and Kenworthy, J (1989), *Cities and Automobile Dependence - An International Sourcebook*, Gower, Aldershott.

28 David Ebgwicht, *Towards an Eco-City: Calming the Traffic*, Sydney, Envirobook, 1992.

29 Ian Manning, *The Open Street: Public Transport, Motor Cars and Politics in Australian Cities*, Sydney, Transit Australia Publishing, 1991, p. 50.

30 C. Shoebridge, "Trams in Waigani, Move people not vehicles", *Post Courier*, 7 October, 1974, p. 2.

31 *Post Courier*, 11 March, 1975, p. 8

32 *Post Courier*, 24 October, 1974 p. 3.

CHAPTER 7 - INDEPENDENCE

Nationalist Spirit

Papua New Guinea's national flag was raised on 16 September, 1975, amid optimism that its citizens would have new opportunities to participate in economic development activities on an equal basis. For the emerging educated elite, centralisation of decision-making in Canberra and Port Moresby had become synonymous with the continuation of colonial rule. This nationalist sentiment became a focus for political debate in the late 1960s and early 1970s. Secessionist sentiments were expressed in Papua and Bougainville, where landowner and church resentment over the mine fuelled powerful anti-government forces, while in the Gazelle Peninsula the Mataungan Association spearheaded a campaign to return alienated lands to local landowners.

A Constitution had been drawn up after extensive consultation involving some 2000 meetings around Papua New Guinea. The Constitutional Planning Committee (CPC), guided by Bougainvillian priest Fr John Momis, recommended that PNG's diverse regional and cultural groups would be best served by a decentralised system of government rather than a single unitary state. The vision was the devolution of decision-making, administration and financial powers to a level where rural populations and their representatives could participate effectively in planning and development. The CPC drafted the Constitution to recognise that districts (later renamed provinces) could choose provincial government if they so desired.

The decision involved significant political and economic costs. National departments and politicians feared reduction of their power and the cost of establishing provincial administrations was seen as excessive.[1] The new Government sought to scrap the provincial government provisions, bringing a swift reaction by the Bougainville Provincial Assembly which unilaterally declared independence on 1 September 1975.

Reconciliation talks between Bougainvillean leaders and central government officials led to the Bougainville Agreement in 1976. Bougainville agreed to remain in PNG if provincial government was re-inserted in the Constitution. This amendment was approved by Parliament in August 1976, through the drafting of a separate *Organic Law on Provincial Government*, which was enacted in March 1977. The Organic Law set the parameters for administrative and financial decentralisation.

When confronted with implementing the process of decentralisation, the Government decided that it would be administratively simpler to devolve uniformly across the 19 provinces than on a piecemeal basis. On 1 January, 1978, substantial financial and administrative powers were transferred to all nineteen provinces.

The Provincial Government Issue

The vision and hopes held at Independence have not stood up well in practice. While the introduction of provincial government generally satisfied regional demands for political represent-ation, the system has been criticised for its inefficiencies and financial mismanagement. In some provinces, the political executive, together with selected public servants, effectively became the *gatekeepers* of the provincial budget. Instead of a mechanism for cooperation and the mutual sharing of power between national and provincial governments, the reality was that the new political structures provided a venue for the interplay of competing interests and institutions.[2] Self-interest and patronage came to be seen as the hallmarks of the provincial government system and

PNG politics in general. Provincial government reforms enacted in 1995 extended the power of national politicians over provincial affairs.

Economic Development: from Village to Mine

Initially, the process of nation-building in PNG was guided by the *Eight Point Improvement Plan*. Its themes were increased participation by nationals in economic activity and equality of opportunity. The reality was very different. Instead of a rural-based, self-sufficient development model, a minerals economy emerged which favoured capital-intensive, enclave activities over labour-intensive, rural-based industries, particularly agriculture.

Over the period 1985 to 1988, exports averaged 40 per cent of GDP and there were high levels of capital inflows into mining and petroleum projects. On average, mining sector investment was equivalent to 8 per cent of GDP during the period 1986-1989 as the Ok Tedi copper mine came into production, new mines were developed at Misima and Porgera and the Kutubu oil fields were developed.

Papua New Guineans played a peripheral role in these large-scale resource development projects. The reality was very different to the hopes of "independence". Problems emerged on Bougainville island where the copper mine dominated the economy and politics. Fundamental differences between landowners and resource developers over land rights, compensation for damage and distribution of benefits fuelled conflict. There were also contradictions within traditional society over responses to the externally imposed changes. Cleavage between local "inheritors" of the new wealth and those who could hope to be dependent beneficiaries became an important factor, while there was political conflict between those who followed orthodox investment paths to profit and populists promoting a distributionist cause.[3] By 1989 Bougainville was enveloped by armed rebellion resulting in the closure of the Panguna copper mine on 15 September.

The result was a period of anarchy and reign of terror for the people of Bougainville which many believe has been more traumatic than the hardship experienced during the Second World War. The economy and infrastructure were destroyed by Bougainvillians themselves and there was significant loss of life.[4] In a short span of time, PNG's most prosperous province was brought back to a factionalised, subsistence society by an anarchic and cargoist revolt which a weak state could not suppress.[5]

The Bougainville crisis and closure of the Panguna copper mine had a dramatic impact on the PNG economy. With World Bank assistance, a program of economic reform was initiated. However, rapid growth in the minerals and petroleum sectors in the early 1990s stimulated expectations of significant wealth. There was also a rush to exploit forest resources and export logs to Asian markets for short-term gain. This resources boom generated high expectations and political pressure to secure and distribute prospective revenues to meet local interests. Uncontrolled government spending on populist activities and the public service resulted without any improvement in productivity. Increasingly, fiscal indiscipline, including wasteful and increasing recurrent expenditure, consistent over-budget expenditure, raids on national savings for short-term consumptive expenditure and disregard for the public debt, has characterised Government perform-ance.[6]

During the mineral boom, capital-intensive production of export commodities and imports were encouraged at the expense of labour-intensive production and domestic supplies. In these circum-stances, the competitiveness of the economy was eroded and unemployment rose.

Since Independence, overall economic performance has fallen short of the aspirations of the people. Employment creation has constantly lagged behind the entry of new job seekers into the labour market and there has been a sharp increase in criminal activity. This in turn has increased transaction costs and further reduced PNGs competitiveness.

Expectations of future wealth stimulated an upsurge in public sector spending on populist activities which could not be sustained. This resulted in the financial crisis of 1994-96 when severe spending cuts had to be imposed and the Government had to turn to international financial institutions for support in the implementation of reforms.

International Rail Revival

PNG has been isolated from the international revival of railways which has occurred since the 1970's. This upsurge is linked to the adaptability of railways to new technology and environmental agenda and major institutional reforms. The technology of steel wheel on steel rails proved to be ideally suited to *new age* micro-electronics. Railways could now apply computer technologies to achieve new standards of operating efficiency and safety. Moreover, the public mood, jolted by the *oil shock* of 1973-74, urban traffic congestion and pollution, took up *limits to growth* and environmental issues. In this new context, the energy and space efficiency of railways became an important advantage.[7] Rail-based urban transport, for instance, requires one-thirtieth the space of private road-based transport and only a fraction of the space for storage (parking) and maintenance.[8] In addition, the high energy efficiency of rail results in less pollution and greenhouse gas emissions than alternative transport.

Heavy investment in railway infrastructure for efficient freight haulage, high-speed railways to link major cities and, within cities, in light rail and underground railway projects has occurred internationally since 1975. More significantly, railway institutions have been reformed to embrace new business cultures in which customer service has first priority and performance is assessed against *world-best* practices.

Reform has not been limited to main-stream public railways. In Australia, heavy haul mineral railways are at the forefront of world-best practice in railway operation. Research and development into canefield railway technology has brought enhanced competitiveness for the Australian sugar industry. Road transport was pushed aside by the efficiencies of modern, computer-controlled railways which move vast quantities of cane at a constant rate from the field through processing mills. By the 1990s, twenty-six mills transported some 30 million tonnes of cane per season over some 3500 km of track, mostly of 610 mm gauge.

Institutional reform has been at the heart of the revival. Internationlly, railway management has thrown off the institutional rigidities which hindered its earlier response to the challenges of the car, the lorry and the bus. In the process, huge bureaucratic empires have been broken up into smaller business groups to achieve international "best-practice" performance standards. In many instances, local communities have revived branch lines or commuter services as small railway operations which can compete where large-scale operators found the service uneconomic. Ironically, many of these new operators began as volunteer groups to preserve and operate closed lines as heritage projects. Through innovation, team-work, basic technical skills and, above all, good management, they have graduated to operate competitive commercial services.

These international trends have bypassed PNG. Within local institutions the response to political demands for expanded transport infrastructure has been viewed within a narrow, traditional framework of roads and airports. The culture was captured by the national airline, *Air Niugini,* in a 1976 advertising slogan, *"who needs trains when We've got planes".*[9]

Bougainville Copper Limited: Drainage Tunnel Railway 1977-1984

Top - Battery -Electric locomotive hauling spoil emerges from the 6.15km tunnel entrance.

Bougainville Copper Ltd.

Middle - 900mm. gauge 10-tonne Gemco battery-electric locomotive No. 2 on the BCL drainage tunnel railway, c. 1980.

Bougainville Copper Ltd.

Bottom - 20-tonne diesel-hydraulic underground locomotive at Panguna, c. 1980.

M. Pearson

Top - Ok Tedi Mining: Ok Mani exploration tunnel adit with construction railway equipment in foreground, 1982-85.

Post Courier

Bottom - A small "cane train" locomotive working on the North Paibuna No. 1 Petroleum Prospecting Licence (PPL 123).

Dick Knox - PNG Resources, July- September 1994.

Mining/petroleum Industry Railways

Exploration and construction activities in the mining and petroleum sectors has stimulated several railway operations. Following the large-scale Panguna copper mine on Bougainville, similar ventures were established at Ok Tedi in 1982, Misima Island in 1986 and at Porgera in 1988. Bougainville Copper Limited commenced construction of a drainage tunnel at their Panguna mine in 1977 using a 900 mm gauge railway.[10] Seven battery-electric and diesel-hydraulic tunnelling locomotives were imported from Australia.[11] The 6.15 km tunnel was completed in 1984.[12]

The discovery of one of the world's largest porphyry copper ore bodies at Mount Fubilan in the remote Star Mountains in 1968 presented PNG nation with a difficult development challenge. The copper ore was capped by a gold-rich zone of ore, but the deposit was located in an isolated region, cut off from the rest of the world by steep terrain and dense tropical vegetation.

Development of the mine commenced in the 1980's and required an investment of K1340 million. Massive landslides in December 1983 and January 1984 resulted in abandonment of the tailings dam at Ok Ma after expenditure of more than K60 million.[13]

Supplies for the project were barged up the Fly River to Kiunga, then transported by road to the mining township at Tabubil. Mining is by open-cut using massive dump trucks. However, railways were employed for an exploration adit and a tunnel at Ok Mani between 1982 and 1985[14]/. Underground diesel-hydraulic locomotives were used.

In 1975, the Department of Transport commissioned a study for the provision of integrated infrastructure to service the Frieda, Ok Tedi and Tifalmin mineral prospects. It recommended use of the existing waterways of the Fly and Sepik Rivers for the mines, supplemented by slurry pipelines and road-barge combinations.[15]. Rail options were examined, but at least 1.5 million tonnes of freight annually was considered necessary to justify construction. Projected transport demand was well below this level.

Harvey Creek

To provide water for the Ok Tedi mine, the company developed a water supply project at Harvey Creek on the Folomian Plateau. Curtin Brothers were contracted to construct a small weir, pump station, pipeline and access tunnel in 1987. Their first task was to push through the tunnel and rail line to give access to the machinery and materials needed for the weir.[16] A 1500 metre funicular railway was constructed through precipitous slopes, unstable ground, constant drizzle and cloud to ferry in the materials. The men building the line had to contend with gradients as steep as 68 degrees and at one point the line plunges almost vertically for over 100 metres near the pump station.

Four pump motors, each weighing over two tonnes, were among the machinery transported over the railway to the site. The construction phase took just over six months. It is understood the railway has been retained to provide access to the pump station and pipeline.

North Paibuna railway

PNG's most recent railway was built in 1993 by the joint-venture partners in Foreland permit PPL-123 to overcome a unique transport problem in the mangrove swamps of the Gulf Province[17]. Previous experience in moving supplies and equipment to exploration wells by road in such swamps had been unsatisfactory. On one occasion, a bulldozer was lost in the slime.

For the North Paibuna No. 1 well, a 300 metre railway was built over the swamp from the river landing to the well site. The steel rails, ties and fittings and two 610 mm gauge flatcars were obtained from Queensland sugar mills. The line was completed in August, 1993. Initially, the flat cars were winched over the line. This proved to be too slow, and a small 4wDM locomotive was obtained second-hand from Queensland. With completion of the well, the railway was taken up in 1995 and the equipment was transported to Port Moresby. It is reported stored in a Curtin Bros. yard.

Agro-Industry Railways

Investment in modern rail technology to move produce at a constant rate from the field through processing mills has played a central role in building the competitiveness of agro-industries in today's global economy. Unfortunately, the necessary security for such long-term investment has been lacking in PNG.

When the viability of a PNG sugar industry was examined by Booker Agriculture International in 1977, it was found necessary to protect the industry behind trade barriers for financial viability. Ramu Sugar Limited was formed in 1978 to establish a 7,500 ha sugar estate and a mill capable of producing 41,000 tonnes of sugar per annum at Gusap in the Ramu Valley. The enterprise, protected by a 150 per cent import tariff, decided to use road transport to move the 300,000 tonnes of cane from the field to the mill each season. Annual cane production has now risen to 400,000 tonnes with a mill throughput of 145 tonnes per hour.

The oil palm industry is export-oriented and therefore must compete on international markets. Nevertheless, the high yields of the pioneer venture at Mosa in West New Britain have encouraged further expansion. However, mill throughput in the range of 60-75 tonnes per hour has been considered too low to justify heavy investment in railways. Accordingly, rail transport has been restricted to the initial movement of fresh fruit bunches through the sterilisers at the mill.

The second oil palm mill, owned by Hargy Oil Palms Pty Limited, was opened at Biala in 1977. A Lister locomotive was used to push wagon-mounted cages into the steriliser over a line about 150 metres in length.[18] This mill has had a chequered history.

Higaturu Oil Palm Pty Limited, a joint venture between the Commonwealth Development Corporation (CDC) and the Government, opened an oil palm mill near Popondetta in Oro Province in 1980. The mill has four 600 mm gauge parallel railway lines, each 250 metres in length, serving the sterilisers.[19] Fresh fruit bunches (FFB) are loaded into cages from the hoppers, then transported to the rail lines by fork-lift trucks. Trains made up of eight cage wagons are pushed into the sterilisers by tractors and then pulled out by winches.[20] There are 250 cages and 40 flat wagons in service, built to standard design by Malaysian manufacturers.

On New Ireland, CDC established Poliamba Pty Ltd to redevelop old German coconut plantations on the Bulominsky Highway to oil palm and cocoa. A K14 million oil palm mill commenced production in 1990.[21] Transport from the fields to the mill is provided by local trucking contractors. Fruit bunches are loaded into standard cage wagons from overhead hoppers for haulage through the sterilisers over a short (150 metre) 700 mm gauge railway.

At their Milne Bay operation, CDC initially tried taking cages to the field and loading them with FFB for transport to the mill. Here the cages were transferred directly onto rail wagons for the sterilisers. However, the experiment proved costly and the company subsequently reverted to traditional road transport, with the FFB loaded into cages and transferred to rail at the mill. A 600 metre circular line with passing loops takes the cages through the sterilisers.

In West New Britain continued expansion of production has resulted in the construction of two additional mills at Kumbango and Kapuia by New Britain Palm Oil Development. The 75 tonnes/hour mills have a similar railway system to that used at Mosa. Large 12-tonne cages have recently been introduced. They are loaded in the field and transported to the mill by road for transfer to rail.

Timber processing has also been a hope for the PNG economy. In response to a new *Forestry Act* passed in 1993, logging companies have established timber processing facilities which employ rail technology. In most cases, second-hand mills have been established and they only process reject logs. Typically, they have breakdown saws to which logs are passed on a rail-based truck (of 1500 or 2000 mm gauge) moved by winch and sophisticated hydraulics. Flitches are then cut into smaller sizes at saw benches and then passed through planers. In both cases, short lengths of rail (of 610 or 762 mm gauge) and feed trucks are commonly used. Sawmills established in recent years employing this technology include Vanimo (x2), Serra, Wawoi-Guave and Stettin Bay.

Building National Infrastructure

The Electricity Commission commenced construction of a K40 million project to build a 10 MW hydro power station at Warangoi, 60 km south of Rabaul, in 1981. Construction was undertaken by the Downer-Kier joint venture who used rail-mounted equipment to construct a 7 km, 4.25 metre diameter tunnel to serve the power station.[22] The tunnel was excavated from both ends. Operations were undertaken on a three shift basis, 24 hours a day for the labour force of 60 Europeans and 600 Nationals.

Battery-electric locomotives were used to place the tunnelling equipment at the face and haul out the spoil. Tunnel break through was on 18 July 1983. The railway continued in operation for tunnel lining operations until completion of the project in November, 1983.

Tunnel work for the Rouna No. 4 power station near Port Moresby used 914 mm gauge construction railways. The Watkins-Kumagai joint-venture imported Japanese-built battery-electric locomotives and rail-mounted tunnelling equipment for the project which was completed around 1988. Four battery locomotives (numbered DBH 86, 93, 95 and 96) from the project were located by authors in a Port Moresby storage yard in late 1993. Two cement hoppers, two rail-mounted hoists, a spoil loader and a rail-mounted cement pump were also at this location. At least 11 4-wheel dump trucks, two cement hoppers and two flat trucks had suffered the indignity of being dumped off the Tatana causeway in Fairfax Harbour in 1994.

Construction of the Ramu sugar mill revived proposals for a railway up the Markham Valley. Heavy traffic on the Highlands Highway and overloading of vehicles was causing rapid deterioration of the road surface, so the potential for railways to provide more efficient transport was examined. A feasibility study was carried out for a standard gauge (1435 mm) gauge railway by Maunsel & Partners in 1981. The price tag of K88 million without the cost of the land, plus K1 million per annum running costs was prohibitive. Nothing came of the proposal.

Urban Development

Since Independence, PNG has seen rapid migration from neglected rural areas to coastal towns and cities. Only 3 per cent of the indigenous population lived in towns in 1960, but, by 1990, this proportion had increased to over 15 per cent and was rising rapidly. Port Moresby's population reached 240,000 in 1990, two-thirds of whom live in informal settlements. These have sprung up as a product of housing shortages and the willingness of local landowners to strike a deal with migrants attracted by employment opportunities and the "bright lights" of the nation's capital. In Lae, the high proportion of informal settlers has made it almost impossible for a reliable census, but the most reliable estimates indicate a population in excess of 160,000.

Public Transport Development

Pre-Independence Port Moresby's public transport needs were served by a bus company using 55- and 72-seater buses on fixed stage routes. With Self Government in 1972 there was pressure to provide business opportunities for Nationals. The licensed public motor vehicle (PMV) had long been a major opportunity for aspiring businessmen in rural areas and it was not long before approval was given for PMVs to operate in the Port Moresby town area. Competition from family-operated mini-buses soon brought the end of the bureaucratic and inefficient Port Moresby Bus Company which went bankrupt in 1981, leaving the needs of the city's commuters in the hands of the ubiquitous PMV. Today, Port Moresby's PMV fleet comprises 800 Japanese-built 25-30 seat mini-buses.

Since 1987, PMVs have been licensed to specific routes.[23] The basic network follows the former bus company network from the village of Hanuabada, on Fairfax Harbour, through the old Government centre of Konedobu to the Port Moresby Town and thence Koki Market, from where the routes branch out to serve the suburbs and settlements on the plateau to the east. As the focus of city activity has shifted away from the older waterside suburbs, new routes have been added to serve these areas. Within the city area there are 24 routes linking the main termini and interchange points at Hanuabada, Konedobu, Town, Koki, Kila Kila, Four Mile (Boroko Shopping Centre), Seven Mile (Jacksons Airport), Hohola, Gordons Market, Tokorara, Morata and Gerehu.

Similar PMV systems operate in Lae, Madang, Rabaul (prior to the 1994 volcano eruption), Wewak, Mount Hagen and Goroka. Over each route, buses compete aggressively for passengers and may offer a door-to-door service in smaller towns. There are no timetables and a flat fare pertains for all journeys. The survival of each operator depends on their ability to maintain the maximum number of passengers in their bus. Accordingly, buses gravitate to where there is the highest passenger demand and many turn-around before reaching a terminal in order to improve their operating efficiency, if not passenger convenience.

The urban PMVs are mostly owned and operated by rural groups. The purchase capital is generally raised from the sale of cash crops such as coffee or from lump-sum payments to individuals or groups (eg, redundancy or compensation payments and, increasingly, Electoral Development Funds Grants from the Government which are intended for rural development). In the 1970s, many of the operators came from the Mumeng area of Morobe Province: today Western Highlanders dominate the PMV trade in Port Moresby. In reality, the low fares mean that few buses recover more than their operating costs and a basic wage for the crew. Buses quickly become dilapidated from intensive use and lose their attractiveness to commuters. As replacement costs are not covered, the group leave the market, to be replaced by new entrants. Thus, the capital cost of buses is a subsidy by rural villagers or other aspiring entrepreneurs to the urban commuter. Only those villagers with a sound economic base, such as the coffee-producing areas of the Highlands, or good access to grant providers can afford to maintain this subsidy.

The rapid increase in PMVs and private vehicles using urban road networks has brought traffic congestion and destruction of roads in PNG towns, particularly in Port Moresby. Air pollution is also rapidly increasing. These problems are aggravated by buses banking up at major PMV stops, blocking streets and the lack of controls over vehicle emissions. The motoring elite regularly vent their frustrations over traffic congestion, potholes and delays on PMV drivers. Others have recognised that the reliance on private cars and mini-buses for urban transport over a restricted road network is rapidly leading PNG's cities toward the urban congestion and pollution of other developing cities. In response to these emerging problems, a number of proposals have been put forward for the introduction of electric light rail for Port Moresby or other rail-based transport systems.[24]. These are reviewed in Chapter 9.

Notes for Chapter 7

1   Axline, WA, *Decentralisation and development policy: provincial government and the planning process in Papua New Guinea*, Port Moresby, IASER Monograph No. 26, 1986, p. 15

2   PNG Parliament, Bi-Partisan Select Committee on Provincial Government, Report of 2 March 1993, p. 23.

3   Griffin, J, "Bougainville - a challenge for the churches", *The Independent*, 17 May 1996, p. 7.

4   *Bougainville: a Pacific solution*, Report of the visit of the Australian Parliamentary Delegation, April 1994, Canberra, AGPS.

5   Griffin, Bougainville - a challenge for the churches", *The Independent*, 24 May 1996, p. 7.

6   Duncan, R and Temu, I, "The need for fiscal discipline", *Saturday Independent*, 9 December 1995.

7   Faith, N, *Locomotion: the railway revolution*, London, BBC Books, 1993, p. 212.

8   Ebgwich, D, *Towards an Eco-city: calming the traffic*, Sydney, Envirobook, 1992.

9   *Post Courier*, 2 April, 1976, p. 10.

10   *Bougainville Copper Annual Report* 1977, p 11.

11   Three 10-tonne Gemco battery locos ex-Mt Lyell Mine, Tasmania (B/No 899, 972 and 2265/6/171/77), two Com-Eng 20 tonne, 4wDH, ex-Mt Isa Mines (B/No. EC4585/1964 and HD 51102/1967) and two EM Baldwin 15-tonnes, underground locos ex-John Holland's Molonglo Tunnels project. Information from John Browning.

12   *Bougainville Copper Annual Report* 1984, p 9.

13   Eagle, M, "Copper mining and the environment in Papua New Guinea", *Post Courier*, 2 September, 1992, p. 18.

14   *The Times of PNG*, 9 April, 1982, p. 15; 20 January, 1984, p. 8.

15   Rendal & Partners, *Integrated infrastructure for Frieda, Ok Tedi and Tifalmin Mineral Prospects*, Port Moresby, November 1975, p. 6-2.

16   *Ok Tedi Nius*, Vol. 2:9, p. 3.

17   *PNG Resources*, July-September, 1994, p. 23-26.

18   N van der Laan, General Manager, Hargy Oil Palms, letter, 24 March, 1981.

19   Field observation, 17 September 1995.

20   A Ayton, General Manager, Higaturu Processing, letter, 30 April, 1981.

21   *The National*, New Ireland feature, 29 June 1995.

22   Briefing notes from Downer-Kier joint venture, comprising Downer & Company of New Zealand and Kier International of the United Kingdom.

23   McKillop, RF, "Public transport and people: a case study of Port Moresby", *Transit Australia*, March 1992, pp. 58-62.

24   *Post Courier*, 21 June 1977, p 2; *Post Courier*, 27 December, 1978, p 25; *Post Courier*, 23 August, 1979, p 4; *Times of PNG*, 17 October, 1986.

Top- The German residence at the Astrolabe Bay tobacco operation c. 1894. The plantation system brought strict class distinctions in which the role of Papua New Guineans was that of servant and unskilled labourer.

Mitchell Library

Bottom - Between 1890 and 1942, plantation railways comprised single lines into the plantation to which animal drawn carts brought the produce for transport to the processing facility. This 1913 view of the Rabaul Botanic Gardens shows buffalo-drawn carts with a tramline in the background.

PNG National Archives

CHAPTER 8. A PNG ECONOMIC HISTORY THROUGH RAILWAYS

The search for economic development has been a constant theme in Papua New Guinea history. This chapter draws on the framework of railway history developed earlier to analyse PNG's economic development experience. It is a history of missed opportunities and "what ifs", particularly in terms of external intrusions. The framework also provides a useful base for understanding the economic problems which have come to dominate PNG's post-Independence experience.

Modernisation

Foreign capitalists, administrators and missionaries came to PNG with confidence that their institutions and belief systems were superior to the societies they encountered at the new frontier. They assumed their task was to improve the lot of the colonised subjects by introducing them to the advanced work habits and social mores of their developed economies.

In the 1960s, the crude approach of the colonialists was refined into a more respectable modernisation theory to explain the concepts of progress and change. Western social thinkers came to see the bridge across "the great dichotomy" between traditional and modern society in terms of the "grand process of modernisation". Sociologists such as Talcott Parsons and David McClelland sought to contrast the features of traditional and modern society. Economic thinking was influenced by Walt Rostow who characterised development as a number of stages linking a state of tradition with mature economies.[1] To Rostow, the introduction of railways was the single most powerful initiator of the *takeoffs* which allowed advanced industrial societies to enhance the living standards of their people.

Counterviews were put forward by Marxist scholars who saw the exploitation of traditional societies by colonial powers as the cause of their underdevelopment and continuing dependence. They in turn influenced nationalists in the colonies who saw railways as symbols of foreign exploitation. It was claimed that railways built under colonial rule inevitably served the interests of the metropolitan power, and only rarely did these coincide with local interests. Such was the theory, but reality turned out to be different. Once countries such as India, China and Korea threw off colonial shackles, they invested heavily in developing their railway networks as the basis for modernisation. Dependency theory, it seems, no longer offers an acceptable understanding of historical trends.

Modernisation theory has made a comeback, albeit with significant revision to account for the rapidly emerging industrial economies of Asia. In Japan, for instance, it is often argued that the traditional feudal system has rapidly transformed into a modern industrial economy without involving the process of "individualism" of the people through breaking out of the cohesive traditional culture. Nevertheless, there has been a dramatic change in their orientation to railway time and the work discipline of modern industry.

But PNG did not gain the infrastructure and social development of the industrial world and its efforts to cope with the modern world has led to frustration among her people. The following sections draw out the key elements from the preceding chapters which provide a fresh understanding of how PNG's past has shaped this response.

The German Era

Under German colonial rule, New Guinea was subjected to powerful external forces prepared to invest in the necessary infrastructure for a modern economy. The *Neuguinea Kompagnie* spent lavishly on plantations, but the hostile tropical environment, disease and inappropriate crops brought initial failure.

Railways were a vehicle for plantation development and a domestic sawmilling industry. While the level of investment in transport infrastructure was high compared with early Australian contributions, it was modest against the grandeur of German efforts in Africa. Some 27 railways have been identified from the German era, mainly light industrial lines serving specific enterprises.

The private sector proved inadequate to the task of colonial administration and the state stepped in to take over administration of the colony in 1899. Significant investment between 1906 and 1914 aimed to establish the basis for a modern transport infrastructure, based on light railways, linking hinterlands with major ports. The outbreak of war in 1914 dashed the achievement of this vision, leaving only a number of embryonic "little railways" which had little impact on the landscape or the local culture.

In the event, German intrusion was restricted to a few enclaves, primarily on islands rather than the mainland. Only a small proportion of the population felt the upheaval of German imperial power. For those who left the village, a term working on a plantation or logging enterprise exposed villagers to a model for a larger-scale industrial society with strict discipline and time-keeping.

Under the plantation system, the management function was reserved for white *mastas,* with New Guineans in an unskilled labouring role. For railway operations their task was to hand-push the trucks or haul logs on bogie trucks. Where locomotives or animal power were employed, the roles of drivers, handlers and mechanics were filled by Europeans or Asians. A number of missionaries, however, deliberately set out to introduce their followers to the technical skills and work discipline of modern industrial enterprise. In these situations, locals were to be found driving the animal-drawn railway trucks.

From the outset, the response of the colonised incorporated fundamental contradictions which remain today. The foreigners - missionaries, recruiters, planters and administrators - brought with them objects, ideas and ways of behaving that were, for the villagers, literally from another world[2]. The indigenous people resented their marginal role in the new order, but were eager for the trade goods of the intruders and impressed with their ways. They hoped to gain access to the superior technology and wealth of the intruders without acknowledging the necessary cultural changes necessary to produce this wealth themselves.

The plantation system provoked deep resentment among those who had their land alienated or were subjected to the indignity of an unequal relationship. On the Gazelle Peninsula and around Madang, this resentment was later to become an important stimulant for nationalist movements.

The plantation system also left an important legacy which was to have significant impacts on the social structure of PNG society. Indentured labourers for plantations were inevitably young men who left the village in search of new economic opportunities. Women remained behind to maintain the family and subsistence production. In villages where out-migration was high, the economy stagnated and malnutrition emerged as a problem as women were unable to produce enough food without a male contribution to agriculture. These communities became dependant on remittances from the external economy.

Top - Cutting on North Coast Road, Gazelle Peninsula, c. 1918. The German administration constructed roads with the intention of future conversion to light railways.

MacKenzie, *Australians at War*, Australian War Memorial, p. 358.

Middle - Victors and vanquished: German residents watch the parade of Australian troops at Mango Avenue, Rabaul in 1914. The replacement of a powerful European power by Australia was to have a significant effect on the future PNG economy.

Bunell, FS, *How Australia took German New Guinea.*

Below: Ploughing on Katea Plantation, Papua, 1912. Hopes for agriculture soon faded.

Staniforth Smith, *Handbook of Papua*, 3rd ed. 1912, p. 32A

Australian Involvement

Australian involvement in Papua and New Guinea was primarily a reaction to the fear of European powers. The Australian colonies (and the new Federation after 1901) were too preoccupied with their own development priorities and few resources were allocated for colonial adventures to the north.

Papua and, later, the Mandated Territory were largely left to themselves to develop infrastructure and social services. There were hopes mining and plantation development would provide the basis for a prosperous economy. But the investment which did take place was ill-suited to the situation and ended in ignoble failure. The reality was that Australian capital in the colony was weak and poorly prepared to cope with the challenge of a tropical frontier and alien culture.

As in German New Guinea, foreign intrusion was restricted to the coastal fringes. No public railway was to open up the interior or discipline Papuans to the rule of the timetable, nor were there large industrial enterprises created where Papuans could learn the skills to operate and manage the most basic of capitalist ventures.

There were, however, significant contrasts between Australian colonialism and the German intervention to the north, reflecting the differing cultures of the metropolitan powers. At an individual level, Australian agents of colonialism brought the values of a new and vibrant settler society which was itself throwing off the yokes of the class structures of Europe. Traders, planters and miners adapted the way they worked to meet the ways of the islanders. They employed local people, advanced money to help them pay government taxes, purchased local produce and, in many instances, entered into relationships with local women. Although the power derived from industrial society continued to set Australians apart from local villagers, there was a strong inter-dependence between the pioneers and the Papuan communities with whom they interacted.

When they came together collectively, however, the settlers brought Australian values about the role of the state in providing infrastructure in support of their endeavours. They were successful in persuading the state to build public railways to Sapphire Creek and on Woodlark Island. After the war, companies who built railways in Misima and at Bootless Bay immediately turned to the government for assistance when faced with financial problems.

The arrival of larger companies also altered the relationship between colonial immigrant and villager. Company operations were directed by engineers who came to reshape the land and its resources to achieve efficient operations. Mine sites and large company plantations became expatriate enclaves where individuals remained aloof from the village and looked back to Australia for supplies, news, entertainment and home visits. The relationship with Papuans was that of a powerful employer whose overseers, many of whom were inexperienced in Papuan conditions, directed indentured labour.

Mine or plantation employment was not attractive to local villagers. They found the production of food for sale at local markets or alluvial mining more rewarding pursuits. The majority of labourers who came to the mining fields at Woodlark and Misima came from outside locations, notably the D'Entrecasteaux Islands, Milne Bay and the south coasts, and from the Northern Division.[3] Indentured labourers generally came out of a spirit of adventure, for the wages were meagre. In the early 1920's, underground miners at Misima worked a 44 hour week for 10s a month and keep.

By the mid-1920s the vision of economic prosperity for Papua had faded with the experience of failure for a long list of mining and plantation ventures. The administration, under Lieutenant-Governor Hubert Murray, adopted a protectionist stance. Papuans were protected from ruthless land buyers, from the work exploitation of the indentured labour system and from private expeditions into the inland. In so doing, they inhibited private investment and forces of change which might encourage entrepreneurship among the Papuans. The economy stagnated and with it, the prospects of further railway development faded.

The weakness of Australian capital became more apparent when they extended their control to German New Guinea in 1914. German properties, including the embryonic railway infrastructure, were expropriated. The process stifled investment and rebuilding after the War. Gradually the large Australian trading firms gained control of many properties and planting was expanded.

Plantation railways became a cost-effective and appropriate technology in the New Guinea islands. They were more efficient in their use of space than roads, they could be more easily maintained under tropical conditions and New Guinea labourers were comfortable operating and repairing the equipment. On the island of Bougainville in particular, railways became a part of the plantation way of life.

On the other hand, when the opportunity arose for the government to invest in a railway to link the hinterland at Bulolo with a port, the administration quickly skirted the issue and pleaded lack of funds. Responsibility for solving the transport problem was passed back to the mining company, who decided to by-pass the railway option and selected the *new age* solution of air transport. Thus, although PNG was the *end of the line* for railway transport, it became the birth-place of modern air cargo transport.

It was a decision with significant long-term implications for New Guinea. The Bulolo Gold Dredging Company solution avoided investment in infrastructure which would facilitate general development along its route. Instead, they flew over the villages and agricultural lands, leaving them untouched by outside influences. While the operation of transporting and erecting huge alluvial dredges in the interior was an impressive technological achievement, it was an enclave operation which transferred little in the way of managerial and technical skills to New Guineans. Thousands of labourers, mainly from the Sepik districts, came to work in the goldfields where they were brought in touch with the power and capability of modern industrial society. But they only participated in that process at the margin as unskilled labourers.

A small elite of foreign engineers, pilots and managers achieved the transport task with new machines that demanded high level skills beyond the education base and experience of New Guineans. Not for the last time, miners extracted the wealth of New Guinea in an enclave which had minimal impact on the culture and wider economy.

Apart from the expropriation of land in selected coastal and island locations, the impact of colonialism on the majority of Papua New Guineans was minor. While a proportion of young men tasted something of an external world beyond the village, the vast majority of people maintained their traditional culture and life style.

The War Years

The Pacific War brought a dramatic demonstration of foreign power and technology. Military might rained destruction on the land and it pushed back the jungle to build bases and airstrips. Railways played an important role in this construction and the supply of munitions and stores to army units. Many kilometres of line were built in a short period. For a brief moment in history, the power of industrial discipline and technology was demonstrated before local villagers and labourers.

PNG's war-time railway era lasted less than three years and was primarily a Japanese effort. The social and economic impact of these railways was hindered on two grounds: the Japanese builders were defeated and their military purpose meant they were created in isolation from the local people.

They were the ultimate in enclave activities: built and operated on foreign soil with no reference to local values or involvement. New Guineans only played a minor labouring role in their construction or operation. As artefacts of the vanquished, the Japanese railways were dismantled after the conflict for scrap metal and building materials.

The Pacific conflict was selective in its impact on Papua New Guineans. Coastal villagers had seen their former colonial masters forced to flee in the face of an Asian power, and their labour and cooperation had become a necessary prerequisite for the eventual allied victory. Many suffered dislocation and damage from the heavy bombing. But for the large populations of the inland, the war was an external conflict of little consequence to their isolated world.

Those Papua New Guineans who served in the armed forces found a sense of comradeship. For the first time, they were accepted as equals serving against a common adversary. American troops were favourites due to their generosity in sharing their products (eg, tobacco, sweets and jeep rides) with the locals.[4] Villagers were also drawn outside their local world and for the first time they saw other parts of their country and worked alongside the people from these areas. However, they and their foreign comrades were at the base of the vast hierarchical war machine power structures in which decisions were made by others far removed from the field.

The war provided a dramatic demonstration of the wealth of industrial societies. Ships, aircraft, vehicles, railway equipment, guns, supplies and food arrived on PNG's wharves and beaches in vast quantities and without any logical explanation. It was as if the heavens had opened with an outpouring of industrial wealth had suddenly been directed to PNG. The lesson appeared to be that consumer goods would arrive without the need to invest labour and capital in their production.

Decolonisation

The post-war era saw dramatic changes in the PNG economy and the participation of ordinary Papua New Guineans in development activities. As inland villages were subjected to colonial control external forces began to penetrate into the remotest Highland valleys. Now the majority of ordinary villagers had the opportunity to participate in the development process as small-scale farmers, travellers and social service recipients.

Papua New Guineans made diverging responses to these external forces. On the one hand, the power and wealth of the intruders generated a sense of inadequacy and dissatisfaction with traditional institutions; on the other, many villagers coveted the material goods of the modern world. Some groups sought refuge in spiritual cults to redress perceived inequalities; others enthusiastically adopted new enterprises to earn cash in order to participate in the modern economy. It was in the Highlands areas, where interaction with external economies and cultures was a recent phenomenon, that the response to opportunities to participate in the cash economy was most dramatic. Such was the response in the 1960s, that some observers argued that Highlanders were predisposed to entrepreneurship and had the capacity to leap from the world of traditional exchange to one where business is conducted on a cash basis.[5]

As traditional boundaries were eroded, more Papua New Guineans travelled outside their village and participated in trade. However, the post-war transport system was dominated by the private motor vehicle and the aeroplane. Railways were given little credence by policy-makers and the few railways which were constructed during the period had limited social impact.

On a small number of coconut and cocoa plantations, light railways maintained their cost-effective and environmentally sensitive function which had emerged during the 1920s. Plantation railways were much easier to maintain than roads, required less space, were well adapted to local technical skills and resources, had less environmental impacts and were more robust than tractor-hauled road trailers as rail trucks could still be hand-pushed if the locomotive was unserviceable. However, the plantation era was coming to an end. Maintenance was neglected and the railway systems deteriorated to a point where rehabilitation was no longer seen as viable.

When oil palm, which required transport of large volumes of fruit to central mills, was introduced to PNG, the role of railed transport was restricted to the processing plant. Both here and in the emerging mining industry, road transport was seen as the "modern" solution.

Because of this reliance on private road transport, Papua New Guineans missed the opportunity to gain the discipline and managerial experience of operating a modern, large-scale, industrial institution. Instead, they were sidelined as peripheral *businessmen* operating imported vehicles for small-scale trucking and transport services in a highly competitive environment. They were dependant on the capacity of a central "government" to provide the basic road infrastructure on which they could operate.

Despite the rapid development of village-based cash cropping in the Highlands, most village people found themselves ill equipped to cope with the pace of change imposed by outside forces. Efforts to extend individual efforts to enterprises through cooperatives or business groups inevitably failed, while landowners resented the use of their resources to generate wealth for outside mine and plantation owners. On Bougainville landowners did not accept the government's regulations which precluded them from ownership of minerals found under the surface of their land. Dissatisfaction over the inability of local groups or institutions to play a meaningful role in modern industrial activities was to lead to future conflict.

Independence

The optimism that Independence would generate new economic opportunities for nationals was short lived. The post-Independence era has been characterised by increased reliance on enclave resource projects and a decline in the economic opportunities for the majority of the population. National economic policies worked against labour-intensive industries, particularly agriculture, and rural areas have experienced economic stagnation with deteriorating infrastructure and services. Papua New Guineans play only a peripheral role in large-scale resource development projects. The frustrations generated by economic decline have led to extensive criminal activity which, in turn, has increased commercial costs and reduced the competitiveness of PNG industries.

The only new railways to be constructed in PNG since Independence have been short-term construction lines used by foreign engineering firms to build mining and hydro-electric infrastructure or short industrial lines serving oil palm mills. As such, they symbolise the domination of mining operations in the PNG economy.

Elsewhere, road construction to link rural communities with urban markets and services continues to gain a high political profile. In practice, investments in roads has often had limited development impact. For the Asian Development Bank-funded Hiritano Highway Project located in Central Province, the incentives for food crop production were strong, but the expected levels of economic activity and transport demand did not eventuate.[6] Sealing of the Magi Highway (also in the Papuan region) similarly failed to generate the anticipated economic response.[7]. In practice the majority of target populations chose to use the road for transfer of easily-produced traditional crops and for the satisfaction of social and community needs through family connections in urban areas. In these cases, target income thresholds appear to dominate the preparedness of rural households to expand production.

Traditional culture, particularly the land tenure system, has demonstrated a remarkable resilience to change. Rural communities continue to meet their subsistence food needs and there has been some adaptation to incorporate small-scale cash cropping. But the social mores and obligations required to maintain cultural integrity severely constrain economic productivity. Rural communities have failed to generate the necessary surplus to meet the needs of rapid population growth and the rising aspirations of youth. Economic development within the village culture has reached a plateau and stagnation has set in. Invariably, the gap between aspirations and productivity has generated a drive to gain a share of the wealth produced by others.

Stagnation in rural areas has resulted in migration to towns and cities in search of economic opportunities. An increasing proportion of citizens are now urban dwellers. They rely on public transport to get around low density towns and cities, but the public transport user is very much a second-class citizen who is afforded low priority by the car-orientated urban planners. His or her ability to survive in the high-cost urban economy depends on the unwitting generosity of rural villagers who are willing to subsidise urban commuters for the dubious prestige of operating a PMV. Competition between operators results in a low-cost and flexible service for consumers, but at high cost in terms of congestion and environmental impacts. Unfortunately, PNG has yet to demonstrate a capability to build up and manage the cost-efficient institutions necessary to operate such a system.

Concluding observations

In chapter 1 the central role of railways in building the institutional base necessary for a modern economy was discussed. Through railways, Western economies were able to overcome the problems faced by traditional institutions in achieving secure, low-cost market transactions[8]. With the railway age, new institutions developed to build and maintain the networks, schedule services and regulate contracts on a national scale. These institutions facilitated measurement (quality control) and enforcement of contracts, thereby safeguarding property rights and providing certainty in transactions.

But such institutional development was not to be at the "end of the line" in PNG. Without significant railways, local communities were not enmeshed in the time consciousness and discipline of modern industrial organisations. The public were not educated by railway timetables, workers did not build up the technical skills and work ethics of a modern industrial enterprise and, above all, the managerial skills to achieve the efficient operation of a railway system were not developed. Without these skills and institutional base, traditional groups lacked the productivity to compete with the specialist commercial institutions of the foreign intruders.[9]

In their reliance on road transport and water-based trading, Papua New Guineans were restricted to small-scale enterprises operated at the family level. While an entrepreneurial spirit is apparent in the informal sector, particularly among Highland societies, socio-cultural factors appear to have inhibited the organisation of commercial activity on a scale larger than the extended family unit. The institutional base to build, operate and maintain the large-scale infrastructure and services necessary for a modern economy was not developed. Factionalism, mistrust of outside managers and an emphasis on distribution have hindered the performance of local enterprises. In many cases costly foreign managers were retained to ensure the necessary independence and trust for sustainable operations, thereby contributing to the high-cost status of PNG industries.

In this situation of unequal relationships between clan groups and modern institutions, Papua New Guineans have become *rent-seekers* prepared to sell their resource heritage for short-term gain rather than seeking to produce surplus on a sustainable basis. Initially, this process involved resource owners seeking royalties, equity and compensation in mining and forestry projects. Competing leaders have emerged with claims to represent traditional landowners in negotiations with outside interests. The task of establishing linkages with government agencies and foreign investors tended to favour a new generation of younger, educated people over those who hold leadership through their knowledge of traditional law. But those who followed orthodox investment paths to profits were soon pushed aside by populist ideologies seeking to distrubute the wealth generated by others. Increasingly, "leaders" have served to broker deals and compensation claims between resource-owners and foreign mining and logging interests.

The process has been extended to industry where special deals have been negotiated to establish protected enterprises, often with monopoly status.[10] In the case of food processing industries, this protection has resulted in high domestic prices with economic transfers from poor consumers to richer people. The involvement of politicians in setting up these deals has enabled them to control the allocation of many rents and has led to widespread claims of corruption. The outcome has been an economy based on a resource dependency syndrome in which resource-owners and politicians seek to maximise their take of wealth produced by others.

As property rights and contractual agreements are not subject to coded and time-bound agreements, all developments are dependent on opportunistic political negotiation. This political process seeks to extract benefits in the name of the "resource-owners" and the state. It results in high transaction costs and uncertainty. In these circumstances, commercial risk is high and investment is confined to highly profitable activities, usually of an exploitative and short-term nature. Successful rent-takers in PNG comprise a small segment of the population. Landowners blessed with rich mineral deposits and the political elite have done well; people from resource-poor areas, women and the urban poor have missed out.

As a consequence of poor wealth distribution, PNG now faces a serious law and order situation which impacts on most economic activity and generates unpredictability. The problem has reduced output and competitiveness by destroying or damaging productive capital, raising private security costs, preempting activities for lack of possible insurance cover or fear of attack, and providing PNG with a reputation as a high security-risk nation. In rural areas, lawlessness has contributed to the breakdown in delivery of basic services and caused a contraction in goods markets. The most severe effects of a deteriorating lawlessness are felt by lower income groups, who are least able to protect themselves.

Railway Heritage

Railways in PNG are seen as a foreign intrusion of little significance to Melanesian history. Accordingly, retention and conservation of the artefacts of railway heritage has received low priority. Remnants of the heritage of the *Neuguinea Kompagnie's* tobacco growing ventures at Stephansort remain in the forest. Railway bridges and formation remain intact today, together with the ruins of stables, a sawmill and the headstones of the cemetery, an enduring monument to the colonial men, women and children who became the victims of patriotic fervour.[11]

The role of railways in Papuan economic development was ultimately minor and is largely forgotten. The efforts of colonial masters to establish industrial enterprises and discipline is of minor interest to the national elite. Nevertheless, as they promenade on Port Moresby's Ela Beach on a Sunday afternoon, some local residents may ponder the origins of the straight road lined by majestic casuarina trees which provides the main transport artery between the old town area and the city's spreading suburbs. Possibly someone will remind them that this was the location of preliminary construction work for Papua's first public railway line.

Top - Railway formation converted to road: the Mt. Diamond School road passes through a cutting of the former Bootless Bay-Dubuna railway. Road construction has become a dominant political theme in post-war Papua New Guinea.

Bottom - Railway heritage: the remains of the ore bins at Wai Wai Junction on the Bootless Bay railway where ore from the Laloki Mine was transferred to railway trucks.

Photo - RF McKillop, 1973

On the promenade, a local Rotary club has plinthed a steam engine in homage to the pioneer steam era. The engine was unearthed during construction work for new apartments above Ela Beach in 1986.[12]   Although it is speculated that it was one of the traction engines used for hauling copper ore from the Laloki Mine in 1918, the only authentic information on its origins is that it was originally owned by the Toowong Town Council in Brisbane in 1911. Symbolically for the status of railway and steam heritage in PNG, the unit has been mounted upside down .

More significant icons of railway and industrial heritage can be explored around the sites of the Bootless Bay-Dubuna railway and mining activities. To day, Tahira is a popular marina and ferry terminal to a resort on Loloata Island. The road into Tahira from the Magi Highway follows the old railway formation. Beside the road a large slag heap from the smelting operations poses the challenge to travellers to explore the past of the area. Those who do so will enter a fascinating field of industrial archaeology treasures. On the hills where Papua's largest industrial enterprise and the thriving township of Tahira once stood, the foundations of the smelters and the railway spur line formation can be easily traced. A number of steel remnants - former smoke stacks, building frames, the odd section of railway line - lay rusting away. With the assistance of photographs of the enterprise in its heyday, one can imagine the scene seventy years ago and share the dreams of its founders.

Returning to the Highway, the road has been constructed over the railway formation for about 1.5 km, except for a section of mangrove swamp. Here the railway formation can be easily traced to the north of the road as it winds around the obstruction. Soon a turnoff to the Mount Diamond High School is located. This road is largely located on the old railway formation, including a significant cutting. At Wai Wai Junction, the formation is about 20 metres to the west of the road. Here the foundations of the ore bins and the towers for the aerial ropeway remain in situ. The area is still clear due to impacted soil and the remnants of railway sleepers and even coal for railway use can be readily identified.

Continuing on to the school, a collection of artefacts from the railway and aerial ropeway, including one of the towers and the ropeway winding machinery, have been brought together adjacent to the entrance. Careful observation will pick up the former railway formation continuing northwards from near the entrance for another kilometre or so to the Dubuna mine. Unfortunately, nothing remains of the locomotives and rolling stock. They were swept up in the post-war scrap metal bonanza and sent to Japan.

To day there are few relics left of the turmoil generated by the Pacific War 50 years ago. Two Japanese locomotives have been collected for restoration. In the 1980s, Michael Pearson and students from Buin High School reclaimed and partly restored a Kato Works locomotive (22086/1942) from the Buin railway and rolling stock reconstructed from equipment salvaged from North Bougainville and Kieta. In 1988, the equipment was transferred to Toniva, where the Kieta Lions and ex-servicemen's clubs planned their operation as a tourist railway venture.

The Bougainville Crisis which began in 1989 has brought all restoration plans to a halt. Those involved in the restoration left the Island in fear of their lives. From 1990 to the time of writing the area was under insurgency control and the fate of the locomotive and rolling stock is unknown. Another Kato Works locomotive is exhibited at the Kokopo War Museum, located on the old Ralum Plantation.

Notes for Chapter 8

1   Rostow, WW, *The process of economic growth*, Cambridge, 1960.

2   Burridge, K, *Mambu*, London, 1960, p. 124-6. Describes the impact of German SVD missionaries and recruiters on the villagers of Manam Island.

3   Nelson, H, *Black, White and Gold*, Canberra, ANU Press.

4   Stanner, WEH, *The South Seas in transition*, Sydney, 1953, p. 26.

5   Finney, BR, *Big-men and business: entrepreneurship and economic growth in the New Guinea Highlands*, Honolulu, East-West Centre, 1973.

6   Asian Development Bank, Hiritano Highway Post-evaluation Report, 1987. Incentives for included improved access, lower real cost of transport, frequent vehicle services, growth in Port Moresby population and the high food prices of 1978-83.

7   University of PNG, *Post-Investment Evaluation Study: IBRD Road Project*. UPNG Progress Report, September 1990.

8   North, DC, "Institutions", *Journal of Economic Perspectives*. Vol. 5:1, 1991, p. 101.

9   *Ibid.*, p. 99.

10   Gibson, J, *Food consumption and policy in Papua New Guinea*, Port Moresby, INA Discussion Paper No. 65, 1995, p. 80.

11   Douglas, J, "Taim bilong ol Jeman", *Paradise* (magazine of Air Niuguinea), No, 30, July 1981.

12   *Post Courier*, 6 November 1986, p.1 and 12 November 1986, p.3.

CHAPTER 9. A FUTURE FOR RAILWAYS IN PNG?

New Economic Directions

Papua New Guinea's economic and financial crisis of the 1990's places the nation at a watershed of economic development. Conventional development models which sought to transform the economy from a subsistence-agrarian base to an industrial society have clearly failed and PNG has found its infant industries increasingly uncompetitive in a global economy. The majority of Papua New Guineans have resorted to *rent collection* from resource projects, such as mining, petroleum and forest logging, and their demands have made the investment climate increasingly unstable.

PNG's lack of competitiveness is linked to the high transaction costs of an economy lacking performance-based institutions and secure property rights. For instance, in 1992 PNG's prevailing hourly wages were 300-480 per cent higher than those in competing countries (Indonesia, Philippines and Fiji), the cost of utilities and services were much higher than in competing countries and there had been virtually no increase in productivity in the formal economy per person employed from the early 1970's to the late 1980's.[1].

An economic recovery program was implemented in 1995 with assistance from the World Bank and the International Monetary Fund (IMF). However, there has been strong political opposition to the reforms based on the strong cultural attachment to land in PNG. Land tenure reforms aimed at mobilising land resources for development projects have been set aside and populist causes for the expenditure of public funds have held sway over the economic rationalism of the World Bank and IMF which is rejected as an externally imposed conspiracy.

At the same time, PNG is seeking a place in the emerging global trading and information economy. The dramatic changes of the 1990's have been characterised as a transition to post-industrial economies. Features include:

- a shift of resources from materials and energy to information and knowledge;
- restructuring of employment from manufacturing to service industries, particularly information- and knowledge-based activities ;
- expansion of large firms from local and regional bases to global activities to take advantage of international networks;
- a shift in employment from large firms to small firms as functions are "outsourced" to specialist providers;
- a dramatic expansion of electronic, multimedia forms of communications ;
- rapid increase in information technology capability; and
- confluence of information and communications technologies which are evolving into global information *superhighways* providing access to vast stores of information.

Another trend in Western societies has been rising public concern over environmental degradation and pollution, particularly in urban areas. This is generating fundamental changes in industrial and transport technology. Rail-based transport technologies with low emissions and land use requirements are increasingly seen as an essential element of sustainable development. Computer management systems are also pre-adapted to rail transport and are playing an increased role in enhancing their environmental efficiency.

These global changes impinge on PNG and shape the future directions of the economy. Nevertheless, instability and low competitiveness hinder prospects for industrialisation which might generate employment for the rapidly growing urban populations. PNGs future manufacturing activities will mainly be confined to domestic food processing for urban markets and service industries in the transport sector. Further investment in large-scale resource projects depends on fiscal and social stability to reestablish a favourable investment climate.

Future Transport Directions

The analysis presented in the previous chapters indicates that past failures to establish and sustain substantial railways in PNG has resulted in an inadequate industrial and institutional base for a modern transport system. Moreover, Nationals only play a minor role in the management and ownership of commercial enterprises, including transport. This has generated high levels of dissatisfaction with the current conditions.

Isolation of communities from markets and the high cost of transport continue to be key themes in PNG politics. In 1995 the Government declared that road transport is the cheapest and most convenient means of transporting people, goods and services.[2] Nevertheless, the cost of building and maintaining roads under PNG conditions is very high. In response to this situation, several proposals have been put forward for the introduction of railways to help build the institutional capacity and transport efficiency necessary to compete in the modern world. These concepts are described in the following sections. They fall into two distinct approaches: those which seek to build local management and industrial capacity from the ground-up; and technological approaches which seek to transfer modern overseas railway practice to PNG without consideration of local culture or institutional factors.

The Bougainville Initiative

The closure of the Panguna copper mine on Bougainville island following the outbreak of armed rebellion was discussed in chapter 7. In the resulting anarchy and civil conflict, much of the island's infrastructure was destroyed. The process of pacification and reconstruction commenced in 1993.

As services were gradually restored and the Government set about the task of restoration, the people of Bougainville reviewed the experience of their conflict and pondered their future development options. Many saw the former economic structures, including the foreign mining enclave and the dominance of road transport with its reliance on private vehicle ownership, as contributing factors in their misfortune.

Destruction of transport facilities during the Bougainville Crisis has generated a need for reconstruction of infrastructure. However, some Bougainvillians felt that the high running and social costs of road transport also needed to be addressed. They argued that a transport system based on private vehicle ownership provides special privileges to the wealthy and leads to abuses of the freedom of movement of others. Their vision of the future gave higher priority to public transport solutions in which they could play a more meaningful role.

Michael Pearson assisted this group develop a proposal for the reconstruction of Bougainville on a self-help basis using light railways as an alternative to road transport. The proposal highlights the potential role of rail transport in providing safe, reliable and cost-efficient transport which will unite and build the society with a renewed sense of self-reliance and interdependence.[3] Publicly-owned 610 mm gauge light railways are proposed, with second-hand locomotives from Australian sugar railways and locally-fabricated rolling stock. On lightly-trafficked branch lines, portable track with the use of animal power is envisaged.

The main objective is to provide cheap, safe, reliable, all weather transport to the producers and rural communities of North Solomons Province. A subsidiary objective is to provide jobs for unemployed youth. The scheme would also provide an opportunity for landowners and subsistence producers to be involved in and invest in the development of a transport system which would reduce transport cost, increase productive returns and eventually reduce the dependence on imported fuels. The system would use a high proportion of local materials - timber for sleepers, rolling stock construction and bridges - and develop managerial and industrial skills through construction and operation tasks.

Based on pre-crisis cash crop production, the freight task for the railway is estimated at 54,000 tonnes/annum, while it would also need to meet the local transport requirements of 150,000 people. A full railway network servicing Bougainville and Buka Islands is estimated to require 500 km of light railway, 14 to 21 locomotives, 200 to 300 rail trucks, 20 passenger trucks and four railcars. The estimated capital cost (1992 prices) for a 610 mm gauge permanent system is K25,000/km and for portable track K18,000/km. This compares with K9000/km for graded roads and K60,000/km for 43 mm tar sealed roads. However, annual maintenance costs for graded roads are estimated at K7,200/km compared with K2,100 for the permanent railway and K1,600 for the portable track. More significantly, the light railway would generate many more jobs in the local economy than road construction and maintenance. Estimated freight costs for rail are 22-24 toea/tonne/km compared with 82 toea for graded roads. Comparative passenger costs are K2.20 and K8.20 per 100 km.

The proposal is based on principles which differ markedly from the *modernistic,* free-spending, global and individualistic values which currently characterise the PNG economy. Successful models for such a venture are difficult to find. However, the recent example of Eritrea where the government is rehabilitating its war-damaged railway using local resources, including the labour of demobilised soldiers, rather than relying on external finance and technology has recently captured international attention.[4] The self-reliance philosophy has resulted in the overhaul of old steam and diesel locomotives and the rebuilding of rolling stock using whatever resources are locally available. Unfortunately, there is little evidence that such an austere approach might be enthusiastically taken up in PNG and on Bougainville continued terrorist attacks have hindered the task of reconstruction.

Railways and Environmental Protection

The desire of resource owners in PNG to gain wealth through the rapid exploitation of forest, marine and mineral resources has led to excessive environmental damage. In the forest sector, in particular, this environmental degradation has received considerable international attention.

Of major concern is the environmental damage caused by logging roads and soil compaction by heavy logging machinery. Forest roads require a 40 metre clearing for the road alignment and tracked vehicle access. They are a major source of erosion and sediment discharge into water courses. In contrast to the damage caused by modern logging methods, logging railways operated in PNG for lengthy periods (Chapter 2). Such railways utilise a much higher proportion of local input than road transport - timber rails, home-made trucks and rail-tractors for instance - and are less intrusive on the forest. Rail-based transport minimised the land area required for transport infrastructure and encouraged long-term management practices.

Although, forest railways are normally considered as a high-volume transport mode for large central mills, past operations in PNG demonstrate that low-cost lines built by entrepreneurial operators can play an important role in transporting logs and timber. Environmentally, they minimise the area of land taken over for transport infrastructure, while the opportunity to spread loads over a wide area through the track and sleepers enables railways to transport logs over areas (eg, swamps) where roading is impractical. The use of self-balancing inclines enables railways to operate in steep topography at relatively low cost.

Other advantages of logging railways are the continuous and assured flow of logs to the mill with minimal disruption during unfavourable climatic conditions, reduced wastage of timber in the forest and minimal losses during transport. Initial overhead costs may be high, but operating costs are low where there is sufficient throughput to justify the investment. The reintroduction of logging railways is one option for a more sustainable forest industry.

A major barrier to logging railways in the PNG context comes from the expectation of forest resource-owners that logging will result in construction of road infrastructure, thereby improving their access to services and markets. Until resource-owners come to see railway infrastructure as a superior option from a social point of view, this option is likely to receive limited support.

In the mining and energy sector, the success of the North Paibuna railway in providing safe transport across sago swamps is expected to lead to similar applications elsewhere. For the Nena mine on the border between East and West Sepik, the environmental impact study has identified social and environmental difficulties with the use of the May River as a transport access to the site. The alternative is a 30 km transport corridor from Nena to the Sepik River This route requires the bridging of a considerable area of sago and nipa swamp. A light railway line with adequate capacity to transport containers to the mine site is an environmentally-sensitive option for the project.

Lae-Highlands Electric Railway

An engineer at the University of Technology, Dr Kris Korzeniowski, has drawn on international rail developments to propose a modern electric railway from Lae to Porgera in the Highlands. The proposal is based on the utilisation of the renewable energy resources of PNG's hydro-power system to stimulate development in the areas served by the line.[5] Detailed costing of the 800 km line is said to be proceeding.

The Highlands electric railway proposal is based on modern world engineering practice, particularly recent trends in electric traction in Europe. It assumes that management expertise and the institutional base necessary for successful operation would be imported along with the technology. Although such *modern* technology appeals to the fascination of politicians, economic and social realism is not a strong feature of the proposal. Securing the land corridor and the future infrastructure with adequate security to attract the necessary investment capital appears problematic given the current civil unrest along the proposed route. The necessary economic base to justify the investment remains a pipe dream.

Another grand vision for a railway between Lae and Port Moresby was put forward by Lae MP Hon. Bart Philemon in October 1995.[6] The proposal was prompted by an announcement of increased air fares. It followed a visit by Mr Philemon to mountain railways in Germany and was backed by a submission for a German company to undertake a pre-feasibility study of the route. Again, the economic, institutional and social elements of the project were overlooked.

Urban Railways

The issues of rapid urbanisation in PNG have been addressed in chapters 6 and 7. With a population over 250,000 and rapidly increasing, Port Moresby is experiencing significant traffic problems. In Europe, a number of similar sized cities have recently established light rail rapid transit public transport systems.[7] They include Saarbruken (pop. 180,000), Caen (198,000), Strasbourg (250,000), Laussane, (285,000) and Rouen (392,000). In these cases, public concern over the environment and quality of life issues has resulted in the will to invest in an attractive alternative to the private car for urban commuting which reduced congestion, local noise and atmospheric pollution, while improving safety. However, evaluation of modern light rail operations highlight the following lessons for success[8]:

- political will for long term investment in public transport, backed by strong community support to overcome environmental problems;
- an adequate local financial base (either from tax or private investment) to fund the infrastructure and support ongoing operations;
- adequate capacity of users to pay an economic fare;
- the vital role of institutional or management capacity to ensure that customers are provided with a superior service at reasonable cost;
- secure, long-term land security over rights-of-way for segregated public transport corridors;
- a stable investment climate which encourages investment in long-term projects; and
- public pride in the light rail system which ensures security and care for the infrastructure and rolling stock.

None of these requirements currently exist in Papua New Guinea. While the majority of people in Port Moresby, are dependent on public transport, they have benefited from a system of mini-buses which provide cheap transport, subsidised by rural communities rather than the state. They generate a large source of employment for drivers and offsiders. However, the mini-buses are inefficient movers of large numbers of people, they contribute to road congestion and they rely on imported fuel. Poor maintenance standards result in high levels of exhaust emissions by the mini-buses and other transport. This atmospheric pollution is already a significant contributor to Port Moresby's deteriorating air quality.

With increasing traffic congestion in Port Moresby and the concentration of commuter flows along well defined corridors, the potential for light rail to meet urban commuter needs has been regularly raised in the media. Nevertheless, priority in urban transport planning continues to be given to private cars. A K60 million project to construct the Poreporena Freeway to connect the town area with the airport commenced in June 1995. Media attention has focused on this glamour project which is directed at improving the traffic flow for the small proportion of Port Moresby's population who can afford private cars.

Proposals for a commuter rail system in Port Moresby have recently emerged. In July 1995, the Prime Minister, Sir Julius Chan, publicly urged the National Capital District Commission to commence planning a railway system to connect Port Moresby town to Boroko, Gerehu, 17-Mile on the Sogeri Road and the Tatana/Buruni areas.[9] In March 1996, the Prime Minister again raised the idea in terms of a railway to adjoin a stretch of the new Poreporena Freeway.[10] However, the Governor for the National Capital District expressed reservations about the railway project. These proposals do not appear to be based on an in-depth assessment of the economic and social factors necessary for successful operation in the Papua New Guinea context. The prospects for an urban-based rail revival are therefore not optimistic.

Conclusions

Many observers claim PNG has reached a watershed in its economic and social development. Must the future development of railways await social change and public demand for their construction, or will new railways be built to themselves change the nation's social institutions and development pattern?

Elsewhere, particularly in Europe and Japan, the building of railways dramatically changed the society. In PNG, successive administrations have taken the easy way out and sought *modern* infrastructure without tackling the hard issues such as coded rights, agreement on specified contractual conditions and respect for public and private property.

If the necessary social and institutional change for PNG to compete in the emerging global economy is to occur, then Papua New Guineans may need to go back to the fundamentals. Turning to low-cost, self-help railways, such as those proposed above for Bougainville, can contribute to this fundamental change. As with Eritrea, the conflict which has torn Bougainville society apart may yet provide the basis for a fresh start and low-cost, community-orientated railways could provide the building blocks for a unified and productive society.

Notes on Chapter 9

1   SRI International, *Papua New Guinea Industrial Growth Strategy*, Report prepared for ADB TA No. 1580 PNG, August 1992, p. 70.

2   Baing, A, "Policy speech to National Parliament on Transport", reported in *The National*, 29 March 1995.

3   Pearson, MR, "Use of Railways in PNG", Submission to Minister for Transport, May 1992.

4   *Continental Railway Journal*, No. 105, Spring 1996, p. 342; *SBS World News* 16 March 1996.

5   Peni, E, "Trains: an answer to PNG's transport needs", *PNG Business*, August 1994, p. 17-18.

6   *The National*, 20 October 1995.

7   Wyse, WJ, "Transport and the environment", *Light Rail and Modern Tramway*, February 1995, p. 29.

8   For example, see Buisson, C, "How France has overcome the investment nightmare", *Light Rail and Modern Tramway*, December 1995, p. 408

9   *Post Courier*, 14 July 1995.

10   *The National*, 15 March 1996.

BIBLIOGRAPHY

Books and Articles

Allied Geographic Section, SW Pacific Area Terrain Studies, 1942-43.
Australian Expropriation Board, *Catalogue of New Guinea properties,* , Comm. of Aust., Melbourne, 1927.
Australian Parliament, *Bougainville: a Pacific solution,* Report of the visit of the Australian Parliamentary Delegation, April 1994, Canberra, AGPS.
Australian Parliament, *New Guinea: Report on Expropriated Properties and Businesses.* The Parliament of the Commonwealth of Australia 6/8/1924.
Axline, WA, *Decentralisation and development policy: provincial government and the planning process in Papua New Guinea,* Port Moresby, IASER Monograph No. 26, 1986, p. 15.

Ballard, RD, *The lost ships of Guadalcanal,* London, Weidenfeld, 1993.
Bougainville Copper Annual Reports, 1967 to 1984.
British New Guinea Annual Report, 1889-90 to 1905-1906.
Bullen, J, "Australian Railwaymen at War, 1916-1919", *ARHS Bulletin*, Vol. 46, No. 695, September 1995, pp. 243-256.
Burridge, K, *Mambu,* London, 1960.

Collinson, JW, *Tropic coast and tablelands*, 1941.
Cooke, J, *Working in Papua-New Guinea, 1931-1946*, Lara Publications, 1983.
Cornfield, RS, *Hold hands cobbers, Vol II, 1930-1990*, Melbourne, Brown Prior Anderson.
Coutts, M, *Taim bifor: a selection of old photographs from Papua New Guinea*, Port Moresby, SP Magazines, 1990.

Denoon, D and Snowden, C, "Bootless Bay revisited", *Light Railways*, No. 74, 1981.
Douglas, B, "Mine tramways at Panguna", *Light Railways*, No. 64.

Ebgwicht, D, *Towards an Eco-City: Calming the Traffic*, Sydney, Envirobook, 1992.
Eggleston, FW (ed), *The Australian Mandate for New Guinea*, Melbourne Univeristy Press, 1928.
Ellis, RF, "The steam locomotives of Nauru and Ocean islands", *Light Railways* No. 88, April 1985.

Faith, N, *Locomotion: the railway revolution*, London, BBC Books, 1993.
Fauer, AD (ed), *Coastwatching in the Solomon Islands: the Bougainville reports, December 1941-July 1943*, New York, Praeger, 1992, p. 90.
Firth, S, *New Guinea Under the Germans*, Melbourne University Press, 1983.
Flierl, J, *Wunder der gottlichen Grande Evangelisten aus Menschenfressern*, Tanunda, Lutheran Mission, 1931.
Fremdling, R, "Railroads and German economic growth: a leading sector analysis with a comparison to the United States and Great Britain", *Journal of Economic History*, 37, 1977.

Gash, N and Whittaker, J, *A pictorial history of New Guinea*, Brisbane, Jacaranda, 1975.
Gautier, T, in Jean Dethier (ed), *All Stations,* London 1981.

Hagspiel, B, *Along the mission trail: III New Guinea*, Mission Press, Tech, Illinois, 1926.
Harvey, JY, "War railway timetables", *ARHS Bulletin* No. 685, November, 1994.
Healy, AM, *Bulolo: a history of the development of the Bulolo region, New Guinea,* NG Research Bulletin No. 15, 196-.

Henley, T, *New Guinea and Australia's Pacific Islands Mandate,* Sydney, John Sands, 1927
Hesse-Wartegg, E, *Samoa, Bismardarchipel und Neuguinea: drei deutsche holonien in der sudsee,* Leipzig, Weber, 1902.
Hilder, Capt. B, "The port of Kavieng", *Walkabout,* January 1950.

Idress, IL, *Gold dust and ashes,* Sydney, Angus & Robertson, 1934.
International Bank for Reconstruction and Development, *The economic development of the Territory of Papua and New Guinea,* Baltimore, 1965.

Jacobs, M, "German New Guinea", in P Ryan (ed), *Encyclopedia of Papua New Guinea.* Melbourne Univ. Press, 1974.
Jinks, N, Biskup, P and Nelson, H (eds), *Readings in New Guinea history,* Sydney, Angus & Robertson, 1973.

Kebirger, *Deutich - Neuguinea und meine Ersteigung des Finisterre,* Hugo Zoller, Union Deutishe Verlagsgesellschaft, 1891.
Kreiger, M, *Neu Guinea: bibliothek der landerkunder,* Berlin, Alfred Schall, 1899.

Legge, JD, *Australian colonial policy,* Sydney, 1956.
P. L. Lowenstein, *Economic Geology of the Morobe Goldfield Papua New Guinea,* Volume 1, PNG Dept. Mines, 1982.
Lyng, L, *Our new possessions (late German New Guinea),* Melbourne Publishing Coy, 1919.

MacKenzie, SS, *The Australians at Rabaul,* Canberra, Australian War Memorial, 1932.
Mandated Territory of New Guinea Annual Reports (MTNG AR) 1921-1922 to 1940-41.
McIntyre, WD, *The Imperian frontier in the tropics, 1865-1975,* London, 1967.
McKellar, CD, *Scented isles and coral gardens,* London, 1912.
McKillop, RF, "Papua New Guinea's Bootless Bay railway", *Light Railways* No.47, 1974.
McKillop, RF, "The Misima Island railway", *Light Railways,* No. 51, Autumn 1975, pp. 4-7.
McKillop, RF, "Mosa Oil Palm Mill, West New Britain, PNG", *Light Railways* No.69, 1980.
McKillop, RF, and Firth, SG, "Foreign intrusion: the first fifty years", D Denoon & C Snowden (eds), *A time to plant and a time to uproot: a history of agriculture in Papua New Guinea,* Port Moresby, Institute PNG Studies, nd (1980).
McKillop, RF, "Tramways and oxen: the Neu Guinea Kompagnie tramways of Astrolabe Bay, Papua New Guinea", *Light Railways,* No. 81, July 1983.
McKillop, RF, "Railways in Australian history: a preliminary reconnaissance. Part 3: building institutions." *ARHS Bulletin,* No. 558, April 1984.
McKillop, RF, "Mosquito coast II: Marienberg sawmill and Tramway, Papua New Guinea", *Light Railways,* 110, October 1990, pp. 7-15.
McKillop, RF, "Public transport and people: a case study of Port Moresby", *Transit Australia,* March 1992, pp. 58-62.
Manning, I, *The Open Street: Public Transport, Motor Cars and Politics in Australian Cities,* Sydney, Transit Australia Publishing, 1991.
Moore, CR, *Kanaka: a history of Melanesian Mackay,* Uni PNG Press, 1986.
Mumford, L, *The city in history,* London, Secker, 1961.

Nelson, H, *Black White and Gold,* Canberra, ANU Press, 1976.
Nelson, H, *Taim bilong masta: the Australian involvement with Papua New Guinea,* Sydney, ABC Books, 1982.
Newman, P and Kenworthy, J, *Cities and Automobile Dependence - An International Sourcebook,* Gower, Aldershott, 1989.
Nihal, H, "The Second World War in Morobe District, *Journal of Morobe Historical Society,* 1:1, May 1972.
Nolan, Janette, *Bundaberg: history and people,* Univ. Qld. Press, 1978.
North, DC, "Institutions", *Journal of Economic Perspectives.* Vol. 5:1, 1991.
PNG Parliament, Bi-Partisan Select Committee on Provincial Government, Report of 2 March 1993.
Pearson, MR, "Use of Railways in PNG", Submission to Minister for Transport, May 1992.

Pearson, R, "A railway in Papua", *Light Railways*, No. 20, 1967, p. 21-23.

Rendal & Partners, *Integrated infrastructure for Frieda, Ok Tedi and Tifalmin Mineral Prospects*, Port Moresby, November 1975.
Rhys, L, *High lights and flights in New Guinea*, UPNG Library A919.546, R479.
Richards, J and MacKenzie, JM, *The railway station: a social history*, Oxford University Press, 1988.
Robson, RW, *Queen Emma*, Brisbane, Robt. Brown, 1994.
Rostow, WW, *The process of economic growth*, Cambridge, 1960.
Rowley, CD, *The Australians in German New Guinea: 1914-21*, Melbourne, 1958.

Sack P & Clark, D (eds), *German New Guinea: the annual reports* (GNGAR), Canberra ANU Press, 1979.
Schaffer, B, "Thoughts at Goroka", *New Guinea*, June/July 1965.
Schoeter, H and Ramaer, R, *German colonial railways then and now*, Krefeld, Rohr Verlag, 1994.
Sinclair, J, *Wings of Gold*, Sydney, Pacific Publications, 1978.
Souter, G, *New Guinea: the last unknown*, Sydney, 1963.
SRI International, *Papua New Guinea Industrial Growth Strategy*, Report prepared for ADB TA No. 1580 PNG, August 1992.
Stanner, WEH, *The South Seas in transition*, Sydney, 1953.
Stewart. Robert, *Nuts to You*, Sydney, Wentworth Books, 1977.
Stewart, I, *Port Moresby: yesterday and today*, Sydney, Pacific Publications, 1973.

The British internal-combustion locomotive, 1894-1940.
Townsend, GWL, *District Officer: from untamed New Guinea to take success, 1921-1946*, Sydney, Pacific Publications, 1968.

United Nations, Report of the 1962 United Nations Visiting Mission to the Trust Territory of New Guinea, New York, 1962.
United States Army, *Handbook on Japanese Military Forces*, US War Department Technical Manual, 15 September 1944.
Voyce, A H, *Peacemakers*, 1977.

Wagner, H and Reim, H (eds), *The Lutheran Church in Papua New Guinea: the first hundred years, 1886-1986*, Adelaide, Lutheran Publishing House, 1986.
Walker, J (Ed), *A Story of Christianity in Papua New Guinea*. Liturgical Catechetical Institute - Goroka, Wirui Press - Wewak.
West, F, *Hubert Murray - The Australia Pro-Consul*, Oxford, Oxford University Press, 1968.
Weston, AE, "Pre-War shipping, Huon Gulf, New Guinea", *Journal of the Morobe District Historical Society*, 3:1, July 1975, p. 42-52.
Williams, M and MacDonald, B, *The Phosphateers: a history of the British Phosphate Commissioners and the Christmas Islands Phosphate Commission*, Melbourne Univ. Press, 1985.
Wiltgen, RM, "SVD Catholic mission plantations: their origins and purpose," *The history of Melanesia: proceedings of the Second Waigani Seminar*. Canberra, 1969.
Wyse, WJ, "Transport and the environment", *Light Rail and Modern Tramway*, February 1995, p. 29.

Newspapers and Magazines

Air Niugini *Paradise* magazine
Australian Board of Missions Review, 1930
Black and White, December 1966
Brisbane *Courier* newspaper, 1940s
Highland News, 1973
Deutsches Kolonialblatt, 1899 to 1902.

New Guinea Gazette, 1922 to 1937
North Queensland Register, 1914
Ok Tedi Nius.
Pacific Islands Monthly, 1930 to 1962
Papua-New Guinea Gazette, 1947 to 1960
Papuan Courier, 1924.
Papua Villager, 1936 to 1939.
PNG Business, 1993-1996
Post Courier, 1970-1996.
Queensland Mining Journal, 1910 to 1922
Rabaul Times, 1925 to 1958
Saturday Independent, 1995-96.
South Pacific Post, 1950 to 1968
Sydney Morning Herald, 1923 to 1945
Territory of Papua Annual Report 1907-1908 to 1940-41
Territory of Papua Government Gazette, 1914 to 1932.
The National, 1992-96
The Sydney Mail, 1914.
The Times of PNG, 1982 to 1995
Walkabout, 1934 to 1973

Manuscripts/Unpublished works

Reference Patrol No 3 of 1947, 15th March 1947, R. R. Cole A/Assistant District Officer.
Grabowsky, I, AMF 70, UPNG Library NG Collection, p. 246-248, Part 2, p. 46; 1929
Report of the 23rd Brigade - Brigadier Potts
Jack Reed - Coastwatcher - Manuscript November 1942
Rowley, CD, "The area taken over from Germans and controlled by the ANMEF",

Correspondence

Anonymous, correspondent to Mr Gilbee Brown signing himself "Phil", 7 June 1964, RF McKillop collection.
Australian Army in August 1950 (Dispatch 15293) to AD Lockyer, South Australia
Ayton, A, General Manager, Higaturu Processing, letter to M Pearson, 30 April, 1981.
Fr Birkmann, information provided via Sister Mary Ruth, letter, 7 August, 1981.
Bougin, Francis, clerk at Soraken, Letter to M Pearson, 28 November, 1978.
Bovelt, A, letter to M Pearson, 11 May 1978, plus observations and report on findings at *Gamodaudau*
Brookfield builders list courtesy Ray Graf
Buckland, JL, letter to RF McKillop, 29 May 1987
Cleland, D, General Manager, The British New Guinea Development Co Ltd., Letter to M Pearson, 28 November 1978.
Memorandum by CEH of Lands, Survey & Mines Department of 26 July 1917, plus map supplied by RF Ellis.
ES&A Bank, Melbourne, letter SW:JET of 11 May 1950 to AD Lockyer
Ferguson, Mrs M A, Letters to M Pearson 6 March and 8 Aug 1979
Extract from letter addressed to the Secretary, Lindenhafen Estates Ltd. Sydney from A.H. Gauld, District Plantation Manager, Lindenhafen, New Britain dated 17th December 1932
Gilbee Brown, H, letters 21 August, 26 September 1962 and 13 April 1964, RF McKillop collection
Gill, SMR, letter, 14 April, 1923, Pacific Manuscripts Bureau microfilm PMB40
Hart, M B, Manager , Coconut Products Ltd, letters to M Pearson, 6 June 1978 and 9 March 1984..
Hayes, Robert and Elsie of Newcastle, letters of 23 May 1945 and 4 August 1950 to AD Lockyer, Adelaide
Hodge, Peter to Charles Small, April 1964

Horne, JS, "Diary of visit to inspect Robinson River Plantation, 30/11/1932 to 22/1/1933", UPNG Library, PNG Miscellaneous Documents, 1885-1964, PMB627.

Howley, Br Pat, headmaster, St Xaviers High School, Kairiru report to M Pearson

CJ Levien, letter to director Wells, 6 April, 1925

AMF II, *Industrial Reports of Luteran Mission, Finschaffen, 1920-1939,* (PMB 642); Letter by J Lindner, 20 August 1925

Lonergan, SA, a/Government Secretary, Territory of PNG, letter CA 25/3/54 to AD Lockyer, 22 March 1950

Low, LJ of Bulolo, letters, to M Pearson, 9 June 1978 and April 1984.

Nicklason, N, letter to M Pearson, 1 May 1978.

PNG National Archives Dispatch Schedules G72, Radio July 4, 1916, A Hunt to Murray

PNG National Archives, Lieutenant-Governor's Office, file 15/8.

PNG National Archives G97 Series Box 2407 File 11.

PNG National Archives G74 Despatch Schedules, Dispatch 18/7832 of 6 July 1918 and radio of 18 September 1918

PNG National Archives. G72 External Affairs Despatches Received by Administrator Vol 1

PNG National Archives - Box 1024 Out Stations N8/2 Samarai Wharf & Jetty Tramline

PNG National Archives Box 6592 Correspondence (G120) 1888 to 1906,

PNG National Archives - Box 6441 Series G69 File 31/5 f /?. 26/2/41 Dept of Public Works.

PNG National Archives - Box 6441 Series G69 File 31/4 f 41-134

PNG National Archives, letter from N Imlay, Collector of Customs to Treasurer, 5 May 1925.

PNG National Archives Box 6592 Correspondence, extract from *Melbourne Age* 20th Sept 1901 and *Bulletin* 5/10/01: T. F. Bevan "New Guinea Development Scheme".

PNG National Archives, Access 36 PWD Box 6211 File 60/3/8/2

Prosser, HE, ex-141 General Transport Company, letter to AD Lockyer, 22 May 1947

RA Lister Australia, letter to M Pearson 21 March 1984.

Ryan, ED, letter to M Pearson, 30 October, 1978.

Saunders, V, letter to M Pearson, 1984

Threlfall, Neville, letter to M Pearson, 10 April, 1984

van der Laan, N, General Manager, Hargy Oil Palms, letter to M Pearson, 24 March, 1981.

Voyce, Rev A H, letter to M Pearson, 2 September, 1981

Williamson, RB (Misima mine manager 1919-21), letter to H Gilbee Brown, A Lockyer collection

Willis, Dr Ian, letter to M Pearson, 9 September, 1978

Wundke, ML, manager, Itikinumu Estate, letter to M Pearson, March 1984.

Referees/Interviews

Batze, Adolf, interview Cairns, M Pearson, December, 1979

Maria Bonnet's father, interview at Hanahan, 1982 M Pearson

Cavanaugh, Jim, phone interview R F McKillop, 7/7/1989. R F McKillop

Campbell, Mr, Numa Numa Manager, interview M Pearson, 1981.

Fox, Peter, personal communication with R F McKillop, Goroka, 1968

Gammage, W and Firth, SW with RF McKillop on German plantations.

Gina, Simon, interview, Teop, 1983 M Pearson

Gulewa village, Misima Island, field interviews by Michael Sakiasi for RF McKillop, November 1975

Haileen, interview, Rawa Plt, 1980 M Pearson

Hakena, John, interview Kubu, M Pearson

Hannett, Leo, interviews 1981 and 1995 M Pearson

Havine, M and villagers, interviews along Numa Numa Trail, April 1986. M Pearson

Hoagae and villagers, nterviews Yokomori village, 1983 M Pearson

Ikupa, Andrew, interview, UPNG, 1993 M Pearson

Iseop Jason, interview Kavieng, September 1995 M Pearson
Kanavi, Oliver, interview at Kavieng, September 1995 M Pearson
Koiri, Clement, interview at Buin, 1981 M Pearson
Lusack, W, verbal report, 1992 M Pearson
McConvil, Fr, personal communication, Chabai, 1983 M Pearson
Mesu village, Interview with two old men in September 1995, M Pearson
Michael of Ieta Village, interview M Pearson
Moorehouse, D, interview at Porgera, July, 1987, R F McKillop
Onol, Joachim, interview Bonom village, 16/5/1989, R F McKillop
Brother Pias, interview M Pearson 1983
Rira, James, interview M Pearson at Kavieng, September 1995.
Br Roland, interview CM Angoram, 20/4/1989, R F McKillop
Tabua, George, personal communication, Daru 1978 M Pearson
Takapi, Alfred, interview Kavieng, September 1995. M Pearson
Tabasi, Mario, interview at Tinputz, 1983. M Pearson
Terova, Timothy, interview Saposa Island, 1983 M Pearson
Fr Tschauder, interview SVD, Madang, 1990 M Pearson

Field Observations/Investigations

Alexishafen, Madang Province, M Pearson, 1990; RF McKillop May 1996
Barges Hill incline railway, Numa Numa Trail, M Pearson, April 1986.
Bootlesss Bay-Dubuna railway, R F McKillop and/or M Pearson, 1973, 1979, 1990 and 1994
Bougainville East Coast Plantations, M Pearson, 1980, 1981 and 1983.
Bougainville, north-west coast plantations, M Pearson, 1981, 1983
Buin-Kangu Area, Bougainville, M Pearson, 1980, 1981, 1984-1987
Bwagaoia-Umuna area, Misima Island, M Sakiasi, November 1975
Daru Island, M Pearson, 1977-78
Higaturu Oil Palm, Oro Province, R F McKillop, 17 September 1995
Kavieng and Huris areas, New Ireland, M Pearson, September 1995
Marienberg Mission, East Sepik, RF McKillop, March and May 1989.
Mosa palm oil mill, West New Britain, RF McKillop, 1972
Panguna, Bougainville Copper drainage tunnel, M Pearson, 1981.
Port Moresby public transport system, RF McKillop, 1990, 1991.
Rabaul and Environs, M Pearson, May 1981.
Vanimo-Serra, Sandaun Province, RF McKillop, March 1996
Vunapope Mission, ENB, M Pearson 1980, RF McKillop, May 1991.

Photograph Collections

UPNG Library HAJ Fryer Collection, negative L. 362
Historishes Bildmaterial ous dem Archives des staatlichen Museums fur Volkerkunde, Dresden. Copy held PNG National Library NG Collection. Photos 313/4
National Archives Photograph collection
US Air Force Photo B 25456 A.C
H Gilbee Brown Photos, RF McKillop collection
RF McKillop collection: Bootless Bay, Marienberg, Vunapope, Numa Numa Trail
Mitchell Library, Sydney

APPENDIX: LIST OF PNG RAILWAYS

This list summarises the known information on all the railways known to have operated in Papua New Guinea. Lists are presented for each of the eras covered in Chapters 2 to 7. Information is provided on the name of the railway, the owner, the province in which it was located and technical details, such as gauge, length and mode of operation. Brief notes are provided on each line.

Province Abbreviations.

CP   Central
EHP   Eastern Highlands
ENB   East New Britain
ESP   East Sepik
NSP   North Solomons (Bougainville)
Gulf   Gulf
Mor   Morobe
Mad   Madang
Man   Manus
MBP   Milne Bay Province
NCD   National Capital
NIP   New Ireland Province
Oro   Oro Province (formerly Northern Province)
SP   Sandaun (West Sepik)
WNB   West New BritainWP Western

Operations - Motive power of railway:

A   Animal Powered
H   Hand-pushed or pulled
L-BE   Locomotive: battery-electric
L-IC   Locomotive: IC-engine
L-S   Locomotive: steam
RM   Rail motor
T   Wheeled tractor
W   Winch-hauled

Name	Owner	Prov.	Gauge mm	Km	Dates	Oper.	Notes
Mioko Pltn	DH&PG	ENB	750-1000?	0.15	188?-1900s	H	Pioneer line from wharf to store
Sattelberg	Lutheran Mission	Mor	700?	?	1895-?	H	At Sattleberg hill station
Stephansort	NGK	Mad	600	24	1893-42	A	Railways serving tobacco fields. Operated as 3 systems after 1901 - Erimahafen (1.6 km), Erimabush (5.6 km) and Bogadjim (8 km).
Jomba Pltn.	NGK	Mad	600	4.5	1892-42	L-S/A	Tobacco railway with 2 steam locomotives, then coconut plantation.
Potsdamhafen Pltn	NGK	Mad	600	0.15	?-1930s	H	Wharf to copra store
Herbertshohe	NGK	ENB	600	1.0?	1893-1930s	H	Originally wharf to cotton store
Ralum Pltn.	Forsayth	ENB	600	0.5?	1900-1943	H	Wharf to copra stores; dual lines
Raniolo Pltn	Forsayth	ENB	600	0.5?	1898-1920s	W	Funicular railway.
Kabakaul	Forsayth	ENB	600	0.5?	?-1960s	H	Wharf to copra store. Restored after WW II by Prod. Control Board.
Ulu Pltn	Methodist Mission	ENB	600	0.3	?-1942	H	Wharf to store, Duke of York Islands
Manuan Pltn	Methodist Mission	ENB	600	1.2	?-1995	H	Plantation railway, Duke of York Islands. Still operating 1995.
Pondo Pltn	NGK/CPL	ENB	700?	8-10	?-1970	L-IC	Plantation railway, diesel locomotive and 12 flatcars 1963.
Numa Numa	Buka Pltn	NSP	600	7.0	1910-42	L-S/A	Plantation railway with reported steam locomotive. Lines lifted by Japanese during the War.
Meto Pltn. (Garowe)	Capt. Hansen	WNB	600	4.5	1909-1943	A	Plantation railway on Witu Island. Subsequently extended to Ilia Plantation
St Anna Pltn	SVD	WSP	700	1.6	1903-42	A	Plantation railway, 4 trucks.
Longan Pltn	HR Wahlen	Man	600	0.1	190?-1930s	H	Wharf to store
Pelleluhu Pltn	HR Wahlen	Man	600	0.5	190?-1943	H	Wharf to store
Mole Is.	NGK	Man	?	0.5	1888-91	H	Phosphate mining line, Purdy Group; wrecked by tropical storm
Nauru Island	Pac. Phospate Coy	na	610	12	1907-95	L-S	Taken over by British Phosphate Commission, 1920; converted to 3ft (914 mm) gauge, 1937; diesel locomotives from 1956.
Rabaul Tmy.	NGL/NGK	ENB	750	4.6	1910-37	H	Street tramway system for distributing goods/mails from wharf to commercial houses and government offices.
Kavieng Tmy.	Government	NIP	600	0.5	1906-1942	H	Wharf to stores and customs shed
Toriu River	SHM	ENB	700	?	1902-17	H	Logging railway to sawmill. Transferred to Kurindal.
Kurindal	SHM	WNB	700	?	1917-28	L-S	Logging railway to sawmill. Transferred to Ulamona.
Ulamona sawmill	SHM	WNB	700	10	1928-95	L-S L-IC	Logging railway to sawmill. 2 steam locomotives, 1 conv. to diesel. Logging line closed 1966, but line from sawmill to wharf continues in operation.
Vunapope	SHM	WNB	700	0.6	1930s-80s	H	Tramways serving timber processing and shipbuilding operations. Some lines remain in place.

German New Guinea (Cont.)

Name	Owner	Prov.	Gauge mm	Km	Dates	Oper.	Notes
Alexishafen	SVD	Mad	700	6	1907-42	A/RM	Logging railway serving large sawmill. Rail motor introduced 1920s to provide passenger transport to airfield. Destroyed during War.
Marienberg	SVD	ESP	700	6	1920s-75	A	Logging railway between Sepik River and steam sawmill. Inland line closed 1960s, but lines at post-War sawmill continued operating until 1975. Lines still in place.
Butawung	Lutheran	Mor	?	?	1922-35	A	Logging railway in Morobe Highlands.
Proposed Lines							
Ramu River	Government	Mad	600	65	1913	na	Proposed extension of line from Stephansort to Lower Ramu flats to serve mining area plus extension north to Friedrick Wilhelmshafen.
New Ireland	Government	NIP	750?	180	1911	na	Planned conversion of Bulominski Highway to railway
Rabaul-Keravat	Government	ENB	750	45	1912	na	Conversion of roads to light railway. Tunnel through "Tunnel Hill" at Rabaul constructed for the line.

Chapter 3: Papuan Railways

Name	Owner	Prov.	Gauge mm	Km	Dates	Oper.	Notes
Pt Moresby Wharf	BPs	NCD	1067	0.2	1895-1910	H	BP wharf to store in Port Moresby
Pt Moresby Wharf	Admin.	NCD	610	0.25	1905-42	H	Wharf to store. Double tracked 1912.
Samarai Island	Admin.	MBP	610	0.6	1905-62	H	Tramway system from wharf to stores. Some lines reconstructed after War.
Daru Island	Admin	WP	610	0.5	1917-63	H/T	Wharf to store.
Bomana Pltn	BNGDC	CP	762	?	1912-22	H	Sisal plantation
Fairfax Pltn	Clark & Whitting	CP	762	?	1912-22	H/L-IC	Sisal plantation
Robinson River	BPs	MBP	610	30	1920s-42	H/T	Plantation railway. Trucks pulled by tractors
Orangerie Bay	Admin	MBP	610	0.8	1926-?	H	Plantation railway.
Baibara	?	MBP	610	?	?-1960s	H	Plantation rly.
Hagita & Waigani	Catholic Miss.	MBP	762	6	?-1950s	H/A	Plantation railways linked to wharf at Gabugabuna
Itikinumu	BNGDC	CP	900	0.4	?-1970s	H	Rubber plantation
Eilogo Pltn	?	CP	762	3-4	?-1970s	?	Rubber plantation.
Kenosia Pltn	BNGDC	CP	?	?	?	?	Rubber plantation.
Doa Pltn.	BNGDC	CP	?	?	?	?	Rubber plantation.
Woodlark Is.	WI Proprietry	MBP	762	2.5	1900-60	H/L-IC	Mining Company line to link Kulumandau to jetty.
Woodlark Is.	Admin.	MBP	762	7.5	1915-21	L?	Public railway to Busai mining field.
Kulumandau mine	Kulumandau- WI Coy	MBP	610	0.4	1911-21	H	Adit to crushers
Busai mine	Federation mine	MBP	610	0.3	1911-21	H	Adit to crushers
Bonivai mine	Woodlark King	MBP	610	0.4	1924-42	H	Adit to crushers
Misima Island	Block 10 Coy	MBP	610	11.5	1919-22	L-S	Mining railway from port at Bwagaoia to Ulamona.
Misimi Island	BP/Ryan	MBP	610	0.6	1922-60s	H	Jetty to store
Bootless Bay-Dubuna	NG Copper Coy	CP	1067	10.4	1918-27	L-S	Mining railway; 2 steam locos; maintained until 1931
Buna-Yodda	?	Oro	762	1.6	1914	H	Portable line
Buna Sawmill	Papuan TI	Oro	762	?	1915-?	?	Logging line
Vailala	Anglo Persian	Gulf	610	>2	1915-21	H	Oil rig supply
Popo (funicular)	Anglo Persian	Gulf	610		1921	W	funicular railway
Akoropaira	Anglo Persian	CP	1067	0.3	?	H	River to supply base
Yule Island	SHM	CP	1067	?	1891-37	H	Wharf to store
Kwato Mission	LMS	MBP	?	0.5	1892-94	H	Construction
Dogura Cathedral	Anglican Miss.	Oro	762	1.0	1930-42	L?	Construction
Ononghue	Catholic Miss.	CP	?	1.5		A	Logging line
Sideia Island	Catholic Miss.	MBP	?	?		H	Wharf to mill
Sewa Bay sawmill		MBP	?	0.4		H	Wharf to mill
Proposed Railways							
Sapphire Creek Railway	Admin.	NCD/ CP	610	30	1914	L-S	Construction started, not completed.
Veimauri River sugar mill	Hall Sound Coy	CP	610	21	1901	L-S	Sugar milling proposal
Sangara Plantation	Sangara Pltn.	OP	610	20	1932	L-S	Sugar milling venture - trial plantings only.

Chapter 4: Mandated Territory of New Guinea

Name	Owner	Prov.	Gauge mm	Km	Dates	Oper.	Notes
Rabaul-Rapindik tramway	Administration	ENB	762	3	1922-37	L-IC	Public tramway with passenger train timetable
Malaguna Coal Wharf	Administration/BP	ENB	610	0.3	1930-42	H	Wharf to store
Ah Tams Wharf	Ah Tam	ENB	610	0.15	1920-29	H	Wharf to store, destroyed by fire
Toboi tramway	CPL	ENB	610	0.5	1930-42	H	Wharf to store, double tracked
Soraken pltn.	Choisal Pltns	NSP	610	3-5	1920-42	L-IC	Plantation railway
Kunua Pltn.	Choisal Pltns	NSP	610	3-4	1925-42	L-IC	Plantation railway
Teopasino pltn.	Choisal Pltns	NSP	610	4.1	1920s-60s	L-IC	Plantation railway
Tinputz CM	Marist Bros.	NSP	610	0.1	1930-43	H	Sawmill line
Banio pltn.	Choisal Pltns	NSP	610	5	1920s-60s	L-IC	Plantation railway
Arigua pltn.	Choisal Pltns	NSP	610	3-5	1920s-42	L-IC	Plantation railway, branch line to Kuwina Pltn. (BPs)
Buoi pltn.	BPs	NSP	610	4	1930s-90	H	Plantation rly.
Mabiri Pltn.	Marist Bros	NSP	610	?	?-1960s	H	Wharf to store
Tearouki Pltn.	Marist Bros	NSP	610	?	?-1942	H	Beach to store
Porton Pltn.	?	NSP	610	?	?-1942	H	Wharf to store
Lindenhafen	BPs	WSP	610	8-10	?-1978	L-IC	Plantation rly.
Ilia Pltn.	Catholic Miss.	WNB	610	1.6	?-1990s	H	Plantation rly.
Unea Island	Bali Pltn,	WNB	762	2	?	A	Plantation rly.
Neinduk Pltn	?	ENB	610	6-7	1930s-42	H	Plantation/sawmill railway, timber railed
Wide Bay sawmill	NB Timber & Mercantile	ENB	?	0.8	1926-31	A	Sawmill line
Saunders Wharf	A Saunders	NIP	750?	0.5	1930s-1942	H	Wharf to copra shed
Kalili Pltn.	?	NIP	610	2-3	1920s?-42	H	Plantation railway; may date from German era
Lossu Pltn.	?	NIP	610	?	1920s?-42	A	Buffalo-worked plantation line; may date from German era
Kimadon Pltn.	?	NIP	610	?	1920s?-42	A	Plantation railway; may date from German era
Waramung Pltn	G Cousins	NIP	610	?	?	A/H	Located on Anir Island
Mariba Pltn.	Lutheran Miss	Mor	?	?	?	?	Wharf to store
Sulankaua	Lutheran Miss	Mor	?	?	?	?	Plantation rly.
Lae Railway	BGD Coy	Mor	1435	1.2	1931-42	L-S L-IC	Wharf to airstrip for Bulolo airlift
Salamaua rly.	BGD Coy	Mor	610	2.5	1929-42	H	Wharf to airstrip
Salamaua Airport	B Watson	Mor	610	2	1936-42	L-IC	Airstrip maintentance
Wau-Bulolo	NG Goldfield	Mor	610	?	1935-42	H	Ore transport
Madang Store	Carpenters	Mad	610	0.5	1932-42	A	Store to wharf
Kupei Audit	Catholic Miss	NSP	610	?	1930-42	H	Ore transport
Proposed Railways							
Bulolo Railway	Eilyou Corp.	Mor	610	266	1929	-	Surveyed line to serve Bulolo goldfields from Salamua

Chapter 5: Pacific War

Name	Owner	Prov.	Gauge mm	Km	Dates	Oper.	Notes
Rabaul Barge Tunnels	Jap Imperial Navy	ENB	2000?	0.5-1	1942-45	H	Lines into tunnels for protection of barges
Tobera airstrip	Jap Imperial Navy	ENB	610	?	1942-45	L-IC	Airstrip construction
Vunakanau airstrip	Jap Imperial Navy	ENB	610	?	1942-45	L-IC	Airstrip construction
Lakunai airstrip	Jap Imperial Navy	ENB	610	?	1942-45	L-IC	Airstrip construction
Keravat	Jap Imperial Navy	ENB	610	?	1942-45	?	Airstrip construction
Panapai	Jap Imperial Navy	NIP	610	2-4	1942-45	?	Airstrip construction
Huris	Jap Imperial Navy	NIP	610	4?	1942-45	?	Airstrip construction, Japanese rails noted here 1995
Katu sawmill	Jap Imperial Navy	NIP	610	2-4	1943-45	?	Sawmill line
Buin railway	Jap Imperial Navy	NSP	610	30+	1942-50s	L-IC	Munitions, supply, airstrip construction and timber transport. Large operation with several branches and minimum 7 locomotives.
Kanga Hill funicular	Jap Imperial Navy	NSP	610	0.5	1942-45	W	Funicular, munitions transport
Tonulai Harbour	Japanese Navy	NSP	610	?	1942-45	W	
Kahili	Japanese Navy	NSP	610	?	1942-45	?	Airstrip construction
Chabai airstrip	Jap Imperial Navy	NSP	610	2-4	1942-50s	L-IC	Airstrip construction, food supplies; 6 locomotives
Tarlena	Jap Imperial Navy	NSP	610	2	1942-50s	H	Supplies
Bonis	Jap Imperial Navy	NSP	610	7?	1942-45	H	Airstrip construction
Buka passage	Jap Imperial Navy	NSP	610	2-4	1942-45	L-IC	Munitions, supply, airstrip construction
Lae airstrip	Jap Imperial Navy	Mor	610	1-2	1943-45	L-IC	Munitions transport
Finschaffen	Jap Imperial Navy	Mor	610	?	1942-43	L-IC	Airstrip construction
Alexishafen	Jap Imperial Navy	Mad	610	2-4	1942-45	L-IC	Airstrip maintenance
Boram airstrip	Jap Imperial Navy	ESP	610	1-2	1942-45	L-IC	Airstrip construction
Kairiru Island	Jap Imperial Navy	WSP	610	6-7	1942-45	L-IC	Munitions, supply, sawmiling
Tadji	Jap Imperial Navy	WSP	610	?	1943-45	L-IC	Airstrip construction
Bulldog Trail rly.	Aust. Army	CP	1067	11	1943-44	Jeep	Supplies for road
Barges Hill	Aust. Army	NSP	490	0.75	1945	W	Funicular
Gamodoudou rly.	US Navy	MBP	610	?	1945	?	US Naval base lines
Wanigela Base	US Army	Oro	610	?	1943-45	?	Army base supplies
Lae Army Base	Aust. Army	Mor	610	?	1944-47	L-IC	Army base supplies
Port Moresby Munitions	Aust. Army	NCD	610	?	1942-45	L-IC	Munitions transport at various dumps in Port Moresby area
Rouna Quarry	Aust. Army	CP	610	1.0?	1942-45	L-IC	Quarry operations
Tatana Wharf	US Army	NCD	762?	1.0	1943-45	L-IC	Supply transport

Chapter 6: Post-War Reconstruction

Name	Owner	Prov.	Gauge mm	Km	Dates	Oper.	Notes
Soraken pltn	Choisal Pltn.	NSP	610	21	1951-84	L-IC	Plantation railway
Kunua pltn.	Choisal Pltn.	NSP	610	11.1	1951-90	L-IC	Plantation railway
Aird Hills	Borneo NG Mangrove	Gulf	610	1.3	1954-58	L-IC	Cutch industry
Tsironge	Marist Bros.	NSP	610	0.3	1950-80	H	Wharf to store
Mabiri pltn.	Marist Bros.	NSP	610	?			
Tubiana mission	Marist Bros.	NSP	610	0.1	1950s-90	H	Wharf to store
Skotlan Mission	Methodist Miss.	NSP	610	0.1	1950s-70s	H	Wharf to store
Kieta tramway	Wong You & Co	NSP	610	0.1	1950s-70s	H	Wharf to store
Kaliai mission	SHM	WNB	700	1.5	1960-90	H	Store to beach
Mosa Oil Palm	NB Oil Palm	WNB	600	0.5	1971-74	L-IC	Oil palm mill supply
Mosa Oil Palm	NB Oil Palm	WNB	700	1.6	1974-95	T/W	Oil palm mill supply
Biala pltn.	CPL	WNB	610	1.0	1950s-70s	H	Wharf to store
Bulolo sawmill	Admin.	Mor	610	0.6	1946-66	H	Sawmill operation
Asitavi mission	Marist Bros.	NSP	?	1.0	1950s-60s	H	Sawmill to wharf and logging line
Panguna Adit	Dillingham	NSP	610	1.6	1967-68	L-BE	Tunnel construction, 3 locomotives
Western Adit	Dillingham	NSP	610	2.6	1968-69	L-BE	Tunnel construction, 4 locomotives
Yonki Tunnel	Hyundai	EHP	914	2.4	1972-76	L-IC	Tunnel construction
Suassi mission	LMS	CP	1067	0.05	1950s	H	Airstrip construction
Kupiano	Admin.	CP	1067	0.05	1950-60s	H	Jetty tramway
Proposed Railways							
Bainyik Railway	Admin.	ESP	610	56	1959	L-IC	Proposal, not built
Pt Moresby-Cape Rodney	Admin.	CP	1435	200	1974	L-E	Ward Railway Plan for electric lines
Ok Tedi-Pt Moresby	Admin.	WP-CP	1435	1000	1974	L-E	Ward Railway Plan for electric lines

Chapter 7: Post-Independence

Name	Owner	Prov.	Gauge mm	Km	Dates	Oper.	Notes
Panguna Drainage tunnel	BCL	NSP	900	6.2	1977-84	L-IC	Tunnel construction, 7 locomotives
Ok Tedi mine	Kennicott	WP	?	?	1970s	L-IC	Exploratory adit
Ok Mani Adit	Ok Tedi Mining	WP	914	?	1980s	L-IC	Tunnel construction
Harvey Creek	Curtain Bros.	WP	?	1.5	1987-pres.	W	Funicular for water scheme construction
North Piabuna	Curtain Bros	Gulf	610	0.3	1993-95	L-IC	Equipment transport over swamp
Warangoi Hydro	Downer-Kier	ENB	610	7	1981-83	L-BE	Tunnel construction
Rouna No. 4 Hydro	Watkins-Kumagai	CP	914	4	1983-88	L-BE	Tunnel construction; 5 locomotives
Biala oil palm	Hargy Oil Palms	WNB	600	0.2	1977-95	L-IC	Oil palm mill supply
Sanganga oil palm mill	Higaturu Oil Palm	Oro	600	1.0	1980-95	W-T	Oil palm mill supply
Kumbango oil palm	NB Oil Palm	WNB	700	0.6?	1993-	W-T	Oil palm mill supply
Poliamba oil palm	CDC	NIP	700	0.4	1990-95	W-T	Oil palm mill supply;
Milne Bay Oil Palm	CDC	MBP	700	0.8	1991-95	W-T	Oil palm mill supply.
Proposed Railways							
Freida-Ok Tedi-Tifalmin	GOPNG	WP/ESP	1435	300	1975	L-IC	Dept. Transport study
Markham Railway	GOPNG	Mor	1435	150	1981	L-IC	Study only - not feasible
Port Moresby	GOPNG	NCD	1435	35	1995	E-RM	Proposed light rail system

UNCONFIRMED

Listing of lines claimed by various sources, but not verified by records:

Owner	Location	Province	Notes
	Nonga	ENB	
	Nordup	ENB	
	Tibual (Timbur)	ENB	Could be Herbertshole
	Rapopo	ENB	Could be Japanese airstrip construction line
	Ulabla	ENB	
	Kapkap	ENB	
	Mangan	ENB	
	Bitalova	ENB	Japanese barge tunnels
Sacred Heart Mission	Rakanda CM	ENB	
Turama Forest Industries	Turama River	Gulf	Logging line? (1994?)
	Yagum Mission	Mad	
	Maiwater Pltn	Mad	
	Lorengau	Man	
	Lingo-Lingo	MBP	
	Malapi	MBP	
	Gala Island	MBP	
	Bolubolu Pltn	MBP	
	Giligili Pltn	MBP	
Cheong	Alotau	MBP	
	Raus Laba	MBP	
	Suwau	MBP	
	Timi Island	Mor	
	Retapiok Isl.	Mor	
Burns Philp	Maritsoan Pltn	NIP	
	Kalili	NIP	
Coconut Prod. Ltd.	Kakola	NSP	
	Toiminapu Pltn	NSP	
	Natabu	Oro	
	Kandrian	WNB	
	Gasmata	WNB	
	Iboka	WNB	
	Arawe	WNB	Could be Japanese airstrip construction line
Ribinau Hedja	Wawei-Guave	West	Logging line? (1994?)

INDEX